Spectral America

A RAY AND PAT BROWNE BOOK

Series Editors
Ray B. Browne and Pat Browne

Spectral America

Phantoms and the National Imagination

Edited by

JEFFREY ANDREW WEINSTOCK

THE UNIVERSITY OF WISCONSIN PRESS / POPULAR PRESS

The University of Wisconsin Press
1930 Monroe Street
Madison, Wisconsin 53711

www.wisc.edu/wisconsinpress/

3 Henrietta Street
London WC2E 8LU, England

5   4   3   2   1

Printed in the United States of America

Library of Congress Cataloging-in-Publication Data

Spectral America : phantoms and the national imagination /
edited by Jeffrey Andrew Weinstock.
p. cm.
"A Ray and Pat Browne book."
Includes bibliographical references and index.
ISBN 0-299-19950-9 (cloth : alk. paper) — ISBN 0-299-19954-1 (pbk. : alk. paper)
1. Ghost stories, American—History and criticism. 2. American literature—
History and criticism. 3. Supernatural in literature. 4. Spiritualism in literature.
5. Ghosts in literature. 6. Death in literature. I. Weinstock, Jeffrey Andrew.
PS374.G45S64 2004
813´.0873309—dc22
2003021170

Contents

Acknowledgments

JEFFREY ANDREW WEINSTOCK

Ghosts may be intangible, but books are material objects that require a great deal of time and effort to produce. I am grateful to the contributors for both their marvelous insights and their patience! In addition, I wish to thank Renée Bergland, Lynette Carpenter, and Anthony Magistrale for positive feedback and helpful commentary, as well as Tricia Brock, Sue Breckenridge, Jackie Doyle, and the University of Wisconsin Press for their time and effort. Finally, I wish to thank Astrid and Alan and Madeline Weinstock for their unwavering and unconditional love and support.

Spectral America

Introduction

The Spectral Turn

JEFFREY ANDREW WEINSTOCK

I. SPECTRAL AMERICA

Our contemporary moment is a haunted one. Having now slipped over the edge of the millennium into the twenty-first century, it seems that ghosts are everywhere in American popular and academic culture. Beginning in the 1980s with *Poltergeist* (1982)—directed by Tobe Hooper and produced by Steven Spielberg—and Bill Murray and Dan Aykroyd in *Ghostbusters* (1984), American cinema has witnessed a spate of big-budget ghostly features including *Ghost* (1990) starring Patrick Swayze and Demi Moore, *The Sixth Sense* (2000) starring Bruce Willis, *What Lies Beneath* (2000) starring Harrison Ford and Michelle Pfeiffer, and *The Others* (2001) starring Nicole Kidman.[1]

On television, late-twentieth- and early-twenty-first century programs such as *The X-Files*, *Buffy the Vampire Slayer*, *Ally McBeal*, and, more recently *Tru Calling*, *Dead Like Me*, *The West Wing*, and *NYPD Blue*, more or less regularly featured and continue to include ghosts and supernatural intervention. On cable, *Crossing Over with John Edwards*, a program that features a psychic who communes with the dead, has become one of the Sci Fi channel's most popular programs. In contemporary literature, Stephen King, an author of supernatural tales, remains one of America's—and the world's—most popular authors, while even such "high brow" authors as Toni Morrison, Louise Erdrich, Maxine Hong Kingston, and Gloria Naylor routinely imbricate the spectral realm with the world of profane reality (Morrison's ghost story *Beloved* won the Pulitzer prize for literature in 1988). On the American stage, two 1990s productions featuring ghosts won Pulitzer prizes for drama: August Wilson's *The Piano Lesson* in 1990 and Tony Kushner's *Angels in America, Part One: Millennium Approaches* in 1993.

Contemporary academia has followed suit in this preoccupation with ghosts; while studies of the supernatural in literature and culture are not new to academia,[2] the late 1980s also marked the beginning of heightened interest in ghosts and hauntings in cultural and literary criticism. Concerned specifically with accounts of "real" ghosts, F. C. Finucane's *Ghosts: Appearances of the Dead and Cultural Transformation* was published in 1996; Jean-Claude Schmitt's *Ghosts in the Middle Ages: The Living and the Dead in Medieval Society*, originally published in French in 1994, was introduced in English in 1998; and Gillian Bennett's *Alas Poor Ghost! Traditions of Belief in Story and Discourse* followed in 1999. As concerns ghosts in American literature and film, one can look to the following monographs issued with increasing velocity over the last twenty years: Howard Kerr, John W. Crowley, and Charles L. Crow's edited collection *The Haunted Dusk: American Supernatural Fiction, 1820–1920* (1983); Lynette Carpenter and Wendy K. Kolmar's edited collection *Haunting the House of Fiction: Feminist Perspectives on Ghost Stories by American Women* (1991); Katherine A. Fowkes's *Giving Up the Ghost: Spirits, Ghosts, and Angels in Mainstream American Comedy Films* (1998); Kathleen Brogan's *Cultural Haunting: Ghosts and Ethnicity in Recent American Literature* (1998); Lee Kovacs's *The Haunted Screen: Ghosts in Literature and Film* (1999); Dale Bailey's *American Nightmares: The Haunted House Formula in American Popular Fiction* (1999); and Renée Bergland's *The National Uncanny: Indian Ghosts and American Subjects* (2000).

Perhaps even more intriguing is the "spectral turn" of contemporary literary theory. Because ghosts are unstable interstitial figures that problematize dichotomous thinking, it perhaps should come as no surprise that phantoms have become a privileged poststructuralist academic trope. Neither living nor dead, present nor absent, the ghost functions as the paradigmatic deconstructive gesture, the "shadowy third" or trace of an absence that undermines the fixedness of such binary oppositions. As an entity out of place in time, as something from the past that emerges into the present, the phantom calls into question the linearity of history. And as, in philosopher Jacques Derrida's words in his *Specters of Marx*, the "*plus d'un*," simultaneously the "no more one" and the "more than one," the ghost suggests the complex relationship between the constitution of individual subjectivity and the larger social collective.

Indeed, the figure of the specter in literary and cultural criticism has become so common that one may refer to contemporary academic discourse as, in some respects, "haunted." The end of the millennium witnessed a proliferation of publications focused specifically on specters and haunting, including Jacques Derrida's *Specters of Marx* (1994), Jean-Michel Rabaté's *The Ghosts of Modernity* (1996), Avery Gordon's *Ghostly Matters: Haunting and the Sociological Imagination* (1997), Peter Buse and Andrew Stotts's *Ghosts: Deconstruction, Psychoanalysis, History* (1999), and Peter Schwenger's *Fantasm and Fiction* (1999). And, if one begins to consider contemporary poststructuralist theory more generally—for instance, the recent preoccupation with "trauma" in which the presence of a symptom demonstrates the subject's failure to internalize a past event, in which something from the past emerges to disrupt the present—the ubiquity of "spectral discourse" becomes readily apparent.

The question of *why* American popular culture and academia finds itself in the midst of this spectral turn is complex and, in various ways, the essays included in this volume will each address different aspects of the needs and desires that ghosts fulfill. However, I will briefly suggest here that the current fascination with ghosts arises out of a general postmodern suspicion of meta-narratives accentuated by millennial anxiety.

As I have indicated above, the idea of the ghost, of that which disrupts both oppositional thinking and the linearity of historical chronology, has substantial affinities with poststructural thought in general. The ghost is that which interrupts the presentness of the present, and its haunting indicates that, beneath the surface of received history, there lurks another narrative, an untold story that calls into question the veracity of the authorized version of events. As such, the contemporary fascination with ghosts is reflective of an awareness of the narrativity of history. Hortense Spillers observes that "[Events] *do* occur, to be sure, but in part according to the conventions dictating how we receive, imagine, and pass them on" (176). This is to say that there are multiple perspectives on any given event and one perspective assumes prominence only at the expense of other, competing interpretations. To write from a perspective other than the authorized one and "to write stories concerning exclusions and invisibilities" is, to quote Avery Gordon, "to write ghost stories" (17). The usefulness of the ghost in the revisioning of history from alternate, competing perspectives is one reason why tales of the spectral have assumed such prominence in contemporary ethnic American literature.[3] The ubiquity of ghost stories in our particular cultural moment is connected to the recognition that history is always fragmented and perspectival and to contestations for control of the meaning of history as minority voices foreground the "exclusions and invisibilities" of American history.

It is also no coincidence that the contemporary American fascination with ghosts seems to have reached a high-water mark at the turn of the millennium and has yet to abate. Ghosts, as all the essays in this volume argue, reflect the ethos and anxieties of the eras of their production. In this respect, the spectral turn of American culture should be read as a mark of millennial anxiety. As a symptom of repressed knowledge, the ghost calls into question the possibilities of a future based on avoidance of the past. Millennial specters ask us to what extent we can move forward into a new millennium when we are still shackled to a past that haunts us and that we have yet to face and mourn fully. The millennial explosion of supernatural cultural production thus seems to suggest that what is as frightening as the unknown field of the future is the tenacious tendrils of a past we cannot shake.

And yet it needs to be acknowledged that our ghosts are also comforting to us. They represent our desires for truth and justice (not to mention the American way), and validate religious faith and the ideas of heaven and hell. They speak to our desire to be remembered and to our longing for a coherent and "correct" narrative of history. We value our ghosts, particularly during periods of cultural transition, because the alternative to their presence is even more frightening: If ghosts do not return to correct history, then privileged narratives of history are not open to contestation. If ghosts do not return to reveal crimes that have gone unpunished, then evil acts may in fact go unredressed. If ghosts do not appear to validate faith, then faith remains just that—faith rather than fact; and without ghosts to point to things that have been lost and overlooked, things may disappear forever. How can we get it right if we do not know that we have gotten it wrong?

That ghosts are particularly prominent in our cultural moment indicates that we are particularly vexed by these questions. The ghosts that we conjure speak to these timely, context-bound fears and desires—they can do nothing else.

II. America's Spectral Turn

To be spectral is to be ghostlike, which, in turn, is to be out of place and time. Ghosts, as noted above, violate conceptual thinking based on dichotomous oppositions. They are neither fully present nor absent, neither living nor dead. The ghost is the mark or trace of an absence. As Avery Gordon puts it, ghosts are "one form by which something lost, or barely visible, or seemingly not there to our supposedly well-trained eyes, makes itself known or apparent to us" (8). Phantoms *haunt*; their appearances signal epistemological uncertainty and the potential emergence of a different story and a competing history.

This volume foregrounds the growing interest in the importance of ghosts and hauntings—of spectrality—to American cultural configurations, and it aims to address a salient gap: the absence of any sustained diachronic attention to the role of the spectral in American culture. In the general body of criticism on American literature, attention has historically been paid to the supernatural writings of individual authors, such as Edgar Allan Poe and Henry James, and individual articles have appeared here and there noting spectral motifs in virtually every time, region, and ethnic group in the United States. Studies have also focused on American ghost stories during discrete blocks of time (Kerr), ghost stories written by specific populations (Brogan; Carpenter and Kolmar; Lundie; Neary; Patrick), ghost stories with particular thematic foci or political orientations (Bergland), and cinematic ghost stories (Fowkes, Kovacs).

However, despite the development of what I am tempted to term "spectrality studies" in the 1990s, and the pronounced contemporary interest in ghosts and hauntings, what is lacking in American studies, literary studies, and cultural studies is any sustained approach to the importance of phantoms to the general constitution of North American national identity and consciousness.[4] That is, while there are specific studies of particular authors and bodies of literature, what all these isolated studies point to the need for, and what precisely is missing, is an analysis of the general importance of phantoms and haunting to the constitution of the "American imagination." *Spectral America: Phantoms and the National Imagination* speaks to this gap by assembling scholars who focus on how phantoms and hauntings have exerted their influences in literary and popular discourses across the span of American history and have shaped the terrain of American consciousness. This is an immense topic, of course, and it is not one that any single volume can hope to exhaust. However, it is my hope that the essays contained within this volume will begin to outline broad parameters for future investigation.

Taken together, the essays included in *Spectral America* demonstrate the ways in which phantoms have been a part of American culture since its inception, and the manner in which the preoccupation with the supernatural has been a defining American obsession—but one that has persistently been appropriated and redeployed to accommodate changing American sociohistorical anxieties and emphases. *Spectral America* thus reveals the idea of the ghost as one that has remained consistently vital to American culture, but demonstrates the ways in which particular ghostly manifestations are always constructions embedded within specific historical contexts and invoked for more or less explicit political purposes. What the contributions to this volume confirm is that America has *always* been a land of ghosts, a nation obsessed with the spectral. Part of the American national heritage is a supernatural inheritance—but each generation puts this inheritance to use in different ways and with differing objectives. This is to say that ghosts do "cultural work," but that the work they perform changes according to the developing needs of the living. Phantoms participate in, reinforce, and exemplify various belief structures. To investigate the role of the spectral in American life, therefore, is to engage with changing parameters of religion and science and to explore the ongoing importance of the liminal in the constitution of American subjectivity. Examining our ghosts tells us quite a bit about America's hopes and desires, fears and regrets—and the extent to which the past governs our present and opens or forecloses possibilities for the future.

III. Inclusions

It seems appropriate to begin a collection of essays concerning the importance of the spectral to the American imagination with a consideration of one of America's foundational traumas: the Salem witch trials. Alison Tracy's "Uncanny Afflictions: Spectral Evidence and the Puritan Crisis of Subjectivity" introduces the subject of spectrality as one so deeply ingrained in American culture and consciousness that its roots can be traced all the way back to the Puritans. Indeed, Tracy's essay identifies the Puritans as the original "haunted Americans" and explores the spectral manifestations in Salem in 1692 as representative of larger systemic anxieties pervading not only seventeenth-century Puritan culture, but "the entire American project." Her essay examines documentary historical materials from the Salem witch trials in order to isolate the "prototypically American aspects of the spectral disruptions," particularly their reliance on visual proof. She concludes that the haunted narrative of Salem and our enduring fascination with it demonstrate the ways in which subjectivity is generated and reproduced out of the material consequences of narrative.

In productive tension with Tracy's essay, Jeffrey Hammond's contribution, "Friendly Ghosts: Celebrations of the Living Dead in Early New England," asserts that most studies of Puritan supernaturalism have focused on manifestations of evil or the demonic to the neglect of equally prominent (while perhaps less dramatic) manifestations of good forces. (The spectral, of course, can have both good and evil functions.) Hammond's essay therefore concentrates on the rhetoric of the Puritan funeral elegy that "made the onslaughts of Satan seem more bearable by assuring mourners that the invisible world remained well-stocked with friendly ghosts who longed for the redemption of the living." Readers of elegy, according to Hammond, "found themselves being coaxed to glory not only by Christ and the clergy, but by an ever-increasing company of souls with whom they once shared life's trials." Hammond eloquently concludes that the "friendly ghosts" of the elegized dead "made the highest virtue out of the deepest human necessity: by giving ritual and performative shape to the inevitable act of mourning, the Puritan elegy reconstructed its readers into selves more capable of opposing Satanic forces." In this way, Hammond argues, the spirits of the dead clearly served the needs of the living.

Transitioning from the Puritan beginnings of American spectral consciousness to the blossoming of American narrative in the early nineteenth century, theorist of the uncanny Allan Lloyd Smith opposes in his essay "Can Such Things Be? Ambrose Bierce, the 'Dead Mother,' and Other American Traumas" what he perceives as the entrenched convention of invoking Sigmund Freud and, in particular, his now famous essay "The Uncanny," to analyze literary hauntings. Lloyd Smith instead turns to the more recent psychoanalytical theorizing of Andre Green and his notion of the "dead-mother syndrome," as well as Nicolas Abraham and Maria Torok's work on "phantoms" and "crypts," in order to analyze the recurrent patterns of domestic trauma in early American uncanny fiction. What Lloyd Smith proposes, revising the familiar proposition that early American romancers such as Brockden Brown, Poe, and Bierce merely adapted the European Gothic to American shores, is a complex theory of the American imaginary as "haunted" by specific historical events that can be found repeatedly "encoded or encrypted within fictions of domestic and familial trauma." Lloyd Smith's essay ultimately theorizes a "specifically American 'political unconscious' that becomes visible more particularly within the frame of 'spectral fictions.'" Nineteenth-century supernatural fiction and its recurrent thematics thereby provides an important window into the mechanics of nineteenth-century American identity formation.

In the same way that Jeffrey Hammond's essay on Puritan funeral elegies works productively with Alison Tracy's essay on spectral evidence in Salem to suggest the importance of both the demonic and the holy to America's early colonists, Terry Heller's essay on the spiritual philosophies of nineteenth-century American regionalist Sarah Orne Jewett, "Living for the Other World: Sarah Orne Jewett as a Religious Writer," provides an important counterpoint to Lloyd Smith's emphasis on specters of domestic violence in the uncanny fiction of America's early male romancers. Heller contends that Jewett's postbellum nineteenth-century writing reveals as one of her cultural projects the intention of creating and sustaining the reader's belief in a world in which benevolent spiritual beings appear regularly in mundane human life. Heller maintains that Jewett saw herself as "participating in the cultural work of creating and sustaining a unified and yet also diverse American culture based firmly upon the belief that a benevolent spiritual world intersects and interacts with ordinary life." She concludes that Jewett's "religion of friendship" "contributes to a cultural project shared by many post–Civil War women regionalists, to forward an alternative model that could replace the public culture these writers saw as increasingly characterized by materialism, extreme individualism, impersonal patriarchal institutions, capitalist commercialism, and an appropriating colonialism." In this way, Jewett's manipulation of supernatural conventions is revealed to be political in nature and part of a larger project of nineteenth-century female authors.

John Kucich, in "The Politics of Heaven: The Ghost Dance, *The Gates Ajar,* and *Captain Stormfield*," provides another example of the ways in which supernatural narratives reflect changing cultural anxieties. Kucich argues that the spread of the Ghost Dance among the tribes of the Great Basin and Plains in 1890 precipitated a crisis not only for the United States's Indian policy but for the "social meaning" of heaven as well. His analysis begins by exploring the ways in which the Ghost Dance movement ironically appropriated aspects of the Christian conception of heaven to help preserve threatened Native American traditions. Then, juxtaposing the philosophy of the Ghost Dance with Elizabeth Stuart Phelps's 1870 best-selling feminist utopian vision of heaven, *The Gates Ajar,* and with Mark Twain's revision of *The Gates Ajar, Captain Stormfield Visits Heaven,* Kucich demonstrates the "common imperialist infrastructure" and the contentious politics of representations of the supernatural world during the latter half of the nineteenth century in America. Heaven is in this way revealed to have been a zone of political contestation at the center of nineteenth-century American gender and racial ideologies.

With interesting connections to Alison Tracy's emphasis on "spectral evidence" in her essay on supernatural manifestations at Salem, Sheri Weinstein, in her essay "Technologies of Vision: Spiritualism and Science in Nineteenth-Century America," approaches the phenomenon of nineteenth-century American Spiritualism through an examination of "technologies of vision." Weinstein argues that the Spiritualist movement was not opposed to technological advancement, but was in fact an extension of scientific and empirical discourses of the late nineteenth century: "It aimed to authenticate the immaterial presence of spirits of the dead through 'objective,' observable, and repeated experiences and through a rationalist discourse of 'factual evidence.'" Weinstein concludes that nineteenth century Spiritualism "assuaged individuals' fears of losing their humanity to technology by making the human body itself a type of penetrative and communicative 'technology,' a machine of vision." American culture in the nineteenth century, according to Weinstein, took pleasure in what could not be seen. Spiritualism, in her estimation, was a discourse that worked to redefine the nature of "vision" itself.

In "Flight from Haunting: Psychogenic Fugue and Nineteenth-Century American Imagination," Jessica Lieberman introduces a fascinating discussion of nineteenth-century American incidents of "fugue," disturbed states in which the one affected performs acts of which he or she appears to be conscious but of which, upon recovery, he or she has no memory. Of particular interest to Lieberman are instances of flight, of "sudden uprooting and hasty departure." In the process of analyzing nineteenth-century explanatory causes for fugue states, including possession by spirits, what Lieberman details is the racialized breakdown of psychological diagnosis; while the flight of enslaved Africans and African Americans from bondage was "quickly dismissed as insane behavior unworthy of much study," white flight captured the attention of celebrated thinkers in government, law, medicine, and science. Lieberman's analysis focuses on the case of Ansel Bourne, America's first documented fugue patient who went missing in 1887. According to Lieberman, the Bourne case narrates the pedagogic value of both listening to ghosts and recognizing the importance of the presence of the past in the constitution of American selfhood. Lieberman concludes with the assertion that "flight from haunting" should be understood as a fundamental component of American subjectivity.

Moving us into the twentieth century, Charles Crow, the editor of *American Gothic: An Anthology 1787–1916*, in his "The Girl in the Library: Edith Wharton's 'The Eyes' and American Gothic Traditions" focuses on Edith Wharton's "anxiety of influence" as she negotiated inherited generic conventions of supernatural storytelling. In the same manner that Heller's essay on Jewett attends to the ways in which Jewett's religion of friendship, revealed through the supernatural aspects of her fiction, placed her in opposition to the materialistic ideologies of late-nineteenth-century American culture, Crow writes that Wharton's 1910 short story "The Eyes" "parodies and discredits an aspect of the dominant literary tradition, which is characterized by its clubby, masculine atmosphere and avuncular confidential voice, a tradition Wharton associates with Washington Irving." Crow concludes that "The Eyes" "reveals Wharton's mature awareness of the confining tradition of storytelling that she inherited as a young writer from Irving and other male predecessors" and argues that the tale "memorializes" her escape from her subservience to this tradition. Wharton's ghostly tale is thereby revealed to be a story both indebted to and critical of an American tradition of supernatural storytelling.

Elizabeth T. Hayes's "'Commitment to Doubleness': U.S. Literary Magic Realism and the Postmodern" also focuses on the ways in which authors writing from the margins make use of the supernatural to contest the status quo. Hayes proposes that magic realism, by presenting supernatural events as mundane, de-centers the traditionally accepted Cartesian boundaries between the rationally knowable world and the supernatural world and functions subversively to call into question the binarized thinking of Western culture. Hayes contends that the magic realism of contemporary authors such as Morrison, Naylor, Wilson, and Tan "subverts the conventions of realism and challenges the hegemony of rationalism by interrogating Cartesian binaries, erasing or at least blurring the border between the natural and the supernatural, the living and the dead, the past and the present, the knowable and the unknowable." Through its "commitment to doubleness," magic realism thereby provides ethnic American authors with a powerful tool for sociopolitical critique.

Developing certain ideas first introduced in her book *Giving Up the Ghost: Spirits, Ghosts, and Angels in Mainstream Comedy Films*, Katherine A. Fowkes turns her attention in "Melodramatic Specters: Cinema and *The Sixth Sense*" to the cinematic hit of the same name in order to explore the ways in which cinematic storytelling manipulates filmic and generic expectations in the service of crafting ghostly narrative. Fowkes writes, "There is something inherently ghostly about the photographic image which when combined with narrative and other cinematic conventions makes film an uniquely efficient purveyor of the ghost story." However, what Fowkes's analysis uncovers is that *The Sixth Sense* shares two related themes with other recent ghost movies including *Ghost, Always,* and *Truly, Madly, Deeply* (1991): the difficulty of communication between men and women and the distance or absence of the husband or father in the American family. *The Sixth Sense* is thus revealed to be a film that tells us quite a bit about not only the conventions of ghost movies, but also American anxieties concerning gender relations and the constitution of the family.

In "Stephen King's Vintage Ghost-Cars: A Modern-Day Haunting," Mary Findley fixes her attention on publishing powerhouse Stephen King. In particular, Findley focuses her attention on King's vintage ghost cars in *Christine* (1983) and *From a Buick 8* (2002). Her analysis reveals that, through a curious conjunction of technology and the supernatural, what King captures is contemporary American anxiety concerning the perils of technological progress. According to Findley, King's spectral vehicles from the past disrupt the narrative present and ominously figure a world in which machines have the potential to dominate human beings. King's deployment of supernatural conventions therefore responds to our specific cultural moment and the anxieties pursuant to living in the nuclear age.

In Diana Davidson's contribution to *Spectral America,* "Ghosting HIV/AIDS: Haunting Words and Apparitional Bodies in Michelle Cliff's 'Bodies of Water'," the author explores a very potent and problematic deployment of spectral rhetoric in contemporary American culture: the "ghosting" of individuals living with HIV and AIDS. Davidson's examination of Michelle Cliff's "Bodies of Water" reveals the ways in which the trope of "ghosting" "makes queer and HIV+ bodies absent," with significant political and personal repercussions for individuals living with HIV. What Davidson's essay makes explicit are the political ramifications of naming and the ways in which language is inherently imbued with power relations. In contrast to several of the essays included in this volume that focus on how the spectral can be used as a tool for subversion, Davidson demonstrates that the language of spectrality can also be deployed as a mechanism to exclude and to silence.

Rounding out the collection, Bridget M. Marshall's essay "Salem's Ghosts and the Cultural Capital of Witches" returns the reader again to Salem—this time, however, from a particularly modern perspective. While Tracy and Hammond's essays at the start of the volume consider the importance of supernatural manifestations primarily within the context of seventeenth-century America and as formative of American spectral imagining, Marshall's essay looks at the uncanny aftermath, so to speak, of Salem in terms of contemporary tourism. Ghosts, says Marshall, are big business. However,

Marshall argues that the cultural creation of twentieth- and now twenty-first-century Salem—which purports to recreate the Salem of 1692—in fact blocks access to the historicity of the event and the venue. Presenting a forceful perspective on the ethics of the production and consumption of haunting, Marshall maintains that tourism in Salem becomes an opportunity not for education or contemplation, but for entertainment and a theme-park-style "experience." Salem continues to haunt, but what the commodification of Salem makes evident is the ways in which narratives of history are shaped by the demands of the present. From Marshall's perspective, what truly haunts contemporary Salem is the absence of haunting. In packaging the horrific to make it entertaining, something of the horror of the witchcraft trials has been displaced.

This collection starts with haunted Puritans and ends with Puritan hauntings. While moving forward chronologically, this return to the start at the end signals the dual chronology of the ghost—the fact that it is simultaneously of its time and out of time. The popularity of ghost stories seems perpetual, although the extent may vary from decade to decade. However, as all the inclusions in this volume make evident, the spectral itself changes persistently to accommodate the needs and desires of the living. The essays contained in this volume examine the cultural work that the spectral has executed in the past and continues to perform in the present. Taken together, they demonstrate that America has always been a land populated with ghosts and that the American imagination has always been haunted. To investigate ghosts is to unearth one's heritage and to analyze the competing and evolving ideologies that have more or less explicitly shaped the development of a nation.

NOTES

1. One could supplement this list with Michael Keaton in *Beetlejuice* (1984), Spielberg's *Always* (1989), Kevin Costner in *Field of Dreams* (1989), Brandon Lee in the cult hit *The Crow* (1994), Kevin Bacon in *Stir of Echoes* (1999), big-budget 1999 remakes of both *The Haunting* and *House on Haunted Hill*, the re-release of *The Exorcist*, Tim Burton's version of *Sleepy Hollow* (2000) and *The Ring* (2002), and, depending upon one's interpretation of the ghostly elements, one could include *The Blair Witch Project* (2000).

2. Older studies of the supernatural in literature include Dorothy Scarborough's seminal survey, *The Supernatural in Modern English Fiction* (1917); H. P. Lovecraft's increasingly cited *Supernatural Horror in Literature* (1945), and Julia Briggs's *Night Visitors: The Rise and Fall of the English Ghost Story* (1977). There are also, of course,

studies of the use of supernatural conventions in individual authors such as Poe and Irving and a large body of information on the Gothic novel.

3. See Hayes in this volume, as well as Brogan and Gordon, for studies of contemporary ethnic American ghost stories as forms of political critique. For discussions of feminist ghost stories, see Carpeter and Kolmer, Lundie, Neary, Patrick and Salmonson.

4. Bergland comes closest to this objective in her study of the importance of Native Americans as spectral to the constitution of American cultural identity.

WORKS CITED

Bailey, Dale. *American Nightmares: The Haunted House Formula in American Popular Fiction.* Bowling Green, Oh.: Bowling Green State University Popular Press, 1999.

Bennett, Gillian. *Alas, Poor Ghost! Traditions of Belief in Story and Discourse.* Logan: Utah State University Press, 1999.

Bergland, Renée L. *The National Uncanny: Indian Ghosts and American Subjects.* Hanover, N.H.: University Press of New England, 2000.

Briggs, Julia. *Night Visitors: The Rise and Fall of the English Ghost Story.* London: Faber, 1977.

Brogan, Kathleen. *Cultural Haunting: Ghosts and Ethnicity in Recent American Literature.* Charlottesville: University Press of Virginia, 1998.

Buse, Peter, and Andrew Scott, eds. *Ghosts: Deconstruction, Psychoanalysis, History.* New York: St. Martin's, 1999.

Carpenter, Lynette, and Wendy K. Kolmar, eds. *Haunting the House of Fiction: Ghost Stories by American Women.* Knoxville: University of Tennessee Press, 1991.

Crow, Charles L., ed. *American Gothic: An Anthology 1787–1916.* Malden, Ma.: Blackwell, 1999.

Derrida, Jacques. *Specters of Marx: The State of Debt, the Work of Mourning, and the New International.* Translated by Peggy Kamuf. New York: Routledge, 1994.

Finucane, R. C. *Ghosts: Appearances of the Dead & Cultural Transformation.* Amherst, N.Y.: Prometheus, 1996.

Fowkes, Katherine A. *Giving Up the Ghost: Spirits, Ghosts, and Angels in Mainstream Comedy Films.* Detroit: Wayne State University Press, 1998.

Gordon, Avery. *Ghostly Matters: Haunting and the Sociological Imagination.* Minneapolis: University of Minnesota Press, 1997.

Higley, Sarah, and Jeffrey Andrew Weinstock. *The Nothing That Is: Millennial Cinema and the Blair Witch Controversies.* Detroit: Wayne State University Press, 2004.

Kerr, Howard, John W. Crowley, and Charles L. Crow, eds. *The Haunted Dusk: American Supernatural Fiction, 1820–1920.* Athens: University of Georgia Press, 1983.

Kovacs, Lee. *The Haunted Screen: Ghosts in Literature and Film.* Jefferson, N.C.: MacFarland, 1999.

Kushner, Tony. *Angels in America: A Gay Fantasia on National Themes. Part I: Millenium Approaches.* New York: Theatre Communications Group, 1992.

Lovecraft, Howard Phillips. *Supernatural Horror in Literature.* 1945. Reprint. New York: Dover, 1973.

Lundie, Catherine A. "Introduction." In *Restless Spirits: Ghost Stories by American Women 1872–1926*. Amherst: University of Massachusetts Press, 1996.

Morrison, Toni. *Beloved.* New York: Plume, 1988.

Neary, Gwen Patrick. "Disorderly Ghosts: Literary Spirits and the Social Agenda of American Women, 1870–1930." Ph.D. diss. University of California, Berkeley, 1994.

Patrick, Barbara Constance. "The Invisible Tradition: Freeman, Gilman, Spofford, Wharton, and American Women's Ghost Stories as Social Criticism, 1863–1937." Ph.D. diss. University of North Carolina, Chapel Hill, 1991.

Rabaté, Jean-Michel. *The Ghosts of Modernity.* Gainesville: University Press of Florida, 1996.

Salmonson, Jessica Amanda. "Preface." In *What Did Mrs. Darrington See? An Anthology of Feminist Supernatural Fiction.* New York: The Feminist Press, 1989.

Scarborough, Dorothy. *The Supernatural in Modern English Fiction.* 1917. Reprint. New York: Octagon, 1978.

Schmitt, Jean-Claude. *Ghosts in the Middle Ages: The Living and the Dead in Medieval Society.* Translated by Teresa Lavender Fagan. Chicago: University of Chicago Press, 1998.

Schwenger, Peter. *Fantasm and Fiction: On Textual Envisioning.* Stanford: Stanford University Press, 1999.

Spillers, Hortense J. "Notes on an Alternative Model: Neither/Nor." In *The Year Left 2: An American Socialist Yearbook.* Edited by Mike Davis, 176–94. London: Verso, 1987.

Wilson, August. *The Piano Lesson.* New York: Plume, 1990.

FILMS REFERENCED

Always. Dir. Steven Spielberg. Perf. Richard Dreyfuss, Holly Hunter. MCA/Universal Pictures, 1989.

Beetlejuice. Dir. Tim Burton. Perf. Michael Keaton, Geena Davis, Alec Baldwin, Winona Ryder. Warner Bros., 1988.

The Blair Witch Project. Dirs. Daniel Myrick & Eduardo Sanchez. Artisan Entertainment, 1999.

The Crow. Dir. Alex Proyas. Perf. Brandon Lee. Miramax/Dimension Films, 1994.

Field of Dreams. Dir. Phil Alden Robinson. Perf. Kevin Costner, James Earl Jones. Gordon Co., 1989.

Ghost. Dir. Jerry Zucker. Perf. Patrick Swayze, Demi Moore, Whoopi Goldberg. Paramount, 1990.

Ghostbusters. Dir. Ivan Reitman. Perfs. Bill Murray, Dan Aykroyd, Sigourney Weaver. Columbia Pictures, 1984.

Haunting, The. Dir. Jan de Bont. Perf. Liam Neeson. DreamWorks SKG, 1999.

House on Haunted Hill. Dir. William Malone. Perf. Geoffrey Rush. Dark Castle Entertainment/ Warner Bros., 1999.

Poltergeist. Dir. Tobe Hooper. Perfs. JoBeth Williams, Craig T. Nelson. Prod. Steven Spielberg. Metro-Goldwyn-Mayer, 1982.

Ring, The. Dir. Gore Verbinski. Perf. Naomi Watts. Amblin Entertainment, 2002.

Sixth Sense, The. Dir. M. Night Shyamalin. Perf. Bruce Willis. Hollywood Pictures and Spyglass Entertainment, 2000.

Sleepy Hollow. Dir. Tim Burton. Perf. Johnny Depp, Christina Ricci. Paramount Pictures and Mandalay Pictures, 2000.

Stir of Echoes. Dir. David Koepp. Perf. Kevin Bacon. Artisan Entertainment, 1999.

Truly, Madly, Deeply. Dir. Anthony Minghella. Perf. Juliet Stevenson. Samuel Goldwyn Company, 1991.

What Lies Beneath. Dir. Robert Zemeckis. Perf. Harrison Ford, Michelle Pfeiffer. Twentieth-Century Fox, 2000.

William Peter Blatty's The Exorcist. 1973. USA Reissue. Dir. William Freidkin. Perf. Linda Blair. Warner Bros., 2000.

Uncanny Afflictions

Spectral Evidence and the
Puritan Crisis of Subjectivity

ALISON   TRACY

Few, if any, moments in American Puritanism evoke such continued popular interest as do the witchcraft trials in Salem Village in 1692.[1] At the height of the hysteria that gripped the village and surrounding areas, no one seemed safe from the relentless accusations of a small group of girls and young women who claimed to be tormented—pinched, bitten, and psychologically abused—by "shapes," the spectral or disembodied representatives of others. The trials at Salem Village, and especially the hasty and unsubstantiated convictions and executions of the accused witches there, have come to stand for an abuse of power, an outbreak of social hysteria, or any publicly sanctioned attempt to displace social, cultural, or religious anxiety onto a demonized scapegoat. Such common-knowledge interpretation of the events at Salem is registered in our ongoing use of the term "witch-hunt" to describe rampant persecution, such as the House Un-American Activities Committee hearings under Senator Joseph McCarthy in the 1950s, which inspired Arthur Miller's famous allegorical treatment of Salem Village, *The Crucible* (1953). The events at Salem have been read variously as reflecting economic pressures, as manifesting the threat posed by increased social and economic mobility to a conservative, highly static Puritan theocratic culture, or as resulting from the emotional and hormonal fluctuations of adolescence and their effects on suggestible young women in a repressive and restrictive society. Yet none of these explanations fully accounts for the uniquely destructive power of these particular events, or for the fascination that the trials retain today.[2]

The accusations made, and the trials and executions conducted in Salem near the end of the seventeenth century mark a significant and well-documented low point in the Puritan "errand" into the New England wilderness. Far from representing John Winthrop's "city on a hill," whose moral and spiritual excellence would serve as an exemplar for all of Western Christendom, Salem Village and its witchcraft trials are often seen as revealing the inherent moral bankruptcy, spiritual anxiety, and vindictive superstitiousness of this latter-day and self-appointed new Israel. As Winthrop had predicted, "the eyes of all people" had indeed come to rest upon the Puritan community only to see that by the time of the events at Salem, the idealized, single, spiritual "body" in which that community was metaphorically realized had disintegrated beyond repair.[3]

As numerous scholarly works attest, the trials in Salem responded to a variety of historical and material conflicts that disrupted late seventeenth-century Puritan life, and registered the tremendous forces acting upon the larger Puritan community. The witch-hunts concluded a series of ongoing and interconnected crises. These included the decades-long struggle for Salem Village's autonomy from the more prosperous and established Salem-Town; and troublesome village factions, each with differing affiliations with the town and its mercantile economy. In addition, there was an overarching conflict between a conservative, socially and economically marginal group of villagers who maintained allegiance to an earlier form of Puritanism less corrupted by capitalism, and a group of prosperous community members who represented the coming of a new century. According to Paul Boyer and Stephen Nissenbaum's cogent study, *Salem Possessed,* two key families—the conservative, anticapitalist Putnams (whose daughter was one of the first afflicted, followed shortly by her sickly and perhaps vindictive mother)[4] and the up-and-coming Porters—represent the irreconcilable attitudes toward the advent of mercantile capitalism that characterized the village factions. In addition, these families can be linked to opposite sides of the conflict concerning their minister, Samuel Parris, whose hiring and upkeep were flashpoints for hostilities between the town and the village.[5] Boyer and Nissenbaum thus suggest that the events at Salem occurred on the cusp of two distinct economic, intellectual, and social epochs: "[W]hat confronted Salem Village [. . .] was a group of people who were on the advancing edge of profound historical change. If from one angle they were diverging from an accepted norm of behavior, from another angle their values represented the 'norm' of the future" (109). These frictions coalesce around questions of Puritan identity and authority—how identity is to be understood and maintained, and by whom.[6] My claim here is that in its severity and the extent of its reach, the Salem witchcraft outbreak demonstrates the particular psychological costs of such threats to the status quo. I argue in what follows that the events in Salem are distinguished by their ferocity—an intensity that reflects the uniquely psychological threat posed by this particular occurrence of satanic meddling. Given the extent to which individual Puritan identity was inextricable from the workings of the larger community, the social disruptions of 1691–1692 both precipitate and register a crisis not only of community and collective identity but also of the individual experience of Puritan selfhood.

The events began with bizarre behaviors among a group of girls (including the Reverend Parris's own daughter, nine-year-old Betty, and her eleven-year-old cousin, Abigail Williams) whose fits, outbursts, and inappropriate speech could not be accounted for by the local physician except as the result of witchcraft. In February 1692 the first three accusations of witchcraft were made; one of these was directed at Tituba, a West Indian slave in the Parris household, who had supposedly taught the girls some small tricks of fortune-telling. While the first three women accused were social outcasts and misfits (as was typical of such outbreaks), the rapidly multiplying accusations leveled by a growing group of afflicted girls and women soon came to include established members of the church and community, the town's former minister (George Burroughs), and famous figures from outside Salem. Many of the accused, including Captain John Alden, went unrecognized by their accusers until identified by onlookers during the trials.

Throughout early 1692, those accused were arrested and held but could not be tried because the colony lacked a charter granting proper authority.[7] The pace of accusations continued to accelerate until June, when the first trials and executions took place. The trials and executions continued into September, by which time twenty people had died, many more had been convicted, and hundreds had been accused and imprisoned. What finally ended the trials was not a natural slowing of the hysteria but the concerted effort of a group of ministers, led by the prominent Bostonian Increase Mather, who had objected periodically throughout the trials to the uses and possible misuses of "spectral evidence"—that is, the legal reliance on testimony by the afflicted that specters or "shapes" of the accused were responsible for their torments. Cotton Mather, son of Increase and himself a minister, had been a vocal, if ambivalent, proponent of the trials. Like his father, he had expressed concern over the difference between the testimony-based spectral evidence and the higher standards of legal proof, but unlike his father, he had sporadically urged that the trials continue.[8] This direct confrontation with the bases of the court's convictions (and subsequent executions), along with the failure of the trials to end or even slow the afflictions and accusations, apparently persuaded Governor William Phips. On October 12, he announced that he was forbidding further arrests, and by the end of the month, after formally soliciting advice from an assembly of ministers, he disbanded the Court of Oyer and Terminer. A few months thereafter, he created a special court specifically charged to ignore spectral evidence. The newly appointed court immediately acquitted most of the accused; the few who remained were pardoned by Governor Phips, who ultimately issued a general pardon in spring 1693.[9]

These are the outlines of the events of 1692. In attempting to explain their effects on the community, on individuals, and on the larger Puritan project, I suggest that the witchcraft crisis in Salem is fundamentally *uncanny*—that is, it is best expressed in terms of that particular class of unsettling experiences in which, for example, "the distinction between imagination and reality is effaced" (Freud 244), or "the frightening [. . .] leads back to what is known of old and long familiar" (220). It is, further, characterized by an encounter with the *repressed*, by "an actual repression of some content of thought and a return of this repressed content" (220). I argue here that the trials brought the Puritans into terrifying contact with the necessarily repressed basis of their very existence. In Salem, Puritan attention was distracted from the human project of interpreting the *consequence* of an event by a confrontation with the indecipherability of the *causes*. This indecipherability threatened to expose the divine source of meaning as indistinct from its purported opposite, and thus involved a catastrophic encounter with the contingency of meaning in a society predicated on an absolute, if occasionally obscure, divine order. Reading Salem's historiography as *uncanny*—as haunted not merely by specters but by the doubling, misperception, misrecognition, and threatened dissolution of an entire worldview—integrates these trials into a larger uncanny literary history characterized by confrontations with epistemological uncertainty and the contingency of ideology. The uncanny, which Freud identifies as both a psychological and an aesthetic category, can also help explain our ongoing fascination with Salem itself and with its haunted narrative descendants.

In a letter dated August 17, 1692, and written at the height of the unrest, Cotton Mather articulates the epistemological dilemma confronting those who must determine the guilt of the accused witches. Mather, who shared

the ministry of Boston's powerful Second Church with his more prominent father, Increase, is a key figure in the trials and in contemporary
understandings of them. His *Wonders of the Invisible World* (1693) offered
one of the first accounts and interpretations of the events in Salem. Revi-
sionist versions of the events, particularly Robert Calef's *More Wonders
of the Invisible World* (1700), paint Mather as the trial's primary villain for
his insistence that the executions continue—over the protests of skeptics
and in spite of his own uncertainty about the role of spectral evidence in
the trials. In contrast to his father, whose doubts about the conduct and
outcome of the trials led him to oppose them outright, Cotton Mather
appears as a figure tormented by uncertainty about the trials. In his equiv-
ocations and straw-grasping, the younger Mather thus provides an ideal
representative of the larger crisis in Salem.

Spectral evidence is the topic of Mather's letter to John Foster, a member of the governor's council. Mather is specifically concerned here with
the practice of allowing testimony by the afflicted to attribute the actions
of specters or "shapes" to the accused legally when the apparitions may not,
in fact, genuinely represent the person whose shape they have assumed.
Spectral evidence took on a new significance in Salem, where despite
the express doubts of some of the judges and clergymen, it was not only
allowed but often treated as conclusive. In fact, Nancy Ruttenburg claims
that "the near exclusive reliance upon spectral evidence, to the degree that
it figured prominently in every conviction, appears to be the distinguish-
ing characteristic of the Salem trials" (35). The prominence of spectral evidence should not, however, be read as its unanimous acceptance. Its use
was contested throughout the trials, and ambivalence about its necessity
and its reliability characterizes Mather's accounts.

In the letter, Mather focuses his attention on the legal determination of
the origin and thus the meaning of the spectral shapes, and the degree to
which the witch's voluntary participation in the spectral appearance could
be proved. The potential for discrepancy between the intentions of the
accused and his or her purported deeds is necessarily the arena for legal
and spiritual investigation: "A suspected and unlawful communion with a
familiar spirit is the thing inquired after. The communion on the Devil's
part may be proved while, for aught I can say, the man may be innocent.
The Devil may impudently impose his communion upon some that care
not for his company. But if the communion on the man's part be proved,
then the business is done" (*SVW* 119). As Mather acknowledges, determining the "communion on the man's part" becomes terribly difficult without

a confession. The horrifying and elaborate performances of the afflicted, who during the trials assumed tortured positions, mimicked the movements of the accused, and cried out at being pinched and bitten by the shape of the person before them, demanded legal and theological attention, so the correspondence between their testimony, gestures, and the presence of the accused was initially substituted for more rigorous standards of proof.

For the Puritans of New England, problems of exegesis were familiar and even welcome: Their entire religious project depended upon the interpretation of allegorical signs sent by God (what they termed "the invisible world") acting in the "visible world" of their daily lives. Their interpretation of these signs then determined the presence or absence of God's approval of their conduct. In fact, the entire social order of the Puritan errand in New England depended upon an exact equivalence between their external daily lives and their essential spiritual state; for "visible saints" on a divinely directed mission, sanctity in daily life was not necessarily the condition of salvation, but its manifestation. Church membership and inclusion in the community's spiritual body were exhibited through publicly performed narratives of conversion, at which one expressed not the confidence of salvation, but an appropriate degree of the kind of self-doubt or soul-searching associated with proper Calvinist humility (Ruttenburg 38). In the convoluted Puritan semiological system, God's essential unknowability had been tempered by the terms of the spiritual covenant that had sent them into the wilderness. The terms of this compact suggested that God would allow His manipulation of the natural and supernatural worlds to become "more or less legible to the limited vision of mortal creatures. The rigorously educated theocracy, masters of this system of signs [. . .] maintained that God had agreed to the partial illumination of the space of unknowing through their efforts" (Ruttenburg 39).

The Puritans faced epistemological anxiety every day in, for example, the convoluted logic of "remarkable providences." Ann Kibbey has called remarkable providences "an intrusion of supernatural power into [. . .] otherwise ordinary lives." "What made [such] an event a sign of election," according to Kibbey, "was the perceptible disruption per se, not the consequences of it" (136–37). Asserting the logic of the Jeremiad—i.e., that *chastisement* is proof of God's grace and thus of man's election—the doctrine insisted that earthly setbacks be read as God's "warning chastisements" to his chosen people. In their manifestations and consequences, acts of providence were often indistinguishable from the petty inconveniences or

malicious mischief commonly associated with witchcraft, and the appropriate interpretation could be established only through a retroactive reading of the provenance. As Kibbey suggests, "[T]he dualist opposition
between divine power and witchcraft seems to have been much more fragile, much more vulnerable to reversal, than the occurrence of the trials
and executions might otherwise suggest" (126). She argues that by the late
seventeenth century, the Puritan imagination had become deeply obsessed
by its interpretive project—determining the meaning and provenance of
spiritual interventions, divine or diabolical—and was already demonstrating "deep confusion about [. . .] supernatural influence" (126) by the time
of the trials in Salem.[10] The fundamental threat posed by the fragility and
vulnerability of these "dualist oppositions" underpins the Salem trials,
intensifying the effects of their epistemological ambiguity.

Seventeenth-century New England Puritanism was, of course, already
feeling the strain of social change. Newer generations had lost the spiritual
energy and unity of purpose that characterized the early settlers, while religious tolerance in England threatened to make their errand obsolete and
put the theocracy of the Massachusetts Bay Colony at odds with the
English issuers of its charter. The witchcraft outbreak, in its duration and
its intensity, was perhaps the final blow to the elaborate Puritan theocratic
system. The spiritual legibility of earthly signs, as well as the interpretive
authority of the clergy, are precisely what the events at Salem undermined,
simultaneously calling into question the terms of God's covenant and the
social and spiritual Puritan identity predicated upon it. Writing in 1689,
Cotton Mather had confidently asserted the providential order, suggesting
along the lines of orthodoxy that the effects of a recent outbreak of witchcraft were ultimately to his good and, by example, to the good of the
believers; he had "considered more of God's Goodness in these few weeks
of Affliction, than in many years of Prosperity [. . .]. The Lord help us
to see by this Visitation, what need we have to get shelter under the wing
of Christ" (*Memorable Providences* in Burr 130–31). In contrast to these
doctrinaire interpretations, Mather's depictions of Salem in 1692 are significant precisely because he *fails* to account satisfactorily for the events
there. *The Wonders of the Invisible World*, as well as Mather's correspondence, testify to the very different experiences at Salem. Mather's unsuc-
cessful struggle to make events there correspond to Puritan theology reveals
the intensity of the threat they posed to his worldview.

In his letter to Foster, Mather expresses a sense of futility with respect
to the interpretive project facing authorities in Salem ("for aught I can say,

the man might be innocent," he acknowledges). He expresses his considerable reservations about the role of spectral evidence: "I do still think that when there is no further evidence against a person but only this, that a specter in their shape does afflict a neighbor, that evidence is not enough to convict the [person] of witchcraft." However, he resists the full implications of this position; that is, he refrains from suggesting that the court's work cease, placing his hope instead in "our honorable judges [. . .] so eminent for their justice, wisdom, and goodness, that whatever their own particular sense may be, yet they will not proceed capitally against any upon a principle contested with great odds on the other side in the learned and Godly world" (SVW 118).[11] Six people had already been executed, and more would die shortly after the date of this letter, yet Mather, like others in roles of judicial or spiritual authority, remains confounded by the inscrutability of the "truth," the inadequacy of interpretive mechanisms for the issues at hand. "The odd effects produced upon the sufferers by the look or touch of the accused," he writes, "are things wherein the Devils may as much impose upon some harmless people as by the representation of their shapes" (119). In other words, the specters may represent the "harmless" as well as the guilty. Mather even acknowledges that *he* might be similarly misrepresented: "That the Devils have a natural power which makes them capable of exhibiting what shape they please I suppose nobody doubts, and I have no absolute promise of God that they shall not exhibit *mine*" (118). At issue in the letter, then, is this seemingly insurmountable problem of determining with certainty the source of the apparitions and hence their meaning. The corollary problems are the determination of guilt, which rests on a seemingly impossible assurance in the face of contradictory evidence, and the inscrutability of human nature as manifested in the potential duplicity of the witch. Spectral representations, in their indeterminacy, challenge the very definition of Puritan personhood by severing essence from representation. The possibility of unauthorized representation thus calls into question both the degree to which one is responsible for the actions of one's representation and the notion of consistently accountable public identity. Without the anchoring equivalence between the public representation and the private self, the interpretive process remains unfulfilled and unfulfillable. What matters here is not simply that the Puritans are unsure of the source of their afflictions—human interpretations were understood to be fallible—but that spectral confusion suggests that the source can't be known, and that it is, in fact, unknowable.[12]

In his account of the June 2, 1692, trial of Bridget Bishop, the first witch executed, Mather reports the variety of specters whose actions were attributed to her. John Louder, a neighbor who claimed to have had a disagreement with Bishop "about her fowles," testified that, among other visitations, "he saw a Black thing Jump in at the Window, and come and stand before him. The body was like that of a Monkey, the feet like a Cocks, but the Face much like a Man" (Mather, *Wonders* in Burr 226–27). "[T]his Monster" spoke to Louder, "Whereupon he endeavored to clap his hands upon it; but he could feel no substance" (227). While Loudon's testimony was perhaps the most enthralling, other shapes attributed to Bridget Bishop bore at least a visible resemblance to her: "For instance, John Cook testify'd, that about five or six years ago, One morning, about Sun-Rise, he was in his Chamber assaulted by the Shape of this prisoner: which Look'd on him, grin'd at him, and very much hurt him with a Blow on the side of the Head" (224). The Puritans could not doubt the mysterious presence of the invisible world in their daily existence but were unsure how to attribute such variable and inconsistent representations. One option was to grant these "shapes" a separate existence, but that was to acknowledge that these specters were not, in fact, subject to the providential order, which contradicted the Puritan belief that even diabolical affliction was a manifestation of divine will—or, perhaps, divine displeasure. Dispensing with spectral evidence entirely, however, would undermine the essentially interpretive nature of Puritan existence (if God's signs were indeed fundamentally unintelligible, then the very terms of the covenant were broken, and New England was seriously bereft indeed). Accepting testimony and attributing the shapes to the prisoner currently in the dock meant acknowledging that a fellow saint's life might not, in fact, be reliable evidence of his or her spiritual state. While this must have initially seemed the least cataclysmic conclusion, the ambiguity it introduced into a closed system of absolutely dichotomous categories was devastating.

In Bishop's case, spectral evidence was *not* in fact forced to bear the sole weight of her conviction. Yet it figures prominently in Mather's report on her trial, demonstrating the extent to which spectral representations and the necessary distinctions between neighbor or church member and shape, specter, devil, or witch occupied his mind, despite the additional evidence against her. Along with her spectral crimes, Bridget Bishop was convicted on the basis of having left proxy images of her victims in a former house: "several Poppets, made up of Rags and Hogs Brussels, with Headless Pins in them, the Pins being outward. Whereof she could give

no Account unto the Court, that was Reasonable or Tolerable" (Burr 228).
During the course of the trial, "a Jury of Women found a preternatural
Teat upon her Body; but upon a second search, within Three or four
hours, there was no such thing to be seen" (Burr 228–29); such "witches'
teats" were commonly assumed to confirm witchcraft, and their mysterious disappearance often operated to confirm their supernatural origins.[13]
This purported material evidence seems to have made the conviction
and execution of Bridget Bishop less spiritually trying for her judges than
later cases, many of which relied almost entirely on the testimony of the
afflicted. Yet Mather devotes his fullest attention to the testimony and
behavior of Bishop's alleged victims:

> There was little Occasion to prove the Witchcraft, it being Evident and
> Notorious to all Beholders. Now to fix the Witchcraft on the Prisoner at the
> Bar, the first thing used, was the Testimony of the Bewitched; whereof, sev-
> eral Testify'd, That the Shape of the Prisoner did oftentimes very grievously
> pinch them, choak them, Bite them, and Afflict them; urging them to write
> their Names in a Book, which the said Spectre called, Ours. (223)

According to testimony, the shape of Bridget Bishop refers to the "Book"
she wants her accusers to sign (presumably the "devil's book," a sort of
witches' registry) with the ambiguous pronoun "Ours." This pronoun is the
very site of contestation: Does the plural pronoun indicate Bridget Bishop's
voluntary communion with the specter, or not? The provenance of the
shape is no clearer for the testimony heard. The "communion" on Bishop's
part, to use Mather's phrase, remains frustratingly indecipherable—although in this particular case, circumstantial evidence and Bishop's history of legal transgressions tipped the scales of justice. The ambiguities
apparent in her trial, however, reveal not simply a troubling matter of exegesis, but the confutation of meaning itself. Even as the effects of her
witchcraft emerge hyper-visibly on the bodies of the accusers, they resist
definitive "reading" by the court.

   Mather, however, insists that the "Testimony of the Bewitched" is verified by the visible effects of witchcraft upon the bodies of the afflicted:

> It was Testify'd, that at the examination of the Prisoner before the Magis-
> trates, the Bewitched were extremely tortured. If she did but cast her Eyes
> on them, they were presently struck down; and this in such a manner as
> there could be no Collusion in the Business. But upon the Touch of her

Hand upon them, when they lay in their Swoons, they would immediately
Revive; and not upon the Touch of any ones else [*sic*]. Moreover, upon some
Special Actions of her Body, as the shaking of her Head, or the Turning
of her Eyes, they presently and painfully fell into the like postures. (Burr
223–24)

In this excerpt, spectral harm is transmitted across discrete bodies, erasing
the space between them. This "communion" is not, however, a realization
of the metaphorical body of the community of saints, but an intolerable
transgression perpetrated by a shape whose very suggestion undermines that
metaphorical communion. Bridget Bishop's crime is at once horrifically
visible in the writhings and suffering of the afflicted, and *indecipherable*.

Witchcraft posed a clear threat to the public life and to the social and
spiritual institutions of the Puritans of Salem Village. By undermining
the very foundations of public life and community order, however, witchcraft posed an equal if not greater threat to the individual Puritan psyche.
Mather claims that the realm of private, individual intention, what he
calls "the communion on the man's part," is the crux of the public act of
interpretation. Thus, the potential for misrepresentation—what Nancy
Ruttenburg calls "a reconceptualization of human personality as possessed
of a spectral dimension" (23)—presents the most substantial threat to Puritanism. As Boyer and Nissenbaum suggest, the events in Salem mark a
transition from a collectively understood social and religious identity into
what will become the particularized individual subjectivity associated with
the Enlightenment, a subjectivity characterized by private, internal authority over the self. They cast this transition in terms of the "private will," a
space of internal indecipherability unknown to the Puritans, or, more
accurately, one unarticulated except in terms of obedience or disobedience
to God's will and to the communal body of saints. According to Boyer and
Nissenbaum, "In an age about to pass, the assertion of *private will* posed
the direst possible threat to the stability of the community; in the age about
to arrive, it would form a central pillar on which that stability rested" (*Possessed* 109).

According to Ruttenburg, the use of spectral evidence both *refuses* to
accept and ultimately *reveals* the fundamental unknowability of the human
soul that confounds Puritanism: "In place of the cosmological binarism
of visible and invisible realms, the theory of spectral evidence effectively
posited a third realm—the domain of hybridic specters where contact
between spiritual and embodied beings (devil and witch, specter and

victim) could occur—that supplanted the space of unknowing fundamental to Puritan theology" (20–21). Spectral evidence makes that liminal spectral space "present" in a way that makes evident its presence as *absence* in
the prevailing Puritan epistemology. For Ruttenburg, the spectral presence
that makes explicit this absence is "the hidden realm of individual imagination and desire, simultaneously elicited and rejected in the performance
of spectral possession" (23)—Boyer and Nissenbaum's "private will," and
what I argue can best be identified as a crisis of self-identification that
anticipates Enlightenment subjectivity. But to read this moment as marking a shift in the very constitution of subjectivity is, as I will discuss below,
to read it in terms of the *uncanny*: both writ large in the threatened collapse
of the public system of signification, and in private terms as a fundamental threat to the structures of individual subjectivity and Puritan identity.

In seventeenth-century Salem, the crime of witchcraft is redefined.
Where once the primary concern in convicting witches had been collecting
compensation for the consequences of petty household inconveniences
or wrongful injury, the courts at Salem focused on the accused's voluntary signing of "the black man's book." This act inscribed an individual's
contract with the devil and his consent to allow the devil to represent him
spectrally: "The crime lay in the initial compact by which a person per-
mitted the devil to assume his or her shape, or in commissioning the devil
to perform particular acts of mischief" (*Possessed* 11).[14] Such *intentional*
diabolical misalliance, as well as the presence of the spectral "doubles" it
generated, specifically contradicted the necessary equivalence between the
"essence" and the "appearance" of Puritan identity, and thus threatened to
expose the inherent instability of that equivalence across other situations.
In the documents of Salem witchcraft, recognition of the self, of one's
fellow saint, or of divine acts of intervention oscillate uncannily with the
potential for *mis*recognition inhering in the witch, the spectral representation of a fellow saint, or the devil. Visual evidence is undermined by
legal and, more fundamentally, epistemological uncertainty. For example,
Bridget Bishop's "Shape" may resemble her and be thus readily "recognizable" (although, of course, that resemblance could be a devil's trick), or it
may resemble an inhuman "Monster"; the "effects" of her alleged witchcraft are highly *visible* in the postures and mimicry of the afflicted, but
remain illegible. Spectral evidence, and more specifically, the possibility of
specters assuming the shapes of the innocent as well as the guilty, subverts
the divine order that is the presumed basis of Puritan identity. The private and indecipherable space between public acts and private identity is

revealed through the twin threats of misrepresentation and misrecognition and, more fundamentally, through the threat that (mis)recognition *is* recognition, that the essential distinction does not in fact exist except by virtue of the Puritans' investment in it.

As manifested in Salem, spectral affliction involves a doubling of the spectral representation in its ambiguous connection to the person represented. Simultaneously, it erases the boundaries between the witch and the victim as the "shape" or specter transmits injury across discrete bodies, marking the witchcraft on the very body of his or her victim. Such contradictory manifestations exemplify the severity of Salem's dilemmas in Mather's account of the trial of former Salem minister George Burroughs. His account, in its reliance on completely contradictory visual evidence, is perhaps no less remarkable than the events he describes:

> [I]t was Remarkable, that whereas Biting was one of the ways which the Witches used for the vexing of the Sufferers, when they cry'd out of G. B. biting them, the print of the Teeth would be seen on the Flesh of the Complainers, and just such a sett of Teeth as G. B.'s would appear upon them, which could be distinguished from those of some other men's. (*Wonders* in Burr 216–17)

Burroughs's witchcraft makes grotesquely literal the material consequences of witchcraft and realizes its invasion of the metaphorical body of the Puritan community. Despite their hyper-legibility and correspondence to Burroughs's own teeth, however, the bite marks on the victims' bodies nevertheless cannot confidently be "read" as evidence of his signature in the devil's book.

In Freudian terms, the double is uncanny because it poses the threat of misrecognition: "The subject identifies himself with someone else, so that he is in doubt as to which his self is, or substitutes the extraneous self for his own" (234). In Salem, both the subject and his or her fellow saints, whose very identities are premised on being able to distinguish the false self from the true self (or, at least, premised on the belief that the two *are* fundamentally distinguishable), are "in doubt" as to the identities, hence the source or meaning, of both the spectral representations and the "saints" with whom they are associated. The specters themselves defy consistency: Some appear only in the material traces of invisible or disembodied forces, while others are visible (Bridget Bishop's "Monster" or her recognizable shape) and yet have "no substance" in the material world.

While Mather, in describing Burroughs's trial, struggles to reassert an equivalence between what is *seen* (the print of the teeth) and what is *known*, he fails, as the trials themselves failed, to reestablish the relationship between the signifiers and the signified of witchcraft, or to defend the fortress of Puritan theology from the looming specter of indecipherability. In attempting to establish an unarguable correspondence between Bridget Bishop's actions—the "special actions of her body"—and the postures of her accusers, as in linking spectrally transmitted bite marks to George Burroughs's "sett of Teeth [. . .] which could be distinguished from those of some other mens," Mather reveals his desperate desire to reassert the validity and viability of Puritan interpretation. But mere visible evidence, however damning, was unsatisfying without corresponding but ultimately impossible "invisible" proof.

By virtue of their binary and dichotomous representation of the world and the absolute distinctions on which their worldview relies, the Puritans anticipate that crisis of the subject that Mladen Dolar associates with the irruption of the Lacanian "real" (what is external to the subject/psyche or the symbolic order) into the everyday—the crisis of subjectivity named by the uncanny.[15] Dolar suggests that "the great philosophical pairs—essence/appearance, mind/body, subject/object, spirit/matter, etc.—can be seen as just so many transcriptions of the division between interiority and exteriority" (6) and that their threatened convergence evokes the uncanny. Lacan's term, *extimité*, the "extimate," is "simultaneously the intimate kernel and the foreign body," and is "located there where the most intimate interiority coincides with the exterior and becomes threatening, provoking horror and anxiety" (Dolar 6). In Salem, the presence of alien or external specters within the intimate communal body of the believers evokes the quintessential horror characterized as *extimité* and helps explain the violence with which even formerly respected townspeople were persecuted and condemned. The uncanny anxiety in Salem is thus produced by the convergence of the fundamental oppositions or distinctions on which identity is predicated, as well as by the collapse of the stable categories of meaning that once protected the Puritan body. The crisis at Salem threatens to reveal not only the potential misrepresentations staged by the witches in their midst but also the Puritans' more fundamental misrecognition of themselves as one side of an artificially absolute dichotomy that is maintained by their investment in it—a *mis*recognition that is, in psychological terms, the very mechanism of that identity.

In Lacanian theory, identity is created by means of representation or reflection or, more accurately, through a mechanism of *mis*recognition of that representation as the self. Subjectivity is created through the (mis)recognition of the mirror image, or *imago*, as a coherent fiction of mastery that is always provisional and potential, "an exteriority [. . .] more constituent than constituted" (Lacan 2). In his reading of Lacan, Dolar claims that "[t]he image is more fundamental than its owner: it institutes his substance, his essential being, his 'soul'" (12). The image provides a unifying fiction of the self that organizes and represents the individual as distinct from and yet acting within reality. The provisional nature of that subjectivity, however, "will always remain irreducible"—that is, *repressed*—by the individual, whose totalizing coherence *as* self is precisely what the uncanny threatens. The dependence of identity on the (mis)recognition of its own coherence—a relationship so threatening that it must be repressed—is suggested by Freud's "The Uncanny" (1919) as well. As Priscilla Wald has suggested, Freud's footnoted encounter with an "elderly gentleman," whom he fails to recognize as his own reflection, "locates uncanniness [. . .] in the experience of an altered [or unrecognized] self that calls the fundamental assumptions of what the self is and whence it derives into question" (7). These fundamental assumptions—"what the self is and whence it derives"—are precisely what witchcraft in Salem calls into question. The Puritan identity crisis at Salem thus anticipates a new and modern subjectivity as it unsettles the premise of the old one. By calling into question the repressed *fictitiousness* of the basis of Puritan identity— the Puritans' complicity in the fictional coherence of their faith-based universe—these trials permanently undermined the coherence of the Puritan way of life.

The uncanny *experience* in Salem is therefore the intimation, however fleeting, of the fundamental instability of the categories on which meaning and existence are based. Freud names the uncanny as "the return of the repressed"; that is, as the reemergence of "everything [. . .] that ought to have remained secret and hidden but has come to light" (225). His definition echoes the terms of Salem's crisis: He posits the uncanny moment as one in which two ostensibly opposing figures, elements, or definitions appear to coalesce, or in which one is mistaken for the other, revealing the fundamental instability of their distinction.[16] In Salem's unique historiography, however, the uncanny returns not only as a crisis of the individual subject but also as a threat to the mechanism of misrecognition by which Puritan society (mis)understands its own communal consensus as fixed and divinely ordained.

Mather's account, in which he claims to "Report matters not as an Advocate but as an Historian" (Burr 214), attempts to reassert the certainty of the Puritan order, yet fails to convince us, or perhaps himself, that the conventional Puritan explanations fit the troubling occurrences. His imposed certainty rings false, particularly in light of his own struggles with the meaning and legality of spectral evidence. He struggles to erase any lingering uncertainty as to the accuracy of the official verdict by presenting the trial's outcome and meaning as self-evident: The witchcraft had "little Occasion" to be proved, "it being Evident and Notorious to all Beholders." Mather further claims that "there could be no Collusion in the business" of Bridget Bishop's agency in the victims' afflictions, although nothing at the trial has precluded that possibility. Mather's narrative presents Bishop's guilt as a foregone and incontrovertible conclusion—yet it is largely his narration that works to establish that inevitability, merely by insisting upon it.

Most significant in these accounts is Mather's reluctant contribution to the meaning he expects and requires be found in the material. Mather insists on the absoluteness of Bishop's guilt even though the spectral evidence to which he refers is no more conclusive here than elsewhere in the trials; the legal system lacks a means for proving definitively the source of the afflictions beyond the circumstantial evidence provided by the sufferings of the accusers in the presence of the accused. Mather's insistence on the certainty of Bishop's crimes, then, functions as a kind of hyper-denial of his contribution to the meaning of the events unfolding around him; his writings reveal his strained efforts to conform to a Puritan belief structure that ordains his role as purely interpretive. Similarly, in the letter to John Foster discussed earlier in this essay, Mather's assertions about spectral evidence frame theological certitude as publicly derived, as the *absence* of a definitive public or communal objection; the existence of devils and diabolical specters is asserted, tellingly, as something "I suppose nobody doubts." This odd phrase, like Mather's narrative agency in his report of Bishop's trial, reveals the extent to which meaning is in fact predicated on the participation of those who expect to be merely its receivers. Puritan theology and semiology define meaning as unidirectional, emanating from the divine and directed toward a community of believers responsible for deciphering it. Since the primary motivating force in Puritan life is the interpretation of God's providential order, witchcraft not only confounds the *act* of interpretation but also subverts the very premise of interpretive effort. Expressing certainty in terms of the *absence* of public doubt,

Mather inadvertently articulates the fragility of Puritan ideology, whose fixed and absolute oppositions (elect/damned, sacred/diabolical, invisible/visible, saint/witch), are precisely what the competing discourses of witchcraft threaten.

The trials, rather than providing a cathartic experience that could reassert the legibility and viability of the Puritan order, ended instead by order of the governor, acting on the advice of ministers who could no longer tolerate the travesty of spectral evidence. The end of the trials, then, marks not a resolution but a retreat. The crisis at Salem stands as a public, collective experience in which systems of meaning are not only disrupted but *perceived* as imperiled, that is, as a culture's encounter with the contingency of its organizing principles. In this, Salem's fraught acts of interpretation echo the characteristics of the uncanny and thus expose the links between the public crisis and the threat to Puritan subjectivity. The semiological displacements that confounded the Puritan system of meaning threatened to disconnect the mechanism that rendered the invisible world legible via the visible world, and thus threatened the very distinctions by means of which individual subjectivity and the public order were experienced and understood.

The uncanny may also help explain our ongoing fascination with the events in Salem. Freud's essay, in particular, suggests that the uncanny is often an aesthetic experience, a set of effects synthetically or artistically produced: *"There are many more means of creating uncanny effects in fiction than in life"* (Freud 249). In Salem, however, the uncanny is not merely aesthetic; instead, it involves a discomfiting encounter with the necessary fiction of one's own subjectivity. Salem compels us precisely because it is *not* reducible to an aestheticized effect. Instead it stands unique as a genuine historical confrontation between a society and its fundamental fragility—the fictitiousness of the terms by which a community understands and experiences itself. Salem's trial documents record an encounter with the tenuous terms of Puritan existence. By extension, they provide us with an intimation of the precariousness of our own subjectivity, albeit buffered by three hundred years.

The enduring fascination of Salem suggests that what makes such events truly scary is their capacity to reveal and thus undermine the terms by which we experience and understand ourselves. Further, these events redefine a haunting or an uncanny experience as one that involves both the potential dislocation or even erasure of individual subjectivity and a threat to the social, political, and epistemological order by which that subjectivity is experienced. The Puritan crisis (re)produces for its modern readers a pleasurably chilling version of a seventeenth-century encounter with the contingency of selfhood even as it evokes for its audience the intimidation of a less pleasurable encounter with the fragility of our own identities. Salem continues to fascinate not simply because of its witchcraft, or even because it represents some sort of encounter with the supernatural, but because it offers a glimpse of a society's encounter with meaninglessness, and thereby confronts us with the necessity of our individual participation in the consensual fictions that create and maintain meaning. Haunted narratives like that of Salem instruct us in making fictions real, by demonstrating that we ourselves produce reality by our participation in its overarching fictions. Salem reminds us that subjectivity is inevitably haunted by its own insubstantiality and that we ourselves are produced and reproduced through the material consequences of the fictions in which we believe.

NOTES

1. Throughout the essay, I have used the modern-year designations. At the time of the events in Salem, the calendar year began in March, so that January and February—the final months of 1691, and the first months of Salem's troubles—would actually have fallen in 1692, by our reckoning.

2. There are several narrative accounts of the events in Salem. Marion L. Starkey's *The Devil in Massachusetts* is perhaps the most familiar to nonhistorians; her study of the hysterical, delirious, or deluded conduct of the accusers—a small group of girls and young women living in a patriarchal and highly regimented society—suggests a psychosexual component to the events while emphasizing their narrativity: "I have tried to uncover the classic dramatic form of the story itself, for here is real 'Greek tragedy,' with a beginning, a middle, and an end [. . .]. Most important of all, I have tried to review the records in the light of the findings of modern psychology, particularly of the Freudian school" (xxvii). Paul Boyer and Stephen Nissenbaum's *Salem Possessed* (1974), hereafter cited as *Possessed*, attends to the socioeconomic discrepancies among the accusers and the accused, and to the intimately related power politics of Salem Town and Salem Village. Their work in "deciphering that inner history" (x) of the events also explains the rancorous factional debates over municipal autonomy and the selection and payment of a minister—Samuel Parris, whose daughter and niece were the first afflicted. Nancy Ruttenburg's *Democratic Personality* (1998) offers a comprehensive overview of both historical and modern documents; see especially 31–62. Ruttenburg's argument emphasizes the antiauthoritarian effects of the crisis, which "articulated a new understanding of the representational possibilities of human personality as they were illuminated by the establishment of unorthodox relationships to social and theological authority"; she considers these new relationships "the origins of democratic personality" (72). I have drawn on the latter two works for much of the historical overview in this essay. As for contemporary accounts, Deodat Lawson's *A Brief and True Narrative of [. . .] Witchcraft at Salem Village [. . .]* (1692) and Cotton

Mather's somewhat apologetic *Wonders of the Invisible World* (1693) are followed by Robert Calef's *More Wonders of the Invisible World* (1700), which is highly critical of the conduct of the authorities (Cotton Mather chief among them) involved in the trials. Cotton Mather's *Magnalia Christi Americana* (1702) offers a rebuttal in his life of Governor William Phips in the appendix to Book II, "Pietas in Patriam"; see especially 325, ff. For comprehensive collections, George Lincoln Burr's *Narratives of the Witchcraft Cases 1648–1706* (1914) includes an extensive sampling of primary materials; Boyer and Nissenbaum's three-volume *The Salem Witchcraft Papers* (1977) collects verbatim transcripts of the actual trials, materials originally compiled and transcribed in 1938 for the Works Project Administration under the direction of Archie N. Frost. David D. Hall's *Witch-hunting in Seventeenth-Century New England* (1991) includes accounts of bewitchings from 1638 to 1692, while his introduction offers brief discussions of the roles of gender and of interpersonal conflict in the accusations (5–7), as well as a concise account of the events.

3. Winthrop's famous sermon to the Massachusetts Bay settlers, "A Modell of Christian Charity," articulates a working model for the ideal Puritan society, in which the individual members function as parts of a body. The simultaneously hierarchical and organic model enabled by this metaphor comes to symbolize both the good and the bad of the Puritan endeavor. The community is conceptualized as a physical body and an economy of obligation, as well as through reference to Christian imagery in which Christ is the head of the church, while his followers are the body.

4. See Starkey, 15–18, on the Putnams, mother and daughter, and their alienation from others in Salem. See also the discussion of the Putnam family in Boyer and Nissenbaum, *Possessed*, chaps. 5–6:110–52.

5. For a discussion of the factional dynamics at work in Salem Town and Salem Village, especially the conflict over the issues of church membership and concomitant taxation, see Boyer and Nissenbaum, *Possessed*, chap. 4: 80–109, as well as the introduction to their *The Salem Witchcraft Papers*, vol. 1, esp. 5–7, 13–18. As mentioned in the previous note, they also provide a detailed account of the plight of the Putnams and others threatened by the new capitalism, *Possessed*, chaps. 5–6:110–52; chap. 7: 153–78 explores Samuel Parris's reactionary relationship to his ministry and his congregation, as well as his effects on the conflicts in Salem.

6. Mary Beth Norton, in *In the Devil's Snare*, has recently proposed yet another interpretation. Based on the presence in Essex County of many refugees from fierce fighting during King William's War, she asserts a connection between the trauma those settlers experienced and the virulence of Salem's witchcraft episode. Norton observes close parallels between descriptions of wartime raids and atrocities on the Maine frontiers and the activities associated with local witches. In addition, she locates several key figures from the Salem/Essex County trials in the Northern territories at the time of the hostilities—most notably George Burroughs, the erstwhile Salem minister, and Mercy Lewis, the Putnam's maidservant. Her argument is fascinating, and does not contradict my assertion that these public crises were registered in psychological frictions. In fact, her discussion of the discursive similarities between descriptions of the hostile "red men" of the frontier and the "men in black" who haunted Salem's afflicted suggests a future realm for me to explore. The overlap between these spectral and physical enemies reveals the anxiety that characterized the Puritans' response to external

threats and demonstrates the psychological pressure imposed by their allegorical interpretive project.

7. The ambiguity of New England's legal and theological position certainly contributed to the general anxiety of the late seventeenth-century Puritan experience. In 1684 British authorities had revoked the original charter in a dispute over religious tolerance—or lack thereof. The replacement administration was overthrown in 1689, and in the following years the colony had made a considerable effort to have "a new" colonial charter and a recognized legal government instated. Thus at the time of the earliest accusations in Salem, the colony was in a kind of legal limbo, lacking the magisterial authority that would allow it to try cases. Governor Phips arrived in May 1692 with a new charter and created a Court of Oyer and Terminer comprising members of his own advisory council; he named William Stoughton, the lieutenant governor, as chief justice. See *Possessed*, 6–7, as well as Phips's own account; see also the "Letters of Governor Phips," October 12, 1692, and February 21, 1693, in Burr, 196–202.

8. See also *Possessed*, 9–10; Increase Mather's, "Postscript" to *Cases of Conscience Concerning Evil Spirits Personating Men* (1693). Cotton Mather's letter to John Foster (August 17, 1692), in Boyer and Nissenbaum's *Salem-Village Witchcraft*, 118–20, is discussed later in this essay; the source is hereafter cited *SVW*.

9. While this put an end to the frenzy of accusations and executions, it did little to heal the community or resolve the tensions that witchcraft had ignited. Boyer and Nissenbaum suggest that Samuel Parris's replacement, Joseph Green, played a key role in smoothing over the tensions in Salem Town and Salem Village, as did the creation of several new local parishes, which dispersed the two factions and dispelled conflict (*Possessed* 217–21). Reparations were eventually paid to most of the families of those executed; furthermore, at least one chronicler, Charles W. Upham, has suggested in his two-volume compilation that subsequent remorse among the authorities led to the destruction of the trial records, with their damning evidence of judicial fallibility. See Ruttenburg, 407–8 n. 9.

10. Kibbey's essay provides a detailed discussion of the "social and religious significance of the concept of witchcraft in the thought of Puritan men" (129) who, by virtue of the power of the Puritan patriarchal system, "acquired a power commensurate with the witch's" (141). Because the misfortunes of his dependents were read as "one more index to the state of his soul" (140), the actions of the adult Puritan male had the "indirect power [. . .] to literally destroy the lives of people around him" (141). Her discussion is particularly useful in tracing the effects of witchcraft lore and popular knowledge on Puritan theology. She also suggests the centrality of the Putnam family to Salem's events, noting that after a sequence of setbacks culminating in the affliction of his daughter and wife, Thomas Putnam found the possibility of his being even indirectly responsible for their condition "so undesirable or implausible that [he] refused the self-interpretation it offered him, and reverted instead to the older explanation of events as the *maleficia* of witchcraft" (143).

11. Despite the dependence on spectral evidence, the court's burden was eased by the confessions of many of the accused witches. One of the ironies of the trials is that most of those who, out of fear, exhaustion, or confusion, confessed to their crimes were imprisoned and later pardoned. Those who remained confident of their own innocence and expressed the truth of their consciences were likely to be found guilty

and executed anyway. See, e.g., documents from the trial of the respected village matriarch Rebecca Nurse, in *SVW*, chap. 2: 18–35, the brief discussion of her case in *Possessed*, 147–51, or Starkey, 162–69.

12. Nancy Ruttenburg offers a compelling reading of spectral evidence and its impact on Puritan theology and epistemology; see chap. 1, esp. 57–69. While our discussions of Salem are complementary in many ways, her larger project lies in the articulation of democracy and "democratic personality" in "isolation from liberal philosophy." She sees its roots instead in a "distinctive subjectivity" that emerges by "announcing itself through the exercise of an authoritative, public voice unconnected to rational debate." She identifies the origins of "a dynamic symbolic system or theater, historically realized in an untheorized and irrational practice of compulsive public utterance" in the epistemological crisis at Salem and its antiauthoritarian redistribution of social power (3).

13. See, e.g., *Possessed*, 13.

14. Because the notion of the legal contract was central to a Puritan community founded by virtue of its compact, or covenant, with God, the diabolical parody of this contract implicit in "the black man's book" and the compact with the devil had particular and disturbing resonance. It thus functioned as a sort of photographic negative, a reverse image of the contractual basis of Puritan identity.

15. In his explication, Dolar is specifically interested in the Lacanian uncanny as the experience of a post-Enlightenment, Cartesian subject with "*a specific dimension of the uncanny that emerges with modernity*" (7), suggesting that "in pre-modern societies the dimension of the uncanny was largely covered (and veiled) by the area of the sacred and untouchable." Since the basis of uncanny experience, in Dolar's formulation, is the threatened convergence of binary opposites, I argue that the Puritans participate in what is best described as an uncanny crisis, and which thus anticipates the modern subject.

16. He illustrates this through his famous discussion of the German term "*unheimlich*," which means not only uncanny, unfamiliar, or strange, but also secret, or private, and thus familiar, or "*heimlich*." In other words, *unheimlich* and *heimlich* are both antonym and synonym, equivalent and opposite. In their "opposition" inheres the ever-present threat of their convergence, which undermines the distinction between them and destabilizes the system of meaning that affirms or requires their difference.

WORKS CITED

Boyer, Paul, and Stephen Nissenbaum. *Salem Possessed: The Social Origins of Witchcraft*. Cambridge: Harvard University Press, 1974.

———, eds. *The Salem Witchcraft Papers: Verbatim Transcripts of the Legal Documents of the Salem Witchcraft Outbreak of 1692*. 3 vols. New York: Da Capo, 1977.

———. *Salem-Village Witchcraft: A Documentary Record of Local Conflict in Colonial New England*. Boston: Northeastern University Press, 1993.

Burr, George Lincoln, ed. *Narratives of the Witchcraft Cases, 1648–1706*. New York: Charles Scribner's Sons, 1914.

Calef, Robert. *More Wonders of the Invisible World; or, The Wonders of the Invisible World, Display'd in Five Parts*. London: published for N. Hillar and J. Collyer, 1700.

Dolar, Mladen. "'I Shall Be with You on Your Wedding-Night': Lacan and the Uncanny." *October* 58 (Fall 1991): 5–23.

Freud, Sigmund. "The Uncanny." In vol. 17 of *The Standard Edition of the Complete Psychological Works of Sigmund Freud*. Translated by James Strachey, with Anna Freud, Alix Strachey, and Alan Tyson, 218–52. Reprint, 1955. London: Hogarth and the Institute of Psycho-Analysis, 1986.

Hall, David D. *Witch-hunting in Seventeenth-Century New England*. Boston: Northeastern University Press, 1991.

Kibbey, Ann. "Mutations of the Supernatural: Witchcraft, Remarkable Providences, and the Power of Puritan Men." *American Quarterly* 34 (1982): 125–48.

Lacan, Jacques. "The Mirror Stage as Formative of the Function of the I as Revealed in Psychoanalytic Experience." In *Ecrits: A Selection*. Translated by Alan Sheridan, 1–7. New York: Norton, 1977.

Lawson, Deodat. *A Brief and True Narrative of Some Remarkable Passages Relating to Sundry Persons Afflicted by Witchcraft at Salem Village, Which Happened from the Nineteenth of March to the Fifth of April, 1692*. Boston: published for Benjamin Harris, 1692.

Mather, Cotton. "Letter to John Foster, A Member of the Governor's Council (August 17, 1692)" in Boyer and Nissenbaum, *Salem-Village Witchcraft*, 118–19.

———. *Magnalia Christi Americana*. 2 vols. Edited by Kenneth B. Murdock. Cambridge: Harvard University Press, 1977.

———. *Memorable Providences, Relating to Witchcraft and Possessions* (1689). In Burr, 89–143.

———. *The Wonders of the Invisible World* (1693). In Burr, 205–51.

Mather, Increase. "Postscript." *Cases of Conscience Concerning Evil Spirits Personating Men*. Boston: 1693.

Norton, Mary Beth. *In the Devil's Snare*. New York: Knopf, 2002.

Phips, William. "Letters of Governor Phips." In Burr, 196–202.

Ruttenburg, Nancy. *Democratic Personality: Popular Voice and the Trial of American Authorship*. Stanford: Stanford University Press, 1998.

Starkey, Marion L. *The Devil in Massachusetts: A Modern Inquiry into the Salem Witch Trials*. New York: Time, 1963.

Upham, Charles W. *Salem Witchcraft*. 2 vols. 1867. Reprint. Williamstown, Ma.: Corner House Publishers, 1971.

Wald, Priscilla. *Constituting Americans: Cultural Anxiety and Narrative Form*. Durham: Duke University Press, 1995.

Winthrop, John. "A Modell of Christian Charity." In *The Humble Request of the Massachusetts Puritans, and A Modell of Christian Charity by John Winthrop*. 1630. Edited by S. E. Morison, 7–21. Boston: Old South Association, 1916.

Friendly Ghosts

Celebrations of the Living Dead
in Early New England

JEFFREY HAMMOND

The experiential power of the "invisible world" in early New England—
the presumed ubiquity of witches, satanic apparitions, and disturbing
omens—is well known. During the Salem trials the possibility of "spectral
evidence" was never questioned, only its judicial reliability. Given the
modern fascination with such darker wonders as witchcraft, we often forget that the invisible world mirrored the ethical dualism that Puritans also
projected onto its visible counterpart. Although outbreaks of the demonic
were especially dramatic, spectral supporters were also thought to be abroad
in the land, countering Satan's influence and working toward the comfort
and salvation of the faithful.

On the face of it, this seems a highly "un-Puritan" notion. Early New
Englanders, who repudiated such agents of intercession in Roman Catholic tradition, insisted that Christ was the sole source of gracious comfort.
In actual practice, however, they augmented the austerity of *Christus solus*
by creating their own collection of benign spirits based on the belief that
every elect soul was a "saint." Although their theology insisted that the truly
saved soul could not be distinguished with absolute certainty, the passing
of demonstrably pious believers inevitably encouraged their retrospective
canonization. Surely the lives of such souls exemplified sanctified lives—
and just as surely, they continued to work toward the same happy outcome
for their survivors. Indeed, ensuring a constant supply of such spirit guides
was a primary function of one of the most widespread and stylized discursive performances in Puritan culture: the funeral elegy. Elegies made
the onslaughts of Satan seem more bearable by assuring mourners that the
invisible world remained well stocked with friendly ghosts who longed for
the redemption of the living.[1]

Elegy made the invisible world both more tangible and less threaten-ing by representing the dead as otherworldly supporters whose sanctity remained as a stimulus of the inner process by which salvation became possible. The starting point of that process was also the ideal outcome of Puritan mourning: heartfelt repentance. This was the only grief that did any good, the only sorrow that saved—and it consisted of moving the be-reaved from lamenting a particular death to lamenting the sin that caused all death. Richard Sibbes argued that sorrow, if it led to repentance, was actually "an happy estate and condition" because it enhanced the mourner's chances for salvation (268). Redemptive mourning also lightened one's grief. "The more a man can mourn for his sins," Sibbes explained, "the less he will mourn for other matters" (270). The key to instilling the sorrow of repentance was to commemorate not the deceased individual so much as the sanctity that made him or her worth commemorating to begin with. Elegy thus reinforced what was, in the Puritan view, the only defensible justification for lamenting a saint's apotheosis. God's people were to be mourned precisely because they *were* God's people. "*When the Saints die let us mourn*," Samuel Willard proclaimed, "And there is no greater Argu-ment to be found that we should excite our selves to mourn by, then the remembrance that they were *Saints*" (16). The rapid increase of funerary ritual in New England during the latter half of the seventeenth century attests to the efficacy with which mourning promoted this saintly ideal.[2]

Essential to proper commemoration was the portrayal of the deceased in terms of the stylized paradigm of a saved soul who would "live on" as a gracious exemplum to survivors. The elegists' repeated invocations of this paradigm resulted in an endless supply of "ghosts" to be confronted with love and not fear. Who could fail to cherish a soul who was, as Urian Oakes portrays Thomas Shepard II, "Lovely, Worthy, Peerless," "Precious, Pleas-ant," "Learned, Prudent, Pious, Grave, and True," and "a Faithful Friend" (Meserole 213)? What's more, who could resist the chance to *become* such a self? Benjamin Tompson declares that he has "penned" his elegy on sister-in-law Mary "for the imitation of the living" (Murdock 3). Samuel Danforth offers Thomas Leonard as a similar model of piety: "GOD grant that all of his Posterity / May imitate his Virtues, and may say / His GOD shall be our GOD" (Meserole 490). The *imitatio Christi* at the heart of each poem was thus enabled through a more immediate and accessible *imitatio sancti*—holiness exemplified in someone who was once fully human and who thus offered less intimidating precedent. Paul had pioneered this use of a holy life by presenting himself as a means of access to the Savior: "Be ye followers of me, even as I also am of Christ" (1 Cor. 11:1). John Fiske offers John Cotton as just such a supporter from beyond the grave, a guide to the treacherous "passage" though the "worlds ocean": "now grant O G[od that we] / may follow afte[r him]" (Meserole 188). Indeed, the elegiac framing of such figures made it seem that heaven was filling up with well-wishers. With each death and commemoration, the trackless wilderness of the world seemed offset by yet another clearly blazed trail to glory.[3]

Elegists frequently made the dead speak this comfort directly, in otherworldly voices that recall Milton's "Saints above," whose singing dries Lycidas's tears; and the heavenly call—perhaps from Michael and perhaps from Lycidas himself—to "Weep no more, wofull shepherds." Benjamin Tompson has Edmund Davie assert his status as heavenly pathfinder with typical directness: "I'm now arriv'd the soul desired Port," Davie asserts; "I've hitt the very Place I wisht at heart, / I'm fixt for ever: Never thence to part" (Meserole 223). John Wilson has Joseph Brisco, a drowning victim, offer his death as a catalyst for reconsidering, from the perspective of faith, what it really meant to be delivered. "What if I was so soon in Waters drown'd," Brisco asks, God "heard my cry / And lookt upon me with a gracious eye" (Meserole 384–85). Depicted as pioneers to bliss, the dead became celestial comforters who urged their own emulation. Cotton Mather has schoolmaster Ezekiel Cheever "dart his Wishes" for teachers to instill piety in their pupils so "That you like me, with joy may meet them here" (92). Mary Gerrish, John Danforth affirms, only "craves, by Friends here left / for to be Visited," and "would Rejoyce to see them all / at th' Heav'nly Table fed" (Meserole 318). Taylor's Samuel Hooker extends the same hope: "In Faith, Obedience, Patience, walk a while / And thou shalt soon leape o're the parting Stile, / And come to God, Christ, Angells, Saints, & Mee" (*Minor Poetry* 122).

Readers of elegy found themselves being coaxed to glory not only by Christ and the clergy, but by an ever-increasing company of souls with whom they once shared life's trials. Like the drowned Lycidas, poised as the "Genius of the shoar" to aid "all that wander in that perilous flood," the dead were eulogized as localized (dis)embodiments of the Holy Spirit, their continued usefulness ensured as recapitulations of Paul's willing martyrdom: "Yea, and if I be offered upon the sacrifice and service of your faith, I joy, and rejoice with you all" (Phil. 2:17). By textualizing the dead in order to keep them within a community that would continue to benefit from their example, elegy strengthened the survivor's sense of an ongoing dialogue with heaven. Elegists frequently highlighted this exchange by addressing the deceased, as when Taylor tells Charles Chauncy that "thou, where thou wouldst be, art" (*Minor Poetry* 35). Mather made the heaven/earth exchange explicit by dropping the usual one-way speech in favor of a dialogue between Nathanael Collins and his survivors, including "an *Elect Lady*, there / Grov'ling in Ashes, with dishev'led Hair"—none other than "*the Church of* Middletown," "*Set in the* midst of *swoons and sobs and shrieks*" (64–65). Invoking an ongoing communication of piety between heaven and earth, elegy encouraged readers in their struggle against grief and sin by offering foretastes of a joy that only the dead could know. Collins himself speaks the comfort that such words from beyond the grave could bring: "Be *glad* that I am here, and after hye" (73).[4]

The death of every pious soul was a good death. John Wilson proclaimed such peace even for the melancholic William Tompson of Braintree, who voices his own reward "Of joys & Consolations / Unspeakably posest" (Murdock 17). By shifting the pastoral *locus amoenus* from this world to the next, the Puritan elegy celebrated the deceased's translation from a physical state construed as illusory, and thus profoundly "fictive," to a spiritual dimension construed as "real." For Puritan readers, these poems confirmed celestial apotheoses that were taken as literal fact: Although elegists employed clearly recognizable metaphors to describe the saint's victory, the resulting poem was not read metaphorically. The elegist ensured that death had no more dominion over the poem than it presumably had in fact (Rom. 6:9). And because the paradigmatic self that was commemorated in all elegies was potentially nascent in survivors, the dead offered something more than good advice from beyond the grave. At root they offered *selves* from beyond the grave, completed versions of the mourner's hoped-for identity. When Taylor proclaimed death's separation of David Dewey's soul from his body, he was invoking what William Ames called the "double form" of the true believer: "that of sin, and that of grace, for perfect sanctification is not found in this life" (Ames 170). By celebrating the dichotomized dead, elegy encouraged mourners to claim the saintly duality for themselves. To be sure, the fact of death confronted survivors with the unreliability of their own dust, the carnal dimension of selfhood that constantly impeded sanctification. But to hear words like those uttered by Mather's Collins—"Souls, follow me" (73)—was to be reminded, once again, of *another* dimension of identity that echoed Collins's glory, however faintly. After praying for God to "Save ev'ry soul that reads this Elegy," Mather proclaimed, as directly and concisely as possible, how the prayer might come true: "Like COLLINS let us live, like COLLINS dy" (74).

Although saving faith could no be mimicked, elegists helped bridge the
gap between the living and the dead by confirming that the deceased's
experience had been similar to the reader's. When describing how such
saints achieved glory, elegists often took pains to assure survivors that the
dead had struggled too. If the reader's anxious present could be equated,
however tentatively, with the deceased's earthly past, then the deceased's
celestial present could be recast as a hopeful harbinger of the reader's
future. Taylor thus assures his readers that Samuel Hooker, for all his glory,
was once beset by spiritual turmoil as difficult as theirs. The earthly
Hooker's inner life had been "A Stage of War, Whereon the Spirits Sword
/ Hewd down the Hellish foes that did disturb" (*Minor Poetry* 117). Like
the pastoral "Saint" who counsels "Soul" in Taylor's *Gods Determina-
tions,* the dead offered supremely comforting testimony: For all the doubts
that plague the earthly believer, "'Twas so with me" (*Poems* 436). Taylor
records the presence of exemplary turmoil in the saintly Dewey, whose
carnal element was nonetheless "A Seat of Sin, Corruption's nest"—a self
that was, by theological and experiential definition, "True only to Un-
truth, and truthless view, / Unfaithfull, Stubborn, truly all Untrue: / Backward to Good" ("Edward Taylor's Elegy" 83, 84). It was "easier," Taylor
confirms, "to bring / Bears to the Stake" than to make the carnal self "cease
to Sin."[5]

William Tompson's chronic depression provided an especially vivid example of the exemplary struggle with doubt. John Wilson exploited the
opportunity to the fullest when he had Tompson confess that "sumtimes
I did think, / In midst of my temptacions / I utterly should sink." It was
only through God's help, Wilson's Tompson concedes, that "with violenc /
My self I did not kill" (Murdock 14). Troubled readers could take heart:
If so tortured a believer could persevere in his faith, they could surely
sustain the sorrow prompted by his death. As an objection to God's will
in taking a beloved life, grief was a kind of sin. And because a sinless
state was not attainable in this life, elegists did not represent sorrow as a
state that could be completely overcome. The closure normally associated
with elegy was consistently deferred, projected onto the next life and fully
available only to those gracious figures whose obsequies were being performed. Sorrow, after all, was a manifestation of the sin that defined the
human condition. Indeed, merely to exist in the world was to be in a state
of mourning: Sorrow had less to do with loss than with the mere fact of
being alive. Elegy thus redirected the mourner's search for comfort toward
an anticipated cessation of what Puritans saw as a deeper grief: the larger

healing of a self that was, like Taylor's Dewey, *already* "spoild" and rent "asunder" by sin ("Edward Taylor's Elegy" 83).

New England's friendly ghosts modeled a gracious perspective not just on death but on dying. Many elegies contain stylized accounts of peaceful deaths that offered a dehortative contrast to the grief-stricken panic of the living. In a popular manual on preparing for death, Edward Pearse confirmed the widespread belief that "in a Dying Hour the Devil is most fierce and terrible in his Assaults and Temptations upon the Soul" (10). The elegist's report of a "good death," which proved that the saint had withstood this final onslaught, was sufficiently common to find its way into a satirical elegiac recipe that Benjamin Franklin published in his brother's newspaper as the deceased's "last Words" and "dying Expressions" (22). In depicting his sister-in-law Mehetabel Woodbridge's passing, Taylor presents just the sort of utterance that Franklin satirized: "Come, one more Pray're, & Then.—said shee as tho' / She should be where she would bee. Ending so" (*Minor Poetry* 126). Whether they spoke at the point of death or from the lofty perspective of heaven, the dead were made to demonstrate their fluency in the "New Words" that Taylor anticipated at his own death and glorification (*Poems* 49). As an anonymous poet has Lydia Minot confirm, "New Light, new Love, new Joy me now do fill, / New Robes I have, new Company, new Skill / To sing th' new Song" (Winslow 7). Deathbed utterances dramatized the saint's transition to this celestial way of speaking. Taylor records Dewey's response to strong winds as evidence of his pious readiness to leave the world: "*The Wind is high*, quoth thee, / *But by to Morrow I'st above it be!*" ("Edward Taylor's Elegy" 83). Taylor provides similar witness to the final hours of Samuel Hooker, whose otherworldly perspective emerges in his "holy Counsill" and "Death Bed Charges." Looking down at his numb hands and arms, Hooker proclaims "They are Dead, you see, and I / Have done with them" (*Minor Poetry* 119).

Nicholas Noyes's poem for Abigail Mather clarifies the didactic function of the good death as an *ars moriendi* performed for the benefit of survivors. After thirty weeks of illness and "*Fervent Pray'r*," Mather's "*Faith* and *Patience* t'was to Try, / And Learn *Us* how to *Live* and *Dy*" (Meserole 284). This gracious manner of dying—the eager embrace of an identity already "dead"—invested deathbed speech with prophetic status. Cotton Mather took immense comfort from his wife's final words: "I faint, till thy last words to mind I call; / Rich Words! Heav'n, Heav'n will make amends for all" (44). In a headnote to John Wilson's anagram on William Tompson, William's son Joseph claims that his father's dying words were "love the lamb, love, love the lamb" (Murdock 12). Elizabeth Tompson's last words, as recorded by Benjamin Tompson, provide equal witness to a gracious leave taking: "Sweet mother, close mine eyes & turn aside, / My Jesus sends for me" (Murdock 11). And John Cotton attributes similarly comforting words to his daughter Sara: "Pray, my Dear Father, Let me now go Home!" (Meserole 382).[6]

These vignettes of deathbed stoicism, even joy, brought obvious comfort to readers fearful of what Philip Pain called "So great a Change" (Meserole 290). With deep feeling and evident pride, the elder Thomas Shepard recorded in his diary that his second wife "continued praying until the last hour of her death," clear evidence that "she was fit to die long before she did die." Joanna Shepard's last words, as Shepard preserved them, were "Lord, though I [am] unworthy; Lord, one word, one word" (71). When John Saffin's son Simon died of smallpox at thirteen, his father followed an elegy he entered into his journal with the assertion that what "Crowneth all the Rest" of his son's gifts was better expressed in "his own language" (21). Near the end, when the doctor asked Simon Saffin "how he did," the boy replied, "never better in all my life." When asked why, he answered, "Because I shall be blessed to all Eternity"—a claim he defended by saying that "Jesus Christ hath told me so." Saffin reports with obvious pride that his son "continued with Soul-Ravishing Expressions till his speech faild him" (22). An anonymous poet confirmed similar peace for the venerable John Alden of Plymouth and Duxbury, who "with St. *Paul,* his *course* now *finished,* / Unclothed, is quietly put to bed [. . .] His Family and Christian friends he blest / Before he did betake himself to rest" (Winslow 13). The explicit link with Paul's assertion that "I have finished my course, I have kept the faith" (2 Tim. 4:7) reflects a deathbed conflation of personal and biblical subjectivities that is common in these poems. A striking example appears in Taylor's elegy for Zecharia Symmes, "this aged Nazarite" who utters the deathbed cry, "my Head! me head!" (*Minor Poetry* 22). Although these words hardly constitute an affirmation of peace, Taylor could not have missed their precise echo of the words spoken by the Shunammite's son, stricken in the fields and raised by Elisha (2 Kings 4:19). It is impossible to know whether Symmes actually spoke these words that Taylor then quoted for their biblical overtones, or whether the poet assimilated Symmes's words to the biblical text. But elegy, like the Gospels, spoke to spiritual rather than literal reality: Taylor's readers would have considered that the poet had gotten the resurrective significance of the passing exactly right.

Such scenes underscore the ambiguous relationship between the "real" and the "fictive" in these poems, an issue that emerges with particular clarity in elegies written in the deceased's voice. In Wilson's poem for William Tompson, for instance, the poet allows the celestial perspective to be conveyed through an authoritative voice represented as issuing directly from beyond the grave. "Do not acount me lost," Tompson proclaims, "in his righteousness I stood / Before my father just" (Murdock 15, 17). To frame an elegy as the deceased's self-elegy was, of course, a device that no reader would have taken literally. But Puritan mourners would not have seen the poem as a "fiction" either. They would have regarded it as a real message from the real Tompson—words he would surely say if he could be heard. Ironically, the credibility of Wilson's poem was enhanced by its frank artifice, by the ploy of a dead man's talking. The monitory advantage of having the dead speak their own obsequies was clear: Who better to articulate the salvific reversal of life and death?

Samuel Torrey embodies the gracious inversion in the figure of William Tompson: "Wele not lament his timely Death, for why / Twas death to live, his life to dye" (Silverman 144). Building on Paul's statement that for the believer death had no sting and the grave no victory (1 Cor. 15:55), Edward Pearse confirmed that for the redeemed death was transformed utterly, from the "King of Terrors" to a "King of Comforts" (149). Taylor, who owned a copy of Pearse's treatise, dramatized this perceptual shift by calling the standard iconography of death a sham: "The Painter lies who pensills death's Face grim / With White bare butter Teeth, bare staring bones, / With Empty Eyeholes, Ghostly Lookes." While the skull retained full appropriateness for an unregenerate understanding of death, the elect soul saw death as "Tamde, Subdude, Washt fair" by the power of Christ's sacrifice: "For thou hast farely Washt Deaths grim grim face / And made his Chilly finger-Ends drop grace" (*Poems* 55). In the same poem Taylor proclaims the grave to be "a Down bed now made for your clay," an image recalling the "bed Christ did perfume" in Anne Bradstreet's "As Weary Pilgrim" (295). Survivors who could achieve this perspective—and elegy helped them do so—found that their thinking had already moved closer to that of the commemorated dead. This was the perspective of someone, as Pearse confirmed, who "has all things ready for a dying hour." Such a person "sees Death to be a conquered Enemy, an Enemy conquered by the Death of Christ; and so is carried above the fear of it" (22).[7]

Death's terror to the natural sensibilities was invoked easily enough, and elegists encouraged the survivors' repentance by exploiting the fear shared by all earthly pilgrims. Pain underscored the key element of all Puritan treatments of mortality. "Could I in greatness farre surmount the skie," he attests, "Great, Fair, Rich, Wise, all in Superlatives: / Yet if I were still mortal, there would be / A debt still to be paid to death by me" (Meserole 289). Pain's list of "Superlatives," an echo of elegiac portraiture, reconfirmed the curse accruing to even the best of humanity. Even the saintly Thomas Shepard, Oakes proclaims, had to pay his debt to sin. If a "Holy Life" sparkling with "Deeds of Charity" and "Grace illustrious [. . .] Could have brib'd Death, good *Shepard* had not di'ed" (Meserole 214). Death and sorrow confronted survivors with the most telling quality of the self that elegy exposed for indictment: the mere fact of mortal existence. As Taylor's Hooker consoles his widow, "When we did wed, we each a mortal took; / And ever from that day for this did look / Wherein we parted are" (*Minor Poetry* 122). "All things on Earth do fall alike to all," Wilson reiterated at the passing of Brisco, "To those that do Blaspheme his Holy Name, / And unto those that reverence the same" (Meserole 385). In this, the urgency of elegy. "The Raising-Day hastens apace," John Danforth proclaimed in his poem for Mary Gerrish, and although the poet concedes that Gerrish's death was unexpected, "Yet ben't surpriz'd to see that Dead, / you always knew was Dying" (Meserole 318). Elegy presented the saint's death as a proto-eschatological event, a situational precursor of doomsday. It was also, of course, a precursor to the survivor's private doomsday—telling reconfirmation of Donne's statement that every bell tolls for us. Voicing the chief mandate for all whom death had passed by, Pain insists that "We have no License from our God to waste / One day, one hour, one moment." He prays that God "spare me yet a little, that I may / Prepare for Death, and for the Judgement-day" (Meserole 290).

As reminders of the "great change" coming to all, Puritan elegies presented death as a situational intersection of fear and hope. On the one hand, the death of a saint posed a grim reminder that earth was not heaven. On the other, it proved that the terrifying space between the two realms could be bridged—that it indeed *had* been bridged, and by someone who once walked among us. An anonymous elegist depicts John Alden in just such terms, underscoring his liminality as a latter-day Moses who stood on Pisgah: "and *Canaan* view'd, / Which in his heart and life he most pursu'd." After a lifetime of soaring "on wings of Contemplation" and sending "up many a dart," the old man truly "desir'd to die" (Winslow 13). By urging a redeemed perspective on the deceased's life, the elegy, like the funeral sermon and the jeremiad, indicted readers for such declension as the death witnessed even as it reinforced their identification with a holy people destined, like the deceased, to transcend all such affliction. Further, by urging readers to assess their faith in light of the saintly self who had just gone to glory, the elegy offered a situational replication of the convicting and consoling properties of Scripture itself. Like the law and the gospel, the dead—and the texts that offered them for contemplation—simultaneously condemned and encouraged survivors. Although elegists repeatedly told survivors that they were not at all like this saintly soul, those who persevered in an effort to emulate the deceased might find themselves, like Milton's "uncouth swain" and Lycidas, gloriously twinned with the saint in heaven.

Elegists intensified this identification with the dead by situating them firmly within the pages of Scripture. When Benjamin Tompson called his father a thundering "Textman" (Silverman 145), he suggested the deceased's role not only as an advocate of the Bible but as its anthropomorphic restatement. Ichabod Wiswell similarly called Samuel Arnold "a Text-Man large and ready" (Winslow 15)—"ready," like Scripture itself, for the survivor's consultation and profit. Mather extended the trope to encompass other, Bible-based texts when he embalmed John Clark as a "*Living Sermon* of the Truths he *Taught*. / So all might *See* the *Doctrines* which they *Heard,* / And way to *Application* fairly clear'd" (85–86). Mather also commemorated John Hubbard as an anthropomorphic text of piety: "His *Life* a *Letter*, where the World might Spell / Great *Basils* Morals, and his Death the *Seal*" (86). Dying sealed the saint's identity as a particularized embodiment of the Word: It was the elegist's task to make such souls readable by unlocking their biblical essence.

Elegists reoriented commemoration around an act of explication, a situational opening of the Word. As Francis Drake proclaimed, Jonathan Mitchell's heart contained "The *Scripture* with a *Commentary* bound" (Meserole 459). Benjamin Tompson attested to the survival of his sister-in-law Mary as a pious text: "Let her example as a Coppy stand / To Childrens Children upon every hand" (Murdock 5). Mather attested that Sarah Leverett's good works offered a virtual "*Gloss*" on the law (82), and Joseph Capen gave the trope occupational appropriateness when he confirmed that although printer John Foster's body had been "laid aside like an old Almanack," he would arise as "A fair Edition & of matchless worth, / Free from Errata" (Wright 163). The deceased-as-text offered a compelling figure—so powerful, in fact, that it outlived its original theological context. Franklin adapted it to worldly ends in the "errata" confessed in his autobiography and in his "Printer's Epitaph," where he expected to "appear once more, / In a new & more perfect Edition, / Corrected and amended / By the Author" (91). Franklin and his Puritan forebears agreed that the successful life was an open book, even if they differed utterly in their reasons for writing and reading it.[8]

A striking example of the textualized deceased occurs in Benjamin Woodbridge's poem for John Cotton. Making explicit a performance central to all Puritan commemoration, Woodbridge anatomizes Cotton as "A living breathing Bible" containing "Both Covenants" and destined to reappear, as the trope demanded, in a "*New Edition*" free from "*Errata's*." Indeed, Cotton's name constitutes a "*Title Page*" and "His Life a *Commentary* on the Text" (Meserole 410–11). These images make especially clear the Puritan tendency to equate an experience of the faith with reading. If the words deciphered in the holy dead echoed the eternal Word, mourners could feel the plotless void of loss being filled by an endlessly repeatable story authored by God himself. Most importantly, the elegiac retelling of the gracious story allowed readers to imagine themselves as products of God's authorship. An anonymous poet confirmed that the preaching of John Reiner of Dover had evinced just this sort of affective power: "His sermons were Experiences, first wrought / On his own Heart, then lived what he taught" (Winslow 11). By making piety clearly legible, elegists sought to transfer the "Experiences" of the dead to living hearts.

In the Puritan view, such radical idealizations simply reflected theological accuracy: In shedding a carnal identity that impeded the perfection of grace, the dead were simply no longer human. Transformed by grace and death, they now resembled their Savior more than they did their former selves—a belief that Taylor underscored when he called Samuel Hooker a "bit of Christ" (*Minor Poetry* 123). In Mather's hands, John Clark becomes a heraldic emblem of grace, the dead saint reduced—or, from the Puritan perspective, elevated—to verbal stained glass. We have already seen Mather's textualizing of Clark as "A *Living Sermon* of the Truths he *Taught*" (85). In a short leap from verbal to visual icon, Clark emerges as a graphic image of the Saved Soul as stylized as any tombstone angel: "*Painter*, Thy Pencils take. Draw first, a *Face* / *Shining*, (but by himself not seen) with *Grace*." Mather imagines the words "MY GOD, in *Capitals*" issuing from the deceased's eye, and "A *Mouth*, from whence a *Label* shall proceed, / And [O LOVE CHRIST] the *Motto* to be Read" (86). Opposing the "false Heraldry" of wit scorned by John Norton in his tribute to Bradstreet (Meserole 462), Mather invokes a similar device in his poem for

Sarah Leverett. After lamenting the fact that portrait painting had not been invented in time to record the faces of biblical women, Mather declares that in Leverett "there is an end of all complaints; / ONE Matron gives a sight of *all* the *Saints.*" Leverett, "a curious Draught," is "what an one! by what fine Pencil wrought" (80).

Such frank acknowledgments of representation conceded the inadequacy of language to describe the celestial saint. These stylized portraits also offered powerful antidotes to a fear of death that was as "natural" as it was fallen. Such fear could be overcome, in some measure, if survivors were willing to follow the inner scripts that the textualized dead extended to them. "We should be so affected with the death of such," Nathanael Appleton urged in a sermon for Harvard president John Leverett, as to be "*more careful than ever, to imitate all that we saw great & excellent in them*" (202). As the sole point of entry into such greatness, death invested such souls with enormous exemplary status. In their perceived capacity as "gap-men" who buffered survivors from divine wrath, the holy dead were eulogized as liminal straddlers of what Pain called the "potent fence" dividing sin from sanctity and earth from heaven (Meserole 287). Elegy rendered their piety accessible through the very process of reading and hearing by which the Word itself also yielded its saving secrets. In the call to ponder the earmarks of grace in the deceased, the loss of a saint was transformed into a net gain in sanctity. As John James declared in a poem for John Haynes, death and grief would come to a good end if the deceased's "goodness could in all be found, / And that did circulate around" (Meserole 426). Such recirculation of piety created a parallel textualizing of the living, whom elegy refashioned as selves in closer conformity to the holy dead, as yet more copies of those ultimate texts provided in the Christic *logos* and the Bible. By making the sanctity of the dead available for public assimilation, elegies served not only to alleviate private grief but to transform terror of the spectral world into an embracing of its divine half as a realm more "real" than the physical world. By portraying the deceased in terms of a successful outcome of redemptive processes presumably at work within survivors, elegists repeatedly blurred the line between the living and the dead and reoriented their readers from the seen to the unseen.

Puritan elegies turned the dead into benign phantoms to be welcomed, imitated, and internalized by the living. As a couplet that ends an anonymous broadside elegy for Lydia Minot states, "We'le wait, (Blest Saint) till this Day break, and th' shadows flee: / So shall our wish be crown'd, to have One Lot with thee" (Winslow 7). The Puritan dead thus emerged not only as helpers from beyond the grave but as textualized embodiments of the survivor's most fervently desired self. Ultimately, these "friendly ghosts" could be found within, stimulated by an ever-growing host of spirit guides who knew best how to oppose demonic forces. While elegy kept the invisible world populated with the "living dead" who stood ready to share their redemptive secrets with those who heeded them, it also made survivors feel that they, too, were prepared to leave the visible world—that they were already more akin to the holy dead than to living unregenerates. When Mather had Nathanael Collins urge his survivors to become "Copyes" of him so that "we shall be soon together" (73), Puritan mourners were assured not only of Collins's spectral perpetuation, but of a greater likelihood that they would someday be friendly ghosts too.

NOTES

1. In this goal, the elegy functioned as an accessible and permanent extension of the sermon; since the poems were frequently read aloud and thus experienced as oral performances, they also retained a measure of pulpit orality as localized embodiments of the "living" Word. The prominence of such ritual as that which the elegy represents constitutes a major shift in our understanding of Puritan culture. Hall observes, "Hostile to the magic of the Catholic system, these people reinstated ritual practice at the heart of their religion" (167). Studies correcting the intellectual cast of Perry Miller's Puritans in *The New England Mind* by revealing a rich affective and ritual life in early New England include Pettit, Holifield, Greven, Leverenz, Hambrick-Stowe, Caldwell, King, Cohen, Kibbey, and Delbanco. A parallel development has been a fuller recognition of the depth and complexity of Puritan aesthetic structures; see Scheick (*Design*), Grabo, Rowe, Gatta, Davis, and Hammond (*Sinful Self*).

2. On the elaboration of funerary customs as the seventeenth century progressed, see Stannard (122–26) and Bosco (xii–xiii). The fullest treatments of the Puritan elegy include Draper (155–77), Henson, Pearce (24–41), Silverman (121–32), Tashjian and Tashjian (39–44), Clark, Daly (113–17, 147–51, 162–76), Scheick ("Tombless Virtue"), Schmitt-von Mühlenfels, Schweitzer (41–74), and Hammond (*American Puritan Elegy*). That the ritual and performative dimension of the elegies is rarely discussed (see the Tashjians, Scheick, and Hammond, cited above) reflects the larger fact that occasional verse defies the longstanding critical privileging of the supposedly timeless masterpiece (Hardison 107–08). The insistent cultural and historical contexts of elegy have also frustrated the formalist bias of traditional literary history (Strickland). Indeed, the aesthetic and the historical have always seemed at particularly sharp odds in elegy scholarship (Shaw 11).

3. Rowe comments on a similar role played by Old Testament personal types in Puritan histories and elegies, in which New England's antitypical relation to ancient Israel "allows the contemporary Christian to emulate the *exemplum fidei* without feeling self-defeated by the *exemplum exemplorum* of Christ Himself" (87). The generalized

portraits of the dead have affinities with the Renaissance "character" (Henson 15), as does Puritan biography generally (Piercy 68–75). On stylized elegiac portraiture, see Schmitt-von Mühlenfels (68–92), Scheick ("Tombless Virtue"), Schweitzer (47), and Hammond (*American Puritan Elegy* 92–98, 137–58, 178–84). Bosco (xxvi–xxviii) and Madden discuss similarly idealized portraits in funeral sermons, while Breitwieser relates such stylized depictions to "exemplification" as the central trope of Puritan mourning (53–70). Similar idealizations marked English funeral elegies (Bennett 110–14) and sermons (Lewalski 174–215).

4. As Schmitt-von Mühlenfels points out, Hebrews 11:4 provided biblical precedent for these voices of the dead. By offering a more acceptable sacrifice than Cain's, Abel "obtained witness that he was righteous, God testifying of his gifts: and by it he, being dead, yet speaketh" (98).

5. The sinful/saintly subjective paradigm was ubiquitous in Puritan culture, and in fact extended far beyond mourning. Ultimately, it manifests itself in the widespread Puritan trope of the soul as a "text" to be read for signs of conformity with other pious texts deriving from the Bible. Such texts were indispensable vehicles for disseminating and absorbing ideal patterns of self-experience. As Cohen points out, the individual experience of the faith "acquiesced in the ministry's paradigm of grace" and "ratified the cultural definition of conversion experience" set forth in sermons and treatises (21, 147). On the enormous importance of texts for Puritan devotional practice, see Hambrick-Stowe (157–61), Hall (21–70), King (13–82), Caldwell, and Hammond (*Sinful Self* 3–36, *American Puritan Elegy* 42–68).

6. Affirmations of a "good death" were also standard in English elegies (Bennett 117). On the cultural significance of the exemplary death in early New England, see Schmitt-von Mühlenfels (60–61, 88–92) and Hall (206–09).

7. Death's transformation from the "King of Terrors" points out a sharp contrast between the Puritan theology of death and the traditional images of decay and corruption that continued to appear on broadsides and tombstones. A 1667 sheet for Lydia Minot illustrates this disjuncture between the verbal and the pictorial. Although the cuts feature skulls and crossbones, hourglasses, a funeral procession, picks and shovels, and a skeleton with a scythe, the three anagram-based poems tell a different story by speaking to Minot's embrace by "Happy Death" and her passage to "Life indeed": "O pleasant Lines that thus are fall'n to me! / To make that *Day my Lot* which aye shall be" (Winslow 7). It is the text and not the graphics that anticipates the stylized cherubs and angels that would replace death's heads on tombstones in the early eighteenth century. Dethlefsen and Deetz graph this shift to an iconography more consistent with the optimistic thrust of elegy in the cemeteries of Cambridge, Concord, and Plymouth (505). For photographs of stones illustrating this change and insightful discussions of its significance, see Ludwig and the Tashjians.

8. The most immediate form of decoding a life, of course, was the widespread practice of finding anagrams in the deceased's name. On the transformation of the Puritan dead into pious texts, see Scheick ("Tombless Virtue"), Hammond (*American Puritan Elegy* 145–48, 169–71), and Schweitzer, who notes that the elegist was able to perform the commemorative duty by "giving up writing altogether, to become the reader of divine grace," a shift that offered Puritans "a practical method, consistent with their theology, for the apparent production, rather than the creation, of discourse"

(70, 58). In this challenge to explicate the dead as neobiblical texts, Puritan elegies participated fully in the testing of survivors central to the elegiac tradition generally and to the mourning process that elegy both mirrors and generates. As Sacks observes, the repetitive forms of elegy enable mourners to bring their "loss into language, testing how it feels to speak *and hear* of it in words" (25).

WORKS CITED

Ames, William. *The Marrow of Theology.* Translated by John D. Eusden. Boston: Pilgrim, 1968.

Appleton, Nathanael. *A Great Man Fallen in Israel.* Boston: 1724. In *New England Funeral Sermons.* Vol. 4 of *The Puritan Sermon in America.* Edited by Ronald A. Bosco, 175–212. Delmar, N.Y.: Scholars' Facsimiles and Reprints, 1978.

Bennett, A. L. "The Principal Rhetorical Conventions in the Renaissance Personal Elegy." *Studies in Philology* 51 (1954): 107–26.

Bosco, Ronald A. "Introduction." In *New England Funeral Sermons.* Vol. 4 of *The Puritan Sermon in America 1630–1750.* Edited by Ronald A. Bosco, ix–xxviii. Delmar, N.Y.: Scholars' Facsimiles and Reprints, 1978.

Bradstreet, Anne. *The Works of Anne Bradstreet.* Edited by Jeannine Hensley. Cambridge: Harvard University Press, 1967.

Breitwieser, Mitchell Robert. *American Puritanism and the Defense of Mourning: Religion, Grief, and Ethnology in Mary White Rowlandson's Captivity Narrative.* Madison: University of Wisconsin Press, 1990.

Caldwell, Patricia. *The Puritan Conversion Narrative: The Beginnings of American Expression.* Cambridge: Cambridge University Press, 1983.

Clark, Michael. "The Honeyed Knot of Puritan Aesthetics." In *Puritan Poets and Poetics: Seventeenth-Century American Poetry in Theory and Practice.* Edited by Peter White, 67–83. University Park: Pennsylvania State University Press, 1985.

Cohen, Charles Lloyd. *God's Caress: The Psychology of Puritan Religious Experience.* New York: Oxford University Press, 1986.

Daly, Robert. *God's Altar: The World and the Flesh in Puritan Poetry.* Berkeley: University of California Press, 1978.

Davis, Thomas M. *A Reading of Edward Taylor.* Newark: University of Delaware Press, 1992.

Delbanco, Andrew. *The Puritan Ordeal.* Cambridge: Harvard University Press, 1989.

Dethlefsen, Edwin, and James Deetz. "Death's Heads, Cherubs, and Willow Trees: Experimental Archaeology in Colonial Cemeteries." *American Antiquity* 31 (1966): 502–10.

Draper, John W. *The Funeral Elegy and the Rise of English Romanticism.* New York: New York University Press, 1929.

Franklin, Benjamin. *Writings.* Edited by J. A. Leo Lemay. New York: The Library of America, 1987.

Gatta, John. *Gracious Laughter: The Meditative Wit of Edward Taylor.* Columbia: University of Missouri Press, 1989.

Grabo, Norman S. *Edward Taylor: Revised Edition.* Boston: Twayne, 1988.

Greven, Philip. *The Protestant Temperament: Patterns of Child-Rearing, Religious Experience, and the Self in Early America.* New York: Knopf, 1977.

Hall, David D. *Worlds of Wonder, Days of Judgment: Popular Religious Belief in Early New England.* New York: Knopf, 1989.

Hambrick-Stowe, Charles E. *The Practice of Piety: Puritan Devotional Disciplines in Seventeenth-Century New England.* Chapel Hill: University of North Carolina Press, 1982.

Hammond, Jeffrey A. *The American Puritan Elegy: A Literary and Cultural Study.* Cambridge: Cambridge University Press, 2000.

———. *Sinful Self, Saintly Self: The Puritan Experience of Poetry.* Athens: University of Georgia Press, 1993.

Hardison, O. B., Jr. *The Enduring Monument: A Study of the Idea of Praise in Renaissance Literary Theory.* Chapel Hill: University of North Carolina Press, 1962.

Henson, Robert. "Form and Content of the Puritan Funeral Elegy." *American Literature* 32 (1960): 11–27.

Holifield, E. Brooks. *The Covenant Sealed: The Development of Puritan Sacramental Theology in Old and New England, 1570–1720.* New Haven: Yale University Press, 1974.

Kibbey, Ann. *The Interpretation of Material Shapes in Puritanism: A Study of Rhetoric, Prejudice, and Violence.* Cambridge: Cambridge University Press, 1986.

King, John Owen, III. *The Iron of Melancholy: Structures of Spiritual Conversion from the Puritan Conscience to Victorian Neurosis.* Middletown: Wesleyan University Press, 1983.

Leverenz, David. *The Language of Puritan Feeling: An Exploration in Literature, Psychology, and Social History.* New Brunswick, N.J.: Rutgers University Press, 1980.

Lewalski, Barbara Kiefer. *Donne's Anniversaries and the Poetry of Praise: The Creation of a Symbolic Mode.* Princeton: Princeton University Press, 1973.

Ludwig, Allan I. *Graven Images: New England Stonecarving and its Symbols, 1650–1815.* Middletown, Ct.: Wesleyan University Press, 1966.

Madden, Etta. "Resurrecting Life through Rhetorical Ritual: A Buried Value of the Puritan Funeral Sermon." *Early American Literature* 26 (1991): 232–50.

Mather, Cotton. *Cotton Mather's Verse in English.* Edited by Denise D. Knight. Newark: University of Delaware Press, 1989.

Meserole, Harrison T., ed. *American Poetry of the Seventeenth Century.* 1968. Reprint, University Park: Pennsylvania State University Press, 1985.

Miller, Perry. *The New England Mind: From Colony to Province.* 1953. Reprint, Boston: Beacon, 1961.

———. *The New England Mind: The Seventeenth Century.* 1939. Reprint, Boston: Beacon, 1961.

Murdock, Kenneth B., ed. *Handkerchiefs from Paul.* Cambridge: Harvard University Press, 1927.

Pearce, Roy Harvey. *The Continuity of American Poetry.* Princeton: Princeton University Press, 1961.

Pearse, Edward. *The Great Concern: or, A Serious Warning to a Timely and Thorough Preparation for Death.* Boston: 1705.

Pettit, Norman. *The Heart Prepared: Grace and Conversion in Puritan Spiritual Life.* New Haven: Yale University Press, 1966.

Piercy, Josephine K. *Studies in Literary Types in Seventeenth Century America (1607–1710).* 1939. Reprint, Hamden, Ct.: Archon, 1969.

Rowe, Karen E, *Saint and Singer: Edward Taylor's Typology and the Poetics of Meditation.* Cambridge: Cambridge University Press, 1986.

Sacks, Peter M. *The English Elegy: Studies in the Genre from Spenser to Yeats.* Baltimore: Johns Hopkins University Press, 1985.

Saffin, John. *John Saffin His Book.* Edited by Caroline Hazard. New York: Harbor, 1928.

Scheick, William J. *Design in Puritan American Literature.* Lexington: University Press of Kentucky, 1992.

———. "Tombless Virtue and Hidden Text: New England Funeral Elegies." In *Puritan Poets and Poetics: Seventeenth-Century American Poetry in Theory and Practice.* Edited by Peter White, 286–302. University Park: Pennsylvania State University Press, 1985.

Schmitt-von Mühlenfels, Astrid. *Die "Funeral Elegy" Neuenglands: Ein gattungsgeschichtliche Studie.* Heidelberg: Carl Winter, 1973.

Schweitzer, Ivy. *The Work of Self-Representation: Lyric Poetry in Colonial New England.* Chapel Hill: University of North Carolina Press, 1991.

Shaw, W. David. "Elegy and Theory: Is Historical and Critical Knowledge Possible?" *Modern Language Quarterly* 55 (1994): 1–16.

Shepard, Thomas. *God's Plot: The Paradoxes of Puritan Piety.* Edited by Michael McGiffert. Amherst: University of Massachusetts Press, 1972.

Sibbes, Richard. *Spiritual Mourning* (orig. numbers 14 and 15 of *The Saint's Cordials.* London: 1629). In *Works of Richard Sibbes.* 7 Vols. Edited by Alexander B. Grosart, 6: 265–92. 1862. Reprint, Edinburgh: The Banner of Truth Trust, 1983.

Silverman, Kenneth, ed. *Colonial American Poetry.* New York: Hafner, 1968.

Stannard, David E. *The Puritan Way of Death: A Study in Religion, Culture, and Social Change.* New York: Oxford University Press, 1977.

Strickland, Ronald. "Not So Idle Tears: Re-Reading the Renaissance Elegy." *Review* 14 (1992): 57–72.

Tashjian, Dickran, and Ann Tashjian. *Memorials for Children of Change.* Middletown: Wesleyan University Press, 1974.

Taylor, Edward. "Edward Taylor's Elegy on Deacon David Dewey." Edited by Thomas M. Davis. *Proceedings of the American Antiquarian Society* 96, Part 1 (1986): 75–84.

———. *Edward Taylor's Minor Poetry.* Edited by Thomas M. Davis and Virginia L. Davis. Boston: Twayne, 1981.

———. *The Poems of Edward Taylor.* Edited by Donald E. Stanford. New Haven: Yale University Press, 1960.

Willard, Samuel. *The High Esteem Which God Hath for the Death of His Saints.* Boston: 1683. *New England Funeral Sermons.* Vol. 4 of *The Puritan Sermon in America.* Edited by Ronald A. Bosco, 1–20. Delmar, N.Y.: Scholars' Facsimiles and Reprints, 1978.

Winslow, Ola E., ed. *American Broadside Verse.* 1930. Reprint, New York: AMS Press, 1974.

Wright, Thomas Goddard. *Literary Culture in Early New England 1620–1730.* 1920. Reprint, New York: Russell and Russell, 1966.

Can Such Things Be?

Ambrose Bierce, the "Dead Mother," and Other American Traumas

ALLAN LLOYD SMITH

Through repetitions, unexpected stresses, aporias and elisions, amnesias, and resistance to interpretation, texts often suggest cultural traumas beyond their ostensible motifs and retrievable motives. Uncanny American stories of the nineteenth century, as much as British Victorian fictions, speak of matters beyond or below the textual surface and apparent scope—and their pre-Freudian "innocence" allows perhaps a less defended access to materials than later writers would be willing to admit. Reading against the grain or between the lines of such fictions is a parallel to the psychoanalytic project and may be further enabled by certain post-Freudian formulations and the privileging of suggestiveness over "truth." Detailed readings of particular texts by, for example, Ambrose Bierce, Brown, Dana, or Melville lead to wider speculation about the forces within American culture that may be at play in the production of the uncanny in this period. As in the Freudian project, apparently domestic travails may refer to larger cultural and sometimes national issues.

That domestic trauma should recur as the deep structure of uncanny fictions will not surprise readers of Freud's 1919 essay on the uncanny, in which he argues that this effect can be produced by a defamiliarization of the domestic; Freud describes the *unheimlich* as the strange in the familiar and the familiar in the strange, "everything that ought to have remained [. . .] secret and hidden but has come to light" (354). If other literary examples were needed in addition to his recourse to Hoffman's "The Sandman," Freud might have referenced George Eliot's "The Lifted Veil," along with Henry James's *The Turn of the Screw*, as examples of the same principle.

One difference between the American and the British or European versions of the Gothic and the uncanny may have to do with the comparative absence of aristocratic societal structures and feudal inheritance in
the New World. David Punter has suggested in *The Literature of Terror*
that the imaginative negotiations between an emergent middle class and
these older structures shaped the European Gothic, and Fredric Jameson
relatedly argues :

> The melancholy of disbelief, the nostalgia of the nineteenth-century intel-
> lectual for the "wholeness" of a faith that is no longer possible, is itself a kind
> of ideological fable designed to transform into a matter of individual exis-
> tence what is in reality a relationship between collective systems and social
> forms. Religion has the symbolic value of wholeness, no doubt, but it is the
> wholeness of the older organic society of *gessellschaft* that it conveys. (252)

Without entering into detailed discussion of precisely what was, or was
not, available to the American culture of the new—or in Bierce's case, the
newly tried—republic, it is clear enough that the hypothesized relationship between collective systems and social forms was, at the very least,
much different in the United States than in Europe. Whether in Bierce's
California or the Ohio of his upbringing, or in Brockden Brown's Philadelphia, Poe's Richmond, or even Hawthorne's more rooted Massachusetts, the social structures were less fully formed, and less rooted in the
sanctions of the past than in those of the Old World. An inevitable effect
of this was to privilege the family, and with that, I would argue, the place
of the woman in the family, making her an equal—or, more than equal—
moral arbiter to the male. The conjunction of this positioning, which led
to women's idealization, alongside a parallel hysterical construction of
masculinity in the early period, may underlie the vengeful and misogynis-
tic direction of so many early American fictions of the uncanny and offer
some explanation for the "phantom" that, according to Marek Wilczynski,
haunts these writings:

> In the early nineteenth-century American Gothic [. . .] the intertextual
> matrix of the genre was transmitted from text to text through a recurrent
> plot of assassination—[a] particular repetition compulsion that made the
> male protagonists from *Wieland* to *Pierre* either murder their wives under
> some malevolent agency, or (as in the case of the latter) involuntarily bring
> doom upon all the loved ones. Though no external evidence confirms direct

transmission—Dana read Brown's Gothic romances beyond any doubt, and Allston was fascinated with them, but most probably neither Poe nor Melville knew *Wieland*, or, for that matter [Dana's] "Paul Felton" and [Allston's] *Monaldi*—the perseverance of the same basic motif allows me to put forward a psychoanalytic hypothesis of essential affinity. It is not only that the unconscious of American Gothic characters functions as a hereditary crypt of a "transgenerational phantom" (a term introduced by the psychoanalyst Nicolas Abraham) compelling them to reenact time and again the unsolved plight of the German grandfather of Theodore Wieland, but in consequence of reiteration a kind of generic "textual unconscious" establishes itself to harbor for half a century the gnawing fear of the collapse of the family and hence also of the national community. (Wilczynski 10)

Wilczynski mentions here Nicolas Abraham and Maria Torok's discussion of the "phantom," and I will return to this as potentially useful in determining the relationships between the domestic or familial, and larger cultural issues. But another possibly powerful theoretical framework in this area is suggested by Andre Green's concept of the "dead mother." This is the title of a paper that Green wrote in 1983, in which he develops "a paradigm of the child's response to a traumatic disruption of maternal relatedness in infancy and early childhood" and its "subsequent pathology" (Modell 78). The mother in question is of course emotionally dead rather than actually dead. Green's concept refers to:

an *imago* which has been constituted in the child's mind, following maternal depression, brutally transforming a living object, which was a source of vitality for the child, into a distant figure, toneless, practically inanimate, deeply impregnating the cathexis of certain patients [. . .] and weighing on the destiny of their object libidinal and narcissistic future [. . .]. [The] dead mother [. . .] is a mother who remains alive but who is, so to speak, psychically dead in the eyes of the young child in her care. (Green in "The Dead Mother," quoted in Kohon 2)

Gregorio Kohon elucidates the notion of "blank anxiety" as one of a series of concepts created by Green: "negative hallucination, blank psychosis, blank mourning," all of which are connected to "the problem of emptiness, or of the negative " (3). For Green, Kohon explains, "blankness" is "the result of one of the components of primary repression: massive decathexis of the maternal primary object, which leaves traces in the unconscious in the form of 'psychic holes.'" The sudden loss of love causes a psychical catastrophe and "is followed by loss of meaning; for the child, nothing makes sense any more" (3). One consequence may be an incapacity for love:

> The subject's trajectory evokes a hunt in quest of an introjectable object, without the possibility of renouncing it or losing it, and indeed, the possibility of accepting its introjection into the ego, which is cathected by the dead mother. In all, the subject's objects remain constantly at the limit of the ego, not wholly within, and not quite without. And with good reason, for the place is occupied, in its centre, by the dead mother. (Green, quoted in Kohon 4)

There is, then, no room for anyone else. But "behind the dead mother complex, behind the blank mourning for the mother, one catches a glimpse of the mad passion of which she is, and remains, the object, that renders mourning for her an impossible experience" (Kohon 4). The inability of the mother to recognize the child's inner life can be devastating, as if the mother failed to recognize his or her humanity—in effect as if the mother wished the child did not exist, wished him or her dead: "Believing that the mother withholds permission to exist may result in the conviction that all desires are forbidden, for if one does not have a right to exist, one has no right to have desires, to want anything for oneself" (Modell 78). The mother's unresponsive, expressionless face, without animation, produces an echo in the child: "the flight of animation, a deflation of posture, a fall in positive affect and facial expressivity, a decrease in activation, etc. In sum, the experience is descriptively one of a 'micro-depression'" (Green, quoted in Modell 78). And further, the child "models herself on what she perceives as her mother's unconscious attitudes. This total identification with a dead mother who is incapable of loving, contributes to a corresponding incapacity to love others and to love oneself" (Modell 79). Sufferers of the dead-mother syndrome may be unable to experience pleasure (not feel a masochistic compulsion to seek pain—pleasure is simply missing or felt to be forbidden), and may have great difficulty in "being with the other." "They maintain a corpse-like posture, do not move on the couch [in analysis], and speak in a dead-seeming voice drained of all affective valencies" (Modell 80). But of course there may be different outcomes. Although "a total identification with the mother's affective deadness is the most pathological and malignant," the child may try to compensate for the fear of inner deadness "through a hypersexuality or an addiction to thrills or induced crises" (Modell 84, 85).

Green's identification of this pattern seems potentially instructive in considering one of Ambrose Bierce's most powerful and puzzling ghost stories. In "The Death of Halpin Frayser" (1893), the protagonist dreams of walking along a dusty road and turning into—he does not know why—"a road less travelled," in the ruts of which is a crimson liquid that he takes to be blood. With the red liquid and a twig he writes feverishly in his red-leather pocket book, while he hears a strange low and wild peal of laughter growing nearer.

> [Frayser] had but one thought: to complete his written appeal to the benign powers who, traversing the haunted wood, might some time rescue him if he should be denied the blessing of annihilation. He wrote with terrible rapidity, the twig in his fingers rilling blood without renewal; but in the middle of a sentence his hands denied their service to his will, his arms fell to his sides, the book to the earth; and powerless to move or cry out, he found himself staring into the sharply drawn face and blank, dead eyes of his own mother, standing white and silent in the garments of the grave! (410)

This extraordinary apparition seems to cause his death: In any event he is later found dead, evidently strangled by two powerful hands, his body in a rigid attitude of "desperate but ineffectual resistance—to what?" (415). What is more, he is found dead on the grave of one Catherine Larue, who, it turns out (though this was unknown to him, she having taken a new name through remarriage), was his mother.

As is customary in Bierce's supernatural fictions, the reader is invited toward a realistic explanation: The (we assume real) investigating detectives, on the track of a madman called Larue, assume that he, having killed his wife in his mania, now haunts her grave and has killed Frayser as well. But, as is also customary in Bierce's writing, the possible realistic explanation is only the uppermost layer of a series of deeper insights and ironic alternatives below the surface.

One of these layers ironically addresses the question of the fictionality of the fiction: The writing that Halpin Frayser dreams he is so anxious to finish with his twig dipped in blood (or that he perhaps wrote earlier in his book using red ink) turns out to be a poem in the manner of his ancestor Myron Bayne, a once-famous "Colonial bard"—not unlike Philip Freneau, it would seem, since the poem rather resembles his "The House of Night"—although Frayser, while poetic in inclination, has never actually been a poet. The abruptly broken-off manuscript describes, or foretells, the enchanted wood in which he meets his death, in which "Conspiring spirits whispered in the gloom,/ Halfheard, the stilly secrets of the tomb./ With blood the trees were all adrip; the leaves/ Shone in the witch light with a ruddy bloom" (416). Bierce's interest in the uncanniness of writing itself is reinforced here by his characteristic production of narrative uncertainties as sections on Frayser's subjective experience alternate with a retrospective history of his life and the experiences of the two detectives who find his body.

Within the retrospective section, Bierce investigates the unusually close relationship between Halpin and his once-delightful mother, based in part upon a shared secret admiration for Myron Bayne's poetry, a thing not to be admitted in their practical Southern family:

> Their common guilt in respect of that was an added tie between them. If in Halpin's youth his mother had "spoiled" him, he had assuredly done his part toward being spoiled. As he grew to such manhood as is attainable by a Southerner who does not care which way elections go, the attachment between him and his beautiful mother—whom from early childhood he had called Katy—became yearly stronger and more tender. In these two romantic natures was manifest in a signal way that neglected phenomenon, the dominance of the sexual element in all the relations of life, strengthening, softening, and beautifying even those of consanguity. The two were nearly inseparable, and by strangers observing their manners were not infrequently mistaken for lovers. (15)

As in other Bierce stories, the South offers a paradigm of formal and distant patriarchy within which there seems to be a decadent female over-closeness. Halpin's decision to visit California—where he will be "shanghaied" and thereby lose all contact with his family for many years—is of course opposed by his mother, who in a dream sees Myron Bayne pointing to Halpin's portrait, now painted with a face cloth "such as we put on the dead." Halpin's mother explains, "And I saw below the edge of the cloth the marks of hands on your throat—forgive me, but we have not been used to keep such things from each other. Perhaps you have another interpretation. Perhaps it does not mean that you will go to California. Or maybe you will take me with you?" (411). Halpin's immediate reaction is that the dream "foreshadowed a more simple and immediate, if less tragic, disaster than a visit to the Pacific coast. It was Halpin Frayser's impression that he was to be garroted on his native heath" (411). Given the already anticipated outcome, for "heath" the reader might well be expected to realize the echo of "hearth" and thus find the threat rather nearer to home, especially when Mrs. Frayser complains of her "stiff" fingers and suggests that the medicinal springs in California might be of assistance. While she remains charming as ever, Mrs. Frayser's subtly implied threat, immediately noted by her adoring son, suggests another side to this loving mother. This brings back into focus Andre Green's recent psychoanalytical work on the "syndrome" of the "dead mother" and the way that it might illuminate the story of Halpin Frayser. Here then, is the nature of Halpin's appalling death:

> The apparition confronting the dreamer in the wood—the thing so like, yet so unlike, his mother—was horrible! It stirred no love nor longing in his heart; it came unattended with pleasant memories of a golden past— inspired no sentiment of any kind; all the finer emotions were swallowed up in fear. He tried to turn and run from before it, but his legs were as lead; he was unable to lift his feet from the ground. His arms hung helpless at his sides; of his eyes only he retained control, and these he did not dare remove from the lustreless orbs of the apparition, which he knew was not a soul without a body, but that most dreadful of all existences infesting that haunted wood—a body without a soul! In its blank stare was neither love, nor pity, nor intelligence—nothing to which to address an appeal for mercy. [. . .] For a time, which seemed so long that the world grew grey with age and sin, and the haunted forest, having fulfilled its purpose in this monstrous culmination of its terrors, vanished out of his consciousness with all its sights and sounds, the apparition stood within a pace, regarding him with the mindless malevolence of a wild brute; then thrust its hands forward and sprang upon him with appalling ferocity! [. . .] Borne backward to the earth, he saw above him the dead and drawn face within a hand's-breadth of his own, and then all was black. [. . . A]nd Halpin Frayser dreamed that he was dead. (412)

Halpin's adventurous life, and the hysterical quality of his dream in the woods, fit well enough with Green's point; his apprehension of the threat from his mother before leaving for California suggests that he had penetrated to the "dead mother" behind the benign surface of her smothering intensity. This is not to suggest that Bierce himself should be understood as somehow a victim of the dead-mother syndrome—the biographical evidence is not there—or that he would be in any sense cognizant of a psychoanalytical theory advanced a century after his writing, although the premonitory echo is interesting enough. I am concerned, however, to discuss this thematic in terms of further cultural patterns in early American Gothic and uncanny writing where, as will emerge, the concept of the "dead mother" has a peculiar resonance.

In common with other American Gothicists, most of Bierce's uncanny fiction is grounded in underlying domestic trauma. "The Moonlit Road," for example, accounts for a haunting experience in which a father and his unseeing son encounter an apparition; the ghost is the wife whom the man murdered in a fit of jealousy. Unusually, in this tale, the ghost speaks through a medium: Not knowing who had killed her, the dead woman's spirit has attempted to break through from beyond.

> Their faces were toward me, the eyes of the elder man fixed upon mine. He saw me—at last, at last, he saw me! In the consciousness of that, my terror fled as a cruel dream. The death-spell was broken: Love had conquered Law! Mad with exultation I shouted—I must have shouted, "He sees, he sees: he will understand!" Then, controlling myself, I moved forward, smiling, and consciously beautiful, to offer myself to his arms, to comfort him with endearments, and, with my son's hand in mine, to speak words that should restore the broken bonds between the living and the dead. (79)

Unsurprisingly, the husband is driven to madness by this experience.

"The Secret of Macarger's Gulf" is also generated by a man's brutal murder of his wife, her body having been concealed under the floor of the haunted cabin. "The Haunted Valley" similarly concerns a murder: W'isky Jo Dunfer kills his ambiguously gendered "Chinaman" servant Ah Wee, and a lunatic recounts the story of how "W'isky thought a lot of that Chink; nobody but me knew how 'e doted on 'im. Couldn't bear 'im out of 'is sight, the derned protoplasm!" (151). On the grave Dunfer writes:

> AH WEE—CHINAMAN
> Age unknown. Worked for Jo. Dunfer.
> This monument is erected by him to keep the Chink's
> memory green. Likewise as a warning to Celestials
> not to take on airs. Devil take 'em!
> She Was a Good Egg. (144)

When the narrator shrewdly asks him when *he* went mad, the tale's informant, Gopher, bellows:

> [N]ine years ago, w 'en that big brute killed the woman who loved 'im better than she did me!—me who had followed 'er from San Fransisco, where 'e won 'er at draw poker!—me who had watched over 'er for years w 'en the scoundrel she belonged to was ashamed to acknowledge 'er and treat 'er white!—me who for 'er sake kept 'is cussed secret till it ate 'im up. (154)

Whether Ah Wee should finally be read as male or female perhaps remains open to question, but in any event the pattern of a savage assault on the loved one again constitutes the underlying drive of the narrative, as it does also in "The Middle Toe of the Right Foot."

A striking parallel can also be made between Bierce's "Death of Halpin Frayser" and some of Charles Brockden Brown's productions. In "Somnambulism: A Fragment," Brown introduces both the disturbing reality of dream and the strange, mocking cry or laugh in the wilderness, along with the obligatory death of the loved one. Brown's narrator tells of a late-night journey of the object of his affection and her father through the wilderness of Norwood, their carriage accident, and her mysterious death as she waits beneath a tree for her father's return. The narrator, Althorpe, has insisted that they not make this trip, although he is unable to specify the dangers that threaten them and it seems that his own character and motives are to be questioned. The mocking cry may come from a lunatic who roams wild in the woods, frightening travelers. As far as the narrative proper is concerned, either this wild man, Nick Handyside, has shot the young woman to death, or some other unknown assailant has done so. The preface to the story, however, which outlines a strange case of homicidal somnambulism, would seem to implicate the narrator, although there is no contributory evidence and his motive in that case remains unclear. Like Frayser, he has dreamed a violent and incoherent dream in which he shoots dead the assailant of the unfortunate girl and her father. In fact, not only his dream but the whole of the narrative seems to be a case of "saying makes it so." In outlining his fears for the travelers, Althorpe recalls a large tree that grows in the middle of the roadway, and fantasizes a carriage accident; this is exactly what happens and the carriage smashes against that very tree. Thus, the distinctions between author, narrator, and narrative collapse in the fulfillment of prophetic fantasy, encouraging the reader to think of Handyside as another manifestation of Althorpe's self—

his double—and the tree as a projection of his antipathy to patriarchal authority—in this case, the controlling father.

This fragment seems to have provided Brown with the basis of his novel *Edgar Huntly*, in which not one but two somnambulists are involved. Discovering a man called Clithero behaving peculiarly, Edgar Huntly tracks him in the wild region of Norwalk. Eventually he hears the story of how Clithero unhappily caused the death of his patroness Mrs. Lorimer's brother and deludedly attempted to kill her in order to spare her the distress of that discovery. But mistakenly believing himself to have instead killed her daughter—his own prospective wife—Clithero flees into the wilderness, a maniac of the kind outlined in the other two stories. Huntly, now believing the man repentant and recovered, gives him Mrs. Lorimer's address—at which Clithero immediately sets off again to kill her! These motifs—the lover/mother figure who must be killed, the laugh of the lunatic in the wilderness, the significance of prophetic dreams, the uncertainties of motivation—form an insistent pattern, and one that is repeated in, for example, Richard Henry Dana Sr.'s tale, "Paul Felton." In this tale, Felton's relationship with an idiotic (and demonic) boy, and his wanderings in the accursed wilderness, lead up to his killing his beloved wife. This is the case in Washington Allston's *Monaldi* also, and, with some significant differences, in Washington Irving's "The Adventure of the German Student." Brown's *Wieland*, of course, also combines these figures: Wieland hears the voices produced by Carwin's ventriloquism (Carwin is the wild card or lunatic in this scenario) and interprets them as messages from God instructing him to kill his beloved wife, Catherine, and their children, and subsequently his sister, Clara. The maniac, idiot, or troublemaking trickster seems to be positioned in these stories as an alter ego or doppelganger, as with Althorpe and Handyside in "Somnambulism," Huntly and Clithero in *Edgar Huntly*, Carwin and Wieland in *Wieland*, the boy Abel and Paul Felton in "Paul Felton," and the two Wilsons in Poe's "William Wilson." Each double seems both to critique and enact the wishes of the primary self. These tales, even leaving aside Edgar Allan Poe's variations, seem to justify Wilczynski's identification of a literary repetition compulsion at work through several generations of American Gothicists—however its genesis may be explained.

Poe's work, too, returns us to the concept of the "dead mother," both literally, in terms of familiar assumptions about the origin of his imaginative drive in his own life experience, and figuratively, in respect of the obsessive motifs of the devastatingly altered loved one and the protagonist's doomed attempt to come to terms with the loss. Even "The Murders in the Rue Morgue" suggests the power of this repetition compulsion: The grotesque murder of a mother and her daughter, displaced as the action of a mindless beast and recuperated safely through the agency of Dupin's godlike reason, remains the affective crisis of the piece, however well disguised. The murder of the wife in "The Black Cat"; Morella's reanimation in her daughter—or Ligeia's within the hapless (and also very possibly murdered) Rowena; the live burials of Madeleine in "The Fall of the House of Usher," and the narrator's cousin in "Berenice" all repeat this obsessive structure. In Poe's case alone among Bierce, Brown, Allston, Dana, and Irving one might plausibly infer the existence of Green's "dead-mother syndrome" from the biographical evidence. What remains puzzling, then, is why the pattern should be repeated so insistently among other American Gothic writers. British Gothic writing of the same period does not seem to display these features. Although an element of sadistic threat against women is evidenced in, for example, Ann Radcliffe's romances, it does not result in the heroine's violent, often macabre, death as in the American variant. Godwin, Maturin, even Monk Lewis do not seem to take quite this route, and neither do Shelley, Hogg, Stevenson, or Stoker (although some elements in *Dracula* or *The Lair of the White Worm* do arguably display elements of the syndrome late in the century). There is, it would seem, a cultural difference not to be fully explained by ideas of the adaptation of Gothic to the more obviously different topography of the American landscape and (relative) absence of a usable past. But this is perhaps to risk a too narrow interpretation of the dead-mother pattern, and it may be as well to look again at one or two other aspects of the syndrome described by Green: specifically, the loss of affect experienced by its victims, and their potentially disruptive behavior, as mentioned in the earlier account of this theory. To recap: Although "a total identification with the mother's affective deadness is the most pathological and malignant" effect, the child may try to compensate for the fear of inner deadness "through a hypersexuality or an addiction to thrills or induced crises" (Modell 84, 85).

One of the most striking features of the writing I have been discussing is the use of affectively "dead" settings: impenetrable woods; meaningless or malignant wildernesses; depressive landscapes like that described at the beginning of "The Fall of the House of Usher," which occasion an utter drop of spirits like the withdrawal from opium; or their architectural equivalents, incomprehensible windings and passages in cities of lost souls like the London of Poe's "The Man of the Crowd."

To pursue this, I will return to "Paul Felton," the last story in Dana's *Idle Man* miscellany (1821–22), which immerses the reader in a realm of dread and despair, as is suggested by its epigraphs: "Pray and beware the foul fiend," and "The sick, in my mind, are covetous of more disease" (271). These stand in ironic counterpoise to a panegyric from Wordsworth on the healthy influence of nature, a romantic aspiration overborne by the "foul fiend" on the one hand, and a diseased subjectivity on the other, both of which are possible concomitants of romantic idealism.

After an enthusiastic youth in which Paul communed with nature, he has engaged in introspection to such an extent that nature says nothing to him, and he lives like "a withered thing amid her fresh and living beauty" (275). This state of Wertherian melancholy is dispelled by Esther, who becomes his wife, causing him to feel that what had bound his soul like ice is melting and passing away. Now he again sees the world as "power, and intellect, and love made visible" and feels the "living Presence throughout the whole" (278). But soon we find him hinting at a lurking evil prospect: "When I see you happy," he tells Esther, "you look to me like a star trailing your glory across my gloom, only to fall and go out in it" (292), a threat that is amply fulfilled in the event. The "foul fiend's" realm is the main setting of the story, a desolate heath of sand tracts and scanty yellow grass, which is thought to be accursed because the footprint of neither man nor beast is to be seen there; and he has his human representative in Abel, a crazed boy, regarded locally as belonging to the "Evil One" ever since he went birdnesting in this forbidden place, and who feels an irresistible attraction to this cursed land. Abel thinks he sees spirits moving in the hut—haunted, according to local lore—located at the center of the wasteland, and he comes to believe that the townspeople are right in their judgment of him. Eventually, Felton is led to kill his wife, but perhaps the main point here is the conjunction of the desolate landscape and the crazed Abel: the landscape as objective correlative of the desolation of spirit, and the boy as the alter ego of Felton and the embodiment of those tendencies toward compensatory excess described in Green's syndrome. He, like the other maniacs encountered in these tales, acts out the disturbed and prohibited desires of the supposedly rational protagonist.

Reading with attention to such issues encourages a reappraisal of, for example, the landscape of Bierce's mysterious story "An Inhabitant of Carcosa." In this tale, a wanderer finds himself on a bleak and desolate plain, among strangely shaped rocks that "seemed to have an understanding with one another and to exchange looks of uncomfortable significance" (309).

A canopy of low leaden clouds hangs over the landscape like a visible curse. There are no birds, beasts, or insects, except that a lynx trots past. The oddly shaped stones seem to be of an ancient graveyard. Then, at a distance, a man appears, "half naked, half clad in skins" carrying in one hand a bow and arrow, in the other a blazing torch with a trail of black smoke. It is neither night nor day, but somehow, it is both at once: "I saw even the stars in the absence of darkness" (313). At last, the traveler recognizes his own grave, with a long-ago date of death, "and then I knew that these were the ruins of the ancient and famous city of Carcosa" (314). Now we know where we are: This is the country of the negative Sublime, the occulted landscape of despair of Poe's "Usher" and "Ulalume," Brown's Norwalk, Dana's blasted heath. We find at the end that this landscape is not American, as the account is "imparted to the medium Bayrolles by the spirit Hoseib Alar Robardin." But such places, like Poe's pseudo-European settings, go beyond geography, just as they go beyond the pathetic fallacy; they are more than representations of subjectivity and seem to hold an active malevolence of their own. The land itself is evil, like the setting of Frayser's dream. The affectless or threatening landscape suggests (dead) Mother Nature's implacable gaze.

In place of the diabolical laughter of Frayser's tale, the idiot boy and devil's child Abel in "Paul Felton," or Handyside in "Somnambulism," we find here a silent savage, whose description perhaps brings to mind stereotypes of the Native American. Similarly, Huntly's somnambulism in *Edgar Huntly* results in his bloodthirsty encounter with several Indians, whom he dispatches with extraordinary viciousness in reparation for his parents' deaths in Indian raids, triumphantly planting his musket at the spot as memorial. This suggests that *one* of the meanings of the motif of mysterious loon-like cries or laughter in the wilderness may be a cultural trace memory of the original inhabitants, subject to massive slaughter behind the scenes of the triumphal American republic. The terrifying maniacal or savage figure in the landscape is also, however, an aspect of the self, as Huntly demonstrates by his more than Indian ferocity. Similarly, Handyside in Brown's "Somnambulism" represents Althorpe's alterior self, and Branscom/Larue, the lunatic in "Halpin Frayser," fulfills Frayser's deadly incestuous drive by killing the latter's mother. In this sense, it is the "imp of the perverse" that Poe identified as the opposing Other within the self, implacably choosing destruction for no apparent reason. But it is also in some ways *non*-subjective, an imposition from outside, a phantom with a historical provenance often rooted in family or cultural history. In this respect, it can be discussed in terms of Nicolas Abraham and Maria Torok's theorizing of the phantom as a description of the transgenerational damaging effects of an encrypted secret, producing a negativity that tyrannizes even though it cannot be understood by the subject.

The "phantom" is Abraham and Torok's designation of the unknowing awareness of another's secret that introduces the concept of "transgenerational haunting," a perspective on "the potential configurations of psychic history and on their role in pathogenic processes and symptom formation" (Rashkin 37). According to Abraham:

> The phantom is a formation of the unconscious that has never been conscious—for good reason. It passes [. . .] from the parent's unconscious into the child's. Clearly, the phantom has a function different from dynamic repression. The phantom's periodic and compulsive return lies beyond the scope of symptom-formation in the sense of a return of the repressed; it works like a ventriloquist, like a stranger within the subject's own mental topography. (Abraham in "Notes on the Phantom" 287–92)

In "Notes on the Phantom: a Complement to Freud's Metapsychology," Abraham argues that "what haunts are not the dead, but the gaps left within us by the secrets of others" and that "what comes back to haunt [us] are the tombs of others" (287, 288). This concept of the phantom enables Abraham and Torok to postulate how influences *outside* an individual's consciously lived experience can determine psychic development by linking certain states of mental disarray to the concealment of a secret rather than to that individual's unconscious as a repository of repressed wishes. "Should a child have parents 'with secrets,' [. . .] the child will receive from them a gap in the unconscious, an unknown, unrecognised knowledge, a *nescience*[. . . .] The buried speech of the parents will be (a) dead (gap) without a burial place in the child. This unknown phantom returns from the unconscious to haunt its host and may lead to phobias, madness, and obsessions" (Abraham, "Poetics," 17 n.1). This phantom itself is outside familiar developmental views of human behavior:

> It holds the individual within a group dynamic constituted by a specific familial (*and sometimes extrafamilial*) topology that prevents the individual from living life as her or his own. [. . . I]t occurs when the child's normal processes of individuation or separation from the parent are hindered by the presence of a gap or lacuna within the parent's speech. The unspeakable

secret suspended within the adult is transmitted silently to the child in "undigested" form and lodges within his or her mental topography as an unmarked tomb of inaccessible knowledge. Its presence there holds the child (later the adult) in a pathogenic dual union with the parent, in a silent partnership dedicated to preserving the secret intact. The child's unwitting involvement in this mute pact interferes with the psychic processes leading to successful introjection and inhibits its emergence as an autonomous subject. (Rashkin 27, italics added)

Abraham and Torok propose that such symptoms can occur "when a shameful and therefore unspeakable experience must be barred from consciousness or simply "kept secret" (Rashkin 22). Abraham also notes that another surprising fact gradually emerges:

[T]he work of the phantom coincides in every respect with Freud's description of the death instinct. First of all, it has no energy of its own; it cannot be "abreacted," merely designated. Second, it pursues in silence its work of disarray. Let us add that the phantom is sustained by secreted words, invisible gnomes whose aim is to wreak havoc, from within the unconscious, in the coherence of logical progression. Finally, it gives rise to endless repetition and, more often than not, eludes rationalization. (Abraham, "Notes," 291)

In his account of the strange parallels in some of these American Gothic fictions, Marek Wilczynski points to the larger implications of domestic aberration and argues that "each of the Gothicists who came after Brown inscribed into his work a 'crypt' containing some obscure and horrifying secret which determined the semantics of the Gothic text" (21). What exactly that secret might be is not really the point, but the nineteenth-century American Gothic "seems to have its peculiar historical underpinning, an oblique critical bent directed against the patriotic zeal of the early Republic and the imperial prospects of the quickly expanding United States" (263).

Such narratives also seem to be "haunted" by the specter of racial consciousness and racist oppression (of which the "Chinaman" of Bierce's "Haunted Valley" is but one example; others include the irruption of the Gothic in Crèvecoeur's *Letters from an American Farmer* at the narrator's encounter with the Negro held in a cage hanging from a tree; Poe's "Hop Frog," with its implicit reference to lynching; the colonial racism hidden in "The Murders in the Rue Morgue"; Robert Montgomery Bird's *Nick o' the Woods*; and the Gothic chapter on the Legree plantation in *Uncle Tom's Cabin*). This argument may be further illustrated by the way that race generates the uncanny in such stories as Melville's "The Bell-Tower" and "Benito Cereno," both from the immediately pre–Civil War *Piazza Tales* collection of 1856. "The Bell-Tower" tells of an Italian inventor, Bannadonna, who builds a magnificent clock tower—the noblest in Italy—to contain the great state-bell. The parallels with the American republic and its Liberty Bell are implicit. During the casting of the great bell, Bannadonna strikes and kills one of his workmen, from whom "a splinter was dashed into the seething mass, and at once was melted in" (122). Consequently the bell develops a blemish, seen in the strange features of one of the girls that was molded to represent the hours around its circumference. Una's smile seems "a fatal one." At the hour on which the bell is first struck, while Bannadonna is absorbed in repairing the blemish on Una's face, he is himself crushed by the uncanny mechanical figure designed to strike the hours: "It had limbs, and seemed clad in a scaly mail, lustrous as a dragon-beetle's. It was manacled, and its clubbed arms were uplifted, as if, with its manacles, once more to strike its already smitten victim. One advanced foot of it was inserted beneath the dead body, as if in the act of spurning it" (127).

Displaced to a Hawthornean setting—exotic Italy—Melville's uncanny Gothicism clearly allows anxieties around slavery, such as are suggested by the manacles, to surface. A similar motif of the spurning foot and the equivocal relationship between master and slave emerges in "Benito Cereno," in which the oval stern piece of the *San Dominick* shows two masked figures, one with its foot on the neck of the prostrate other. That the question asked by this enigmatic tableau is "who is the slave and who is the master?" is confirmed in the recapitulation of the image at the end of the diegesis, when the American Captain Delano stands with his foot on the neck of Babo, the insurrectionary slave and evil genius of the violent deception. In this tale slavery is again a potent generator of the uncanny, as is expressed both in the realization of the stern piece's import and in the Gothicism of the sun-bleached, drifting, monastic ship on which the mist-shrouded figures of the black slaves resemble the Dominican monks who controlled the Inquisition; the ship itself seems a monastery or a ruined chateau. There is a Hegelian implication that the masters are themselves enslaved by the institution of slavery, and also that the threat to the naive republic, represented by the gullible Northerner

Delano, is not so much from the old powers of Europe as from the effects of slavery in the New World itself. Melville's implications are no doubt conscious, but, as in his other writings, he speaks of this period in a way that is veiled to his culture, telling obliquely what it will not hear or cannot say for itself.

After the Civil War, suppressed traumas from the internecine conflict persisted, haunting Ambrose Bierce's later accounts of episodes in the struggle. Bierce's uncanny is generally rooted, like Todorov's description of the uncanny, in the psychological and the real, but it also generally, as is the way of the uncanny, produces a vortex of less easily grounded inference or implication. "A Horseman in the Sky" will illustrate; it might indeed reasonably be subtitled "The Dead Father." Carter Druse, on watch duty to protect the federal troops in a valley a thousand feet below him, wakes from inadvertent sleep to see a mounted enemy spy at the edge of the cliff:

> His first feeling was a keen artistic delight. On a colossal pedestal, the cliff— motionless at the extreme edge of the capping rock and sharply outlined against the sky—was an equestrian statue of impressive dignity. The figure of the man sat on the figure of the horse, straight and soldierly, but with the repose of a Grecian god carved in the marble which limits the suggestion of activity[. . . .] Magnified by its lift against the sky and by the soldier's testifying sense of the formidableness of a near enemy the group appeared of heroic, almost colossal size. (99–100)

Druse prepares to shoot this enemy horseman, but, at that instant, his target turns and seems to "look into his very face, into his eyes, into his brave, compassionate heart" (100). As the reader will learn, although not until the end of the story, the horseman is Druse's own father, the Virginian patriarch against whose loyalties he had rebelled in insisting on joining the Union army: "Well, go, sir, and whatever may occur, do what you conceive to be your duty. Virginia, to which you are a traitor, must get on without you" (98). Druse hesitates, but it is evident that the figure must be killed, having no doubt already clearly seen "as at the bottom of a translucent sea" the lines of men and horses below. His father's words "do what you conceive to be your duty" ring in his memory, and with "his nerves as tranquil as a sleeping babe's," he fires his fatal shot—at the horse.

One thousand feet below, a federal officer sees the astonishing sight of "a man on horseback riding down into the valley through the air":

Straight upright sat the rider, in military fashion, with a firm seat in the sad-
dle, a strong clutch upon the rein to hold his charger from too impetuous a
plunge. From his bare head his long hair streamed upward, waving like a
plume. His hands were concealed in the cloud of the horse's lifted mane.
The animal's body was as level as if every hoof-stroke encountered the resist-
ant earth. Its motions were those of a wild gallop, but even as the officer
looked they ceased, with all the legs thrown sharply forward as in the act of
alighting from a leap. But this was a flight!

Filled with amazement and terror by this apparition of a horseman in
the sky—half believing himself the chosen scribe of some new Apocalypse,
the officer was overcome by the intensity of his emotions; his legs failed him
and he fell. Almost at the same instant he heard a crashing sound in the
trees—a sound that died without an echo—and all was still. (103)

The tableau sets off a cascading dialectic of history and myth, the political and the personal, choice and destiny, in which the archaism of the
horseman's figure, his resemblance to Greek archetype, interweaves with
the conflicted allegiances of Carter Druse and his own deeper psychology. Like the paternal imago that Melville describes in the ancient cellar
museum of the Hotel de Ville in *Moby Dick,* the father is given a grandeur
that makes the event of his overthrowing by the son an emblematic action.
As horseman of the apocalypse (or rider of Pegasus) he is displaced into
uncanny psychoanalytical mythicism. Druse, the "babe," rests easy in his
parricide, and the reader is encouraged to think that he has solved his
dilemma by shooting the horse, not the father. But since his father's death
is equally certain, this choice may be seen as rewarding not only aestheti-
cally for the reader—in line with Bierce's appreciation of the surreal element in the fall (he dryly remarks that "the line of aerial cavalry is directly
downward")—but in more personal terms for Druse: The father is brought
down in his full splendor, bizarrely still in control of his flying horse.
There seems to be a "family secret" here accompanying the larger political
"secret" of the Civil War's deep, underlying damage to family, and this
produces the potent charge of uncanniness.

How then might we translate the thematics of Green's "dead-mother
syndrome" or Abraham and Torok's "crypt" or "phantom" within the unconscious into sociopolitical and cultural terms? It seems that the possibility of extra-familial origins for the phantom encourages speculation
about a political dimension. In this respect the rebellion against the mother
country that shaped the early republic, together with the traumatic parallel

of the French Revolution, and the national "family" conflict over race issues and the Civil War, allows for the possibility that such large political events are encoded or encrypted within fictions of domestic and familial trauma. Similarly, the trauma of conflict between settlers and Native Americans, rewritten in a public discourse of triumphalism, might well continue to haunt the American imaginary and surface at least obliquely within Gothic narratives. I would argue that there may be in this sense a specifically American "political unconscious" that becomes visible more particularly within the frame of "spectral" fictions.

A final note on the nature of these arguments: It is not my intention to demonstrate that the personal psychology or inner demons of these writers in the form of the "dead-mother syndrome" or Abraham and Torok's "crypt" and "phantom" of the family (or cultural or historical) "secrets" are the *exclusive* generators of such uncanny reading effects, although in some respects they may be operating to create them. Rather, I think it is a matter of attending to such features as being *reading effects*, which is to say that one way or another they key into the reading responses of their audience. Thomas Weiskel opened the way to such an understanding in his work on the "negative sublime" in which he explores how textual mechanisms can be inferred to work with the more or less successful (more or less damaged) acculturation of the reading individual, and thus with the reader's unconscious. Current thought regarding "self psychology" indicates that variants of affective disorder are likely in most, if not all, people—if not to the extent of the "sick animal" implied by the earlier Freudian model (see Kohut, "Analysis," "Restoration"; and Bragan). Bierce himself may not necessarily have experienced his flying horseman as uncanny (as his dry humor in the tale might indicate). In this, as in other such texts, we should not expect a uniform reader response any more than we should expect to recuperate the specific affective orders or disorders of their authors. Rather, the intention here has been to offer some possible analytical frames, or lenses, through which to enhance our sense of how the spectral or uncanny elements may operate in American fiction, and perhaps in the history of the American culture.

WORKS CITED

Abraham, Nicolas. "Notes on the Phantom: A Complement to Freud's Metapsychology." *Critical Inquiry* 13 (Winter 1987): 287–92.
———. "A Poetics of Psychoanalysis: 'The Lost Object-Me.'" *Sub-Stance* 43 (1984): 3–18.

Abraham, Nicolas, and Maria Torok. *The Wolfman's Magic Word: A Cryptonomy.* Translated by Nicholas Rand. Minneapolis: University of Minnesota Press, 1986.

———. *The Shell and the Kernel: Renewals of Psychoanalysis.* Vol. 1. Translated by Nicholas Rand. Chicago: University of Chicago Press, 1986.

Allston, Washington. *Lectures on Art and Poems, 1850; and Monaldi, 1841.* Edited by R. H. Dana. Gainesville, Fl.: Scholars' Facsimiles and Reprints, 1967.

Bierce, Ambrose. *Can Such Things Be?* 1893. Reprint. Freeport, N.Y.: Books for Libraries, 1971.

———. "The Death of Halpin Frayser." 1893. In *American Gothic: An Anthology 1787–1916.* Edited by Charles L. Crow, 408–17. Malden, Ma.: Blackwell, 1999.

———. *The Eyes of the Panther: Tales of Soldiers and Civilians.* 1928. Reprint. Freeport, N.Y.: Books for Libraries Press, 1971.

———. "The Haunted Valley." *Can Such Things Be?* 1893. Reprint. Freeport, N.Y.: Books for Libraries Press, 1971. 134–54.

———. "An Inhabitant of Carcosa." *Can Such Things Be?* 1893. Reprint. Freeport, N.Y.: Books for Libraries Press, 1971. 308–14.

———. "The Middle Toe of the Right Foot." *Can Such Things Be?* 1893. Reprint. Freeport, N.Y.: Books for Libraries Press, 1971. 235–251.

———. "The Moonlit Road." *Can Such Things Be?* 1893. Reprint. Freeport, N.Y.: Books for Libraries Press, 1971. 62–80.

———. "The Secret of Macarger's Gulf." *Can Such Things Be?* 1893. Reprint. Freeport, N.Y.: Books for Libraries Press, 1971. 44–57.

Bragan, Kenneth. *Self and Spirit in the Therapeutic Relationship.* London: Routledge, 1996.

Brown, Charles Brockden. *Edgar Huntly; or, Memoirs of a Sleep-Walker.* 1799. Reprint. Edited by Sydney J. Krause and S. W. Reid. Kent, Ohio: Kent State University Press, 1984.

———. "Somnambulism: A Fragment." 1805. In *American Gothic: An Anthology 1787–1916.* Edited by Charles L. Crow, 7–18. Malden, Ma.: Blackwell, 1999.

———. *Wieland, or The Transformation.* 1798. Reprint. Edited by Fred Lewis Pattee. New York: Harcourt Brace Jovanovich, 1926.

Dana, Richard Henry. "Paul Felton." In *Poems and Prose Writings of Richard Henry Dana.* New York: Baker & Scribner, 1850.

Freud, Sigmund. "The Uncanny." In *The Standard Edition of the Complete Psychological Works of Sigmund Freud,* vol. 17, edited by James Strachey, 217–53. London: Hogarth, 1955.

Green, Andre. "The Dead Mother." 1983. In *On Private Madness.* Reprint. London: Hogarth and the Institute of Psychoanalysis, 1986.

Jameson, Fredric. *The Political Unconscious: Narrative as a Socially Symbolic Act.* London: Methuen, 1983.

Kohon, Gregorio, Ed. *The Dead Mother.* London: Routledge, 1999.

Kohut, Heinz. *The Analysis of the Self.* London: Hogarth, 1971.

———. *The Restoration of the Self.* 1971. Reprint. New York: International Universities Press, 1977.

Melville, Herman. "The Bell Tower." 1856. In *American Gothic: An Anthology 1787–1916.* Edited by Charles L. Crow, 121–30. Malden, Ma.: Blackwell Publishers, 1999.

————. "Benito Cereno." 1855. In *The Heath Anthology of American Literature*. Vol. 1. 4th Ed. Edited by Paul Lauter, et al., 2598–655. New York: Houghton Mifflin, 2002.

Modell, Arnold H. "The Dead Mother Syndrome and the Reconstruction of Trauma." In *The Dead Mother*. Edited by Gregorio Kohon. London: Routledge, 1999.

Punter, David. *The Literature of Terror*. London: Longman, 1980.

Rashkin, Esther. "Tools for a New Psychoanalytic Criticism." *Diacritics* (Winter 1988): 31–52.

Weiskel, Thomas. *The Romantic Sublime*. Baltimore: Johns Hopkins University Press, 1976.

Wilczynski, Marek. *The Phantom and the Abyss: The Gothic Fiction in America and Aesthetics of the Sublime, 1798–1865*. Frankfurt: Peter Lang, 1999.

Living for the Other World

Sarah Orne Jewett as a Religious Writer

TERRY HELLER

Love isn't blind; it's only love that sees.

—Sarah Orne Jewett, *Letters of Sarah Orne Jewett* (1911, #133)

The Miracles of the Church seem to me to rest not so much upon faces or voices or healing power coming suddenly near to us from afar off, but upon our perceptions being made finer, so that for a moment our eyes can see and our ears can hear what is there about us always.

—Bishop Latour in Willa Cather, *Death Comes for the Archbishop* (1927)

Scholars such as Elizabeth Ammons, Josephine Donovan, Laurie Shannon, and Sarah Sherman have presented a rather full picture of the religious development of Sarah Orne Jewett (1849–1909).[1] In "The Country of Our Friendship," Shannon argues that Jewett's purpose is religious in *The Country of the Pointed Firs* (1896, hereafter *Pointed Firs*). Shannon sees *Pointed Firs* as "a virtual devotional text," illustrating a pilgrimage from acquaintance to a deep intimacy that is an experience of paradise on earth. She compares the novella to Henry David Thoreau's *Walden* (1854); both present a discipline and a practice for living deliberately by drawing spiritual insight and sustenance from contemplating the intimate and quotidian. Jewett links the cultivation of intimacy in friendship with salvation, and she contrasts her practice with the large-scale systematizing of conventional religion that seeks intellectual comprehension of cosmic purpose.[2]

Jewett's religion of friendship pervades her writing, especially after the early 1880s, and a main purpose of her mature writing career seems to be to encourage readers to undertake the spiritual discipline that she so often represents in her fiction. Jewett's religion of friendship forms part of a cultural project—visible in much post–Civil War women's regionalist writing—to advance ideals that could effectively oppose increasing materialism, extreme individualism, impersonal patriarchal institutions, capitalist commercialism, and an appropriating colonialism. To advance this agenda, Jewett gives particular attention to three aspects of intimate friendship that she believes call one's attention to the spiritual dimensions of daily life: mind reading, transfiguration, and communication with the dead.

We should recognize from the outset that these terms are problematic, mainly because Jewett represents each as being on a continuum of experience in which what we think of as natural shades into what she believes is supernatural. Reflecting on her personal experience of seeing apparitions of her deceased friend, Celia Thaxter, Jewett writes: "and yet where imagination stops and consciousness of the unseen begins, who can settle that even to one's self?" (Jewett, *Letters* #62). What is important to Jewett is that she repeatedly experiences such intimations; taken together, they sustain the faith she puts into the mouths of several of her characters, notably Mrs. Todd in "The Foreigner" (1900), that human happiness comes from living in such a way as to join the mortal world with the spiritual world, to live *in* this world but *for* the next. She shares the belief that she has Dr. Leslie express in *A Country Doctor* (1884), when he discusses the intuition that makes a good doctor able to diagnose a patient well:

> But I have long believed that the powers of Christ were but the higher powers of our common humanity. We recognize them dimly now and then, but few of us dare to say so yet. [. . .] If Christ were perfect man, He could hardly tell us to follow Him and be like Him, and yet know all the while that it was quite impossible, because a difference in his gifts made his character an unapproachable one to ours. We don't amount to anything, simply because we won't understand that we must receive the strength of Heaven into our souls; that it depends upon our degree of receptivity, and our using the added power that comes in that way. (chap. 9)

Christ's power to heal, for example, may be truly supernatural or only an extension of natural human powers. What seems natural in everyday life—knowing what another is thinking, the feeling of spiritual unity with a friend, the vivid perception of a deceased beloved—may be the prosaic side of supernatural experiences that should be termed mind reading, transfiguration, and communication with the dead. As perception becomes finer, what is invisible but always there begins to become visible. Love enables vision.

Jewett's representation of mind reading appears in her earliest fiction, beginning at least as far back as *Deephaven* (1877), and it is not unusual for her characters to experience unmediated communication over considerable distance. Such wordless sharing may range from correctly guessing a person's intentions from close observation to knowing the thoughts of a distant person. Over her life Jewett came to view supernatural telepathy with friends as normal. For example, in a 1905 letter to Sarah Cabot Wheelwright, she writes:

> It is not because I do not think of you very often that I have not written; but every day brings its succession of little hurries, and hours when one cannot write. And then I count more and more upon the truth that we can "think" to each other, when we are really friends, much better and oftener than we can write. When they find out all about wireless telegraphy, they are going to find out how the little batteries in our heads send messages, and then we can do it by rule and not by accident. It is very nice now, however, and we aren't *called up* by strangers as we may be in those later and more instructive days. (Jewett, *Letters* #119)

Though playful in tone, Jewett is serious about the ability of true friends to "think" to each other. Louisa Dresel, in an 1892 letter to Jewett, indicates she shares Jewett's belief (Cary 33). Mind reading occurs frequently in her fiction as well as in her letters.

As Marcia Folsom has shown, silent communication, sometimes over considerable distance, is a central motif in *Pointed Firs* (Nagel 76–89). The narrator says of Mrs. Blackett: "Tact is after all a kind of mind-reading, and my hostess held the golden gift. Sympathy is of the mind as well as the heart, and Mrs. Blackett's world and mine were one from the moment we met. Besides, she had that highest gift of heaven, a perfect self-forgetfulness" (chap. 10). The novel can be understood as the narrator's progress, during her summer in Dunnet Landing, in developing friendships that finally make her feel she belongs to this community. Such progress is possible only through the practice of the arts and disciplines of tact and self-forgetfulness in cultivating one's acquaintances and making them into friends. When she is successful, the narrator knows from the sounds in the house in the morning what her landlady, Almira Todd, is planning for the day, reading thought from careful observation and intimate knowledge. Almira and her mother's self-forgetful friendship is apparent in their ability to imagine each other's feelings and intentions, though a bay stretches between them; for one mundane example, Almira somehow knows that Mrs. Blackett wants an onion for her chowder and brings one along on the visit to Green Island (chap. 8). As the narrator comes to know the village, she and her new friends repeatedly read each others' minds, in small ways and large. The narrator and Mrs. Todd become able to communicate by a glance (chap. 12), and the narrator shows "proofs of divination" based on the ordinary sounds Mrs. Todd makes on the morning of the Bowden reunion (chap. 16). Whether this is true telepathy or only a refinement of friendship is not perfectly clear, but the result looks like mind reading.

Mind reading is a healing power, as Ammons says in "Jewett's Witches" (Nagel 174–77). The more perfect one's self-forgetfulness, the more successfully one enters into the minds and hearts of others, the richer the friendships become, and the greater one's power to heal spiritual hurts. The narrator of *Pointed Firs* arrives at Dunnet Landing in need of renewal. She heals as her desire to work in isolation diminishes, and she enters into the spiritual life of the village and into moments of silent intimacy with the living and the dead, including Captain Tilley (chap. 20) and "Poor Joanna" (chap. 15). Jewett more explicitly illustrates the healing power of mind reading and makes it seem more supernaturally telepathic in "An Every-Day Girl" (1892), a story she recommends to her young correspondent, Louisa Dresel (Jewett, *Letters* #87). Mary, the protagonist, tells her boyfriend: "Aunt Hannah's a lovely old woman [. . .]. She always makes me feel so pleasant. She isn't a bit like anybody else. I've heard mother say ever so many times that she always had the gift of coming just when people wanted her. She sort of flies down out of the air" ("An Every-Day Girl"). Like an angel/witch, Aunt Hannah (who is not really Mary's aunt) magically senses Mary's crisis over what to do with herself after finishing school and is drawn into the village to speak with her. Quickly seeing into her problems more clearly than Mary does, Hannah sets Mary on the road to self-confident, self-possessed adulthood.

Hannah has achieved a virtually supernatural wisdom that somehow allows her to know the minds of less-aware people and to cultivate and help them, just as Mrs. Blackett and the narrator cultivate and help people they meet in the Dunnet Landing stories. Seemingly telepathic communication appears in many Jewett stories from *Deephaven* through *The Tory Lover* (1901). Mind reading's powers to bind and heal are seen in "The

Only Rose" (1894), when Miss Pendexter's vision of the rose as a face leads her to help the inarticulate Mrs. Bickford talk through her dilemma. Finally, Miss Pendexter confides the story of her disappointed love, which indirectly helps Mrs. Bickford solve the problem of what to do with her one rose blossom. In "A Dunnet Shepherdess" (1899), the narrator and William Blackett communicate wordlessly as they travel through the countryside; this deepens their friendship, and the narrator discovers William's love for Esther Hight.

Another effect of mind reading is communion, the feeling of being mentally and emotionally one with one's friends, of being bound together as were Jesus and his disciples at the Last Supper (Matt. 26; Mark 14; Luke 22). Some of the most moving moments in Jewett's works occur when mind reading blossoms into communion. John Humma shows how telepathic communication leads to communion in "The Courting of Sister Wisby" (1887). "The Life of Nancy" (1895) and "Martha's Lady" (1897) end in moments of communion. Another such moment is in *Pointed Firs* when Mrs. Blackett invites the narrator to sit in her rocking chair. The narrator sees deeply into Mrs. Blackett's life as she looks upon the objects in the bedroom:

> Those dear old fingers and their loving stitches, that heart which had made the most of everything that needed love! Here was the real home, the heart of the old house on Green Island! I sat in the rocking-chair, and felt that it was a place of peace, the little brown bedroom, and the quiet outlook upon field and sea and sky.
>
> I looked up, and we understood each other without speaking. "I shall like to think o' your settin' here to-day," said Mrs. Blackett. (chap. 11)

In the rocking chair, the narrator finds an intimacy in friendship that begins to move beyond communion to a still more refined vision, when friends look into each other's souls. This is transfiguration.

Transfiguration refers to the biblical story in which three disciples see Jesus transformed into a shining being, and a voice speaks out of a cloud identifying him as "my son." Then, suddenly, the vision is gone, and Jesus appears as merely a man (Matt. 17; Luke 22). On her own birthday, September 3, 1897, Jewett wrote to young Sara Norton about the deaths of friends:

> One feels how easy it is for friends to slip away out of this world and leave us lonely. And such good days as you have had are too good to be looked

for often. There is something transfiguring in the best of friendship. One remembers the story of the transfiguration in the New Testament, and sees over and over in life what the great shining hours can do, and how one goes down from the mountain where they are, into the fret of everyday life again, but strong in remembrance. I once heard Mr. [Phillips] Brooks preach a great sermon about this: nobody could stay on the mount, but every one knew it, and went his way with courage by reason of such moments. (Jewett, *Letters #73*)

The highest experience of friendship is spiritual communion at maximum intensity, a mutual revelation of shining, spiritual selves as children of God.

This account of the meaning of transfiguration is apt as a plot summary for *Pointed Firs,* in which the narrator's summer visit is a journey up a mountain that, like Wordsworth's vision of daffodils, continues "strong in remembrance" to sustain her after she leaves Dunnet Landing. Within that plot are several such journeys into communion with the living and the dead: the trip to Green Island; the pilgrimage to Shell-heap Island; the visit with Captain Tilley and "poor dear," his deceased wife;. and especially the Bowden reunion, which is a "mountaintop" transfiguration of a whole gathering of family and friends (see Shannon). As "the golden chain of love and dependence" that unifies much of the community of Dunnet Landing becomes more visible, it becomes clear that a good community's reason for being is to create and sustain just such a golden chain (chap. 17). This work is the spiritual life of a community. All other communal activities—defense, commerce, government, religion, education, healing, the arts, and especially housekeeping—are *for* creating and sustaining spiritual connectedness. Hence, the Bowden reunion, the result and reward of a year's labor, becomes a transfiguring occasion of spiritual unity. Nearly everyone emits metaphorical light, and the narrator feels she has become a kindred spirit to a family that represents the very idea of human communion (chap. 18). Faces and places that beam and shine mark moments of transfiguration throughout the novel and throughout Jewett's writing.

"A White Heron" (1886) and "The Queen's Twin" (1899) contain transfigurations that may seem more supernatural, growing out of two kinds of friendship: those with "nature" and those with human friends.

In "A White Heron" a young girl experiences a transfiguration of nature. As a result she turns away, at least temporarily, from human communion, choosing instead a life "heart to heart with nature." Nine-year-old Sylvia is rescued from a too crowded urban family by her grandmother, who brings the child to her sylvan hermitage. There Sylvia cultivates intimacy with

animals, especially birds. Into their lives comes an attractive but dangerous young ornithologist. He loves birds, yet shoots them for study. He
befriends and teaches Sylvia, but hopes to exploit her knowledge of the
local wildlife to add the elusive white heron to his collection. She is
tempted to become a selfless woman, who might love him "as a dog loves."
She climbs a landmark pine to spot the heron's nest for him. However,
while looking out from this tree at dawn, she has a vision that closely
parallels Thoreau's vision of the woods as a friend in "Solitude" (88–89),
a vision of unity with the trees, the birds, the heron, and even—within
Jewett's complex rhetoric—with the narrator and the reader (see Heller).
In the light of this vision, she cannot betray the heron: "The murmur of
the pine's green branches is in her ears, she remembers how the white
heron came flying through the golden air and how they watched the sea
and the morning together, and Sylvia cannot speak; she cannot tell the
heron's secret and give its life away." Instead, she chooses to remain under
nature's tutelage, presumably to develop a self that is strong enough to
deal with males as an equal. A shining moment makes Sylvia aware of a
spiritual friendship in nature that speaks to and sustains her own spiritual
self. This awareness does not forbid human communion, but it defines the
terms of an acceptable relationship—that which fosters without exploitation, possesses without using, knows without violence. This story might
well be seen as an allegory of Jewett's resistance, not only to the "realism"
William Dean Howells demanded for the *Atlantic* (Jewett, *Letters* #34),
but also to appropriation and assimilation by a materialism that would
eviscerate her unique identity and spiritual purpose. But this is not merely
defensive, for Sylvia is engaged in positive self-creation, grounded in a
visionary experience of spiritual reality.

Jewett's personal awareness of a spiritual aspect of nature shows up often
in her fiction and poetry, especially in her first-person sketches, such as
"A Winter Drive" (1881), "River Driftwood" (1881), and "The Confession
of a House-Breaker" (1883). In these stories, Jewett sees nature as a *person*,
as transcendentalists such as Thoreau saw it, with a dual, spiritual, and
material aspect. Sylvia's vision of spirit revealed through nature leads her
to consider the birds as "better friends" than the young hunter might have
been. Though being friends with nature is different from being friends
with people, both processes can lead to transfiguration, the experience of
knowing and being known by a spiritual being.

In "The Queen's Twin," a Dunnet Landing story, Almira takes the narrator inland to the isolated home of a widow, Abby Martin, who is Queen

Victoria's "twin." Literal connections between Abby and Queen Victoria, such as the shared birth date, appear coincidental, whereas some, like naming children, were manufactured. Though they are easy to dismiss or ridicule, these links have sustained Abby's "illusion" that she is intimate with the queen, despite the fact that Abby only glimpsed her once, during a brief stay in London. Abby confides her belief that in her old age, Victoria might well like to know "about us," that is, about the "real" connections between her and Abby: "But I've had a great advantage in seeing her, an' I can always fancy her goin' on, while she don't know nothin' yet about me, except she may feel my love stayin' her heart sometimes an' not know just where it comes from." Through poverty and loneliness, Abby has been sustained by a spiritual bond. Though she is perfectly aware that the queen *knows* nothing of her, she hopes that the queen may *feel* "my love stayin' her heart." Abby confesses that she once so longed to share this bond openly that she prepared her house and a meal for an imaginary visit from the queen:

> "[W]hen I see the dark an' it come to me I was all alone, the dream left me, an' I sat down on the doorstep an' felt all foolish an' tired. An', if you'll believe it, I heard steps comin', an' an old cousin o' mine come wanderin' along, one I was apt to be shy of [. . .]. And I went right to meet her when I first heard her call, 'stead o' hidin' as I sometimes did, an' she come in dreadful willin', an' we sat down to supper together; 't was a supper I should have had no heart to eat alone."
>
> "I don't believe she ever had such a splendid time in her life as she did then. I heard her tell all about it afterwards," exclaimed Mrs. Todd compassionately. "There, now I hear all this it seems just as if the Queen might have known and couldn't come herself, so she sent that poor old creatur' that was always in need!"

Abby's fantasy appears foolish, but it resonates with Jesus's parable of the sheep and the goats in Matthew 25: "For I was an hungered, and ye gave me meat." In a moment of enthusiasm, Almira sympathizes and enters into the "fantasy." She theorizes that the queen, unable to appear herself, has "sent" her representative, and this seems as if it must be true. Victoria *has* been present spiritually, even if the literal queen had no detailed awareness of her act. In response to Abby's longing to express her love, Victoria has somehow accepted Abby's seemingly foolish attempt at hospitality. Almira reflects that Abby certainly is not the only person to have prepared

a meal for an absent friend out of pure longing. This produces a deep
silence out of which comes Almira's insight: "Don't it show that for folks
that have any fancy in 'em, such beautiful dreams is the real part o' life? But
to most folks the common things that happens outside 'em is all in all."
Almira's interpretation transforms Abby's strange dinner into a moment
of spiritual presence—a shining moment when the cousin represents the
queen, who represents, for this moment at least, the spiritual connectedness of all who care for each other. The remembered event shines before the
visitors, they glow in its presence, and then they enter Abby's sanctuary.

Jewett reports having such dreams herself in an 1897 letter to Sara
Norton (Jewett, *Letters* #72):

> Just at this moment, instead of going on with my proper work of writing,
> I find that I wish to talk to you. This is partly because I dreamed about you
> and feel quite as if I had seen you in the night[. . . .]
>
> I think of the old house at home as I write this so gayly, and to tell the
> truth, I wish that you and I were there together. If we were there we should
> see the pink hollyhocks in the garden and read together a good deal. I wish
> that my pretty dream were all true! but one finds true companionship in
> dreams—as I knew last night.
>
> Dear child, I shall be so glad to see you again. I have missed you sadly
> this summer in spite of your letters,— in spite of time and space counting
> for so little in friendship!

For Jewett, as for Almira, there is a sustaining truth in these "beautiful
dreams." They are the *real* part of life, because they reveal each other's souls
and, therefore, point toward the spiritual foundations of happiness. This
may be connected as well with Jewett's belief that "the writer's job is to make
one dream; that is, to make one aware of another realm, a transcendent
realm, by means of images drawn from earthly, everyday reality" (Donovan "Sarah Orne Jewett's Critical Theory" 216; see also Jewett, *Letters* #94).

In "The Queen's Twin," it avails not that a material basis for intimacy
between Abby and the queen is lacking, any more than time and space
can stand between Walt Whitman and his readers in "Crossing Brooklyn
Ferry." In Abby's experience Almira can see reasons to believe that, without being conscious of it, Victoria shares in this connection. These experiences of friendship—mind reading, communion, and transfiguration—
fill life with meaning. Furthermore, they finally point beyond mortality to
another life, for, in Jewett, some friendships overcome the barrier of death.

Jewett's personal views on mortal contact with the spirit world were circumspect. She had felt the presence of the dead, and she reported spiritual communication with parents and friends after their deaths, for example, in her first poem to her father and in another poem, "Assurance" (*Verses*; see also *Sarah Orne Jewett Letters* 105, and Silverthorne 148, 174). According to Blanchard, Jewett was interested in Spiritualism but became at least mildly skeptical about mediums' communications with the dead (158). Central Spiritualist beliefs are that the dead are benevolent and that they can speak to the living from a spirit world that is continuous with the physical world. Historians of Spiritualism emphasize its general egalitarianism and sympathy with women's rights. Such ideas parallel Jewett's, but as Ann Braude shows in *Radical Spirits*, Spiritualism as the adult Jewett would have seen it tended toward sensationalism and scandal. In her fiction, Jewett evinces no interest in mediums or trance circles, perhaps because they represent a ritualistic coercion of communication that Jewett probably found as distasteful as being "called up by a stranger." Playing with Spiritualism causes suffering in "A Sorrowful Guest" (1879), and Jewett even lampoons aspects of Spiritualism in Deacon Brimblecom, a character in "The Courting of Sister Wisby." Contact with the dead should arise spontaneously from the deepest intimacy of friendship. Though one may receive messages from the beloved dead, the experience is not to be sought through a medium, but only accepted, with gratitude and recognition of its mystery. Her careful analysis of her experience of seeing Celia Thaxter after her death in 1894 is characteristic:

It seems as if I could hear her talking, and as if we lived those June days over again. Most of my friends have gone out of illness and long weeks of pain, but with her the door seems to have open[ed] and shut, and what is a very strange thing, I can see her face,—you know I never could call up faces easily, and never before, that I remember, have I been able to see how a person looked who has died, but again and again I seem to see her. That takes me a strange step out of myself. All this new idea of Tesla's: must it not, like everything else, have its spiritual side, and yet where imagination stops and consciousness of the unseen begins, who can settle that even to one's self? (Jewett, *Letters* #62)

The new idea to which she refers is probably wireless communication, one of Nikola Tesla's (1856–1943) projects. Thaxter's unexpected death affects Jewett strangely; she "sees" Thaxter as she has not seen her other beloved

dead. She wonders because she cannot distinguish a line between imagination (the wish to see) and vision (the actual presence of the dead one).
But she is sure that "consciousness of the unseen" begins somewhere along
this continuum, that there *is* a point at which imaginative vision becomes
sufficiently refined to perceive the invisible.

Jewett's fiction consistently embodies a certainty that contact with
the dead occurs, combined with uncertainty about how to tell *when* it
occurs—just as her characters are not always certain whether they have
imagined or experienced mind reading, even though they know they have
communicated without speech. Her biblical touchstone for this experience is the story of Emmaus, told most fully in Luke 24. After his death,
Jesus joins a pair of the disciples on the road to the village of Emmaus, but
they do not recognize him. He comforts the grieving men as they walk.
When he later breaks bread with them, they see who he is, and he van-
ishes. Jewett typically identifies with the disciples' point of view, unsure
about the circumstances of such visions, but still persuaded and com-
forted by the overall experience. Transfiguration reveals the spiritual self
of a living friend; seeing a ghost as Jewett saw Thaxter extends transfiguration to include *dead* friends and points to another level of communion
beyond mortal life, in which souls may mingle completely and eternally.
This realm appears benign, and its influences are benevolent.

This view of ghosts is clearly expressed in "The Foreigner," another of
the Dunnet Landing stories. Almira tells the story of Mrs. Captain Tolland,
who, after much suffering, finds herself exiled in Dunnet Landing. Mrs.
Tolland is a French woman among New Englanders, a Catholic among
Protestants, a warm Latin temperament in a cold country, a gay and artis-
tic personality among Yankee Calvinists, and perhaps a mulatto among
exclusive whites (Schrag). At Mrs. Blackett's insistence, Almira befriends
the lonely woman and then nurses her through her last illness. On the
night of Mrs. Tolland's death, they see a ghost.

The sleeping Mrs. Tolland suddenly rises up in bed and extends her
arms toward the door. Almira glimpses an unexpected face in the darkness. She blacks out momentarily in the presence of "somethin' that made
poor human natur' quail," not from terror, though, but from fatigue and
strain: "I saw very plain while I could see; 't was a pleasant enough face,
shaped somethin' like Mis' Tolland's, and a kind of expectin' look." When
Mrs. Tolland begs with her last breath for confirmation that both have
seen a person she identifies as her mother, Almira responds, "*Yes, dear, I
did; you ain't never goin' to feel strange an' lonesome no more.*" Almira says

that seeing a ghost did not seem "beyond reason": "You know plain enough there's something beyond this world; the doors stand open." Then she quotes her doctor, paraphrasing Jewett's favorite passage from Sir Thomas Browne's "Letter to a Friend": "There's somethin' of us that must still live on; we've got to join both worlds together an' live in one but for the other."

Her acquiescence in her mother's request to befriend Mrs. Tolland brings Almira a bountiful inheritance: a little money and land as the widow Tolland's heir, an improved knowledge of herbs and cooking, a greater tolerance of difference that includes a better understanding of the idea that "there might be roads leadin' up to the New Jerusalem from various points," an intimation of her own immortality, and an assurance that the next life will heal divisions so one will feel "strange an' lonesome no more."

There are many other instances of apparent contact with the benevolent dead in Jewett's fiction. In "A Second Spring" (1893), the ghost of Israel Haydon's first wife appears to bless his second marriage:

[S]uddenly they both felt as if there were a third person present; their feeling toward one another seemed to change. Something seemed to prompt them to new confidence and affection, to speak the affectionate thoughts that were in their hearts; it was no rebuking, injured presence, for a sense of great contentment filled their minds.

In "Miss Tempy's Watchers" (1888), the deceased Temperance Dent seems to hover around the two women she has asked to watch over her body before her funeral. Though, like the friends at Emmaus, they sense her only uncertainly, Tempy acts upon them as a spiritual presence, or perhaps from within them as a shared memory, or perhaps in both ways. In any case, she helps the wealthy but constitutionally stingy Mrs. Crowe to become more like the person she wants to be by making the poor but generous Sister Binson her guide in charitable activity. Their sympathy with Tempy is transformed into a deeper sympathy for each other.

In "An Every-Day Girl," Mary—under the influence of Aunt Hannah—receives help from the spirit world in general rather than from a particular dead person. On the afternoon after her graduation from high school, Mary wonders what to do with herself:

[W]ith a sudden impulse she knelt down and rested her forehead on the window sill. She never had longed to be good and happy and not to make

mistakes as she did just then, and for the first time in all her life there came
to her a sense of help and presence, a warmth of sympathy and love, as if
somebody heard and assured her in her bewildered and trusting little prayer.
[. . .] She knew now for herself that there was a love unseen, and another
life, and that there was light in dark places. All this was known in a wordless way; it was all felt in the silence of the summer evening, in the happy
peace of her young and troubled heart, and Mary Fleming ran down stairs
with shining eyes and went to find her mother.

Jewett wants readers to take seriously Mary's later statement: "There is
something wonderful that comes and helps us the minute we really try to
help ourselves."

More examples of the helpful dead and the benevolence of the spiritual
world appear in *Deephaven* (1877), "Lady Ferry" (1879), "Tom's Husband"
(1882), *A Country Doctor* (1884), *A Marsh Island* (1885)—in which most
of the main characters experience some form of contact—"The Only
Rose" (1894), and "The Tory Lover" (1901). There are, in Jewett, examples
of "gothic" stories, in which the spirit world seems more threatening: "A
Sorrowful Guest," "The Landscape Chamber" (1887), and "In Dark New
England Days" (1890). However, these stories probably do not contradict
Jewett's view that supernatural powers are uniformly benign or helpful.
Whiston's evil ghost in "A Sorrowful Guest" *is* an illusion, and the rather
problematic narrator of that story makes Whiston's subjection to it the
occasion for a meditation on theodicy. The narrator of "The Landscape
Chamber" disputes the miserly father's fixed idea that he suffers from a
hereditary curse. The Knowles sisters of "In Dark New England Days"
become the main victims of the curse they call down upon Enoch Holt
and his family, punished not supernaturally, but rather withered naturally
by their own anger and guilt.

Jewett's representations of mind reading, transfiguration, and ghosts
imply a coherent religious system. She asserts in her correspondence and
demonstrates in her fiction that the mental and emotional intimacies of
friendship are the highest human goods. There are arts and disciplines
of friendship that can bring friends into a kind of mystical telepathic communion. At its deepest and most intense, this communion becomes transfiguration, when the friends know each other spiritually. Also transfiguring
is contact between the living soul and the souls of the dead. Taken together
these religious experiences intimate the existence of a spiritual world of
the benevolently helpful dead through which all people are connected.

Experiences of aid from this other world further intimate that the goal of human life is to cultivate friendship, to live in such a way as to join the mortal world with the spiritual realm.

Articulating Jewett's religion of friendship in this way speaks to the controversy over how Jewett and women's regionalism are implicated in the formation of American national identity after the Civil War. Arguments that Jewett was uncritically involved in this cultural project have appeared in Richard Brodhead's *Cultures of Letters* and in several essays by other critics. Brodhead characterizes regionalism as a tool by which an emerging late nineteenth-century leisure class fashioned itself. Seeking to explain a burgeoning market for regional fiction after the Civil War, Brodhead notices the main demand in magazines like *Atlantic*, *Century*, and *Harper's*, in which much women's regionalist writing and Jewett's best-remembered fiction appeared. These magazines served a developing leisure class as instruments of self-definition (chap. 4). In this market, regional stories mingled with other pieces describing vacation worlds in which the upper classes could meet for the pleasures of conspicuous consumption and where they might contemplate a myth of their origin. Arguing that regional literature was not simply an effort to memorialize disappearing local cultures after the Civil War's assertion of national unity, he says that regional literature's "public function was [. . .] to purvey a certain story of contemporary cultures and of the relations among them," to absorb "local cultures into a history of their supersession by a modern order now risen to national prominence" (121). As Sandra Zagarell develops this line of argument in "Troubling Regionalism," an emerging elite "regionalized" rural cultures by creating a self-legitimizing historical myth that located the origins of the ruling class in a benevolent, hierarchical, past society. Brodhead argues that Jewett's participation in this market led to presenting rural Maine as "a place healed of the alienations that prevail in the world of social mobility and mass-produced commodities" (147). In "*Country's* Portrayal of Community and the Exclusion of Difference," Zagarell points out the racial exclusiveness of Dunnet Landing society. In "Material Culture, Empire, and Jewett's *Pointed Firs*," Elizabeth Ammons argues that Jewett is as uncritical about growing American imperialism as she is about the emergence of class hierarchies and the racial exclusiveness of nineteenth-century nativism. In this view Jewett's fiction generally serves an American leisure class that is defining and legitimizing itself as a white Anglo-Saxon Protestant empire, characterized by racist exclusion, colonialist appropriation, and the rights to own and dominate.

This view opposes the widely shared interpretation of Jewett as a central figure in a project of women regionalist writers to reform American culture. In *Women's Fiction,* Nina Baym characterizes *pre*–Civil War women's writing as sharing a concern to feminize culture, to extend a Christian domestic model of life into the public sphere. Evidence can be seen in, for example, Harriet Beecher Stowe's "The Minister's Housekeeper" (1872) and Rose Terry Cooke's "Freedom Wheeler's Controversy with Providence" (1877), both reprinted in *American Women Regionalists.* Baym sees women writers who came of age *after* the war as shifting toward depicting a woman-centered culture as an alternative to the increasingly materialistic and commercial public culture (chap. 2). An example, in addition to Jewett, is Mary Wilkins Freeman's "A Church Mouse," also reprinted in *American Women Regionalists.* Insofar as Jewett understood her cultural situation, saw herself as presenting a feminist alternative to a dehumanizing public culture, and took seriously her religion of friendship, she would have had to reject major features of an imperialist national identity. Her religion of friendship may be seen as a critique of and remedy for all social forms of exclusion, appropriation, and domination.

Brodhead seems aware that a leisure-class appropriation of Jewett's regional writing is not the same as Jewett's full and uncritical cooperation with this appropriation, and he cautions that Jewett's fiction is not simply reducible to "the social habits and anxieties that attach to this group at this moment in its history: its cross-cultural cosmopolitanism; its anxious nativism; its acquisitiveness and sense of its right to own; its care for literary art" (149). A number of critics have taken up this caution. Zagarell believes that *Deephaven* resists turning locals into fantasy figures for leisure-class myth. Jacqueline Murphy and Laurie Shannon, along with several contributors to Kilcup and Edwards's *Jewett and Her Contemporaries*—notably Marjorie Pryse, Mitzi Schrag, and Alison Easton—also show ways in which Jewett's work resists, evades, and corrects post–Civil War ideologies. However, one does not escape the cultural atmosphere in which one lives, for it always precedes and envelops one's thoughts. Brodhead shows how Jewett benefited professionally from the interests of the emerging cultural elite that found her fiction "charming." She benefited socially from being taken into this elite by Annie Fields and others. Jewett was especially sympathetic with the views of literary art that the new elite had developed (173–74). Still, her religion of friendship opposes practices of exclusion, appropriation, and dominance.

Arguments that Jewett "regionalizes" Dunnet Landing depend upon the incorrect view that she presents the village as an idyllic haven for the exercise of leisure-class "touristic" impulses. The religion of friendship is not merely a local phenomenon, nor is the need for its "consolations" exclusively urban or upper class. The narrator goes to Dunnet Landing on an individualist quest, very much as a tourist, to find a hermitage in which she can finish a piece of writing among what she expects will be simplified social relations. But soon her quest changes into a pilgrimage, for she finds rich possibilities for social intercourse. Instead of appropriating and exploiting the place, she becomes part of it, just as Jewett implies members of the elite who move into rural retreats permanently should do, for example, in "The Life of Nancy." To do this, she must practice disciplines and arts of friendship that are by no means exclusive to rural life. Indeed, she arrives with the skills already developed, and as she comes to know local people, she rises to the delicate challenge of drawing them out. She almost loses Littlepage's story when she starts to find it dull (chap. 5) but earns Almira's deepening trust by tactfully helping the old captain talk and coming to appreciate him as a friend, despite his tedious "epics" (chap. 7, and see Shannon).

As the narrator is converted from tourist to religious pilgrim, so the village comes to seem not a tourist haven, but a typical human community, with plenty of conflict, pain, and suffering (see Mobley, esp. chap. 2). This pattern of an urban character discovering complexity that leads to a critique of "touristic" impulses shows up several times in Jewett, as we have seen in *Deephaven* and "A White Heron," and also notably in *A Marsh Island*, "The King of Folly Island" (1886), and "The Life of Nancy" (1895). Indeed, this motif runs through regionalist literature from that of Mary Noialles Murfree and Kate Chopin through the works of Willa Cather and Eudora Welty. Because the Dunnet Landing narrator's experiences are so rich and positive, a reader might forget that people need friendship in mortal life *because* of failures, losses, and suffering, as shown by characters such as "Poor Joanna" and Santin Bowden or, in the sequels to *Pointed Firs*, Mrs. Tolland and Mrs. Hight. Actually, the country mirrors the city: "One sees exactly the same types in a country gathering as in the most brilliant city company. You are safe to be understood if the spirit of your speech is the same for one neighbor as for the other" (*Pointed Firs* chap. 18; see also Jewett's preface to the 1893 edition of *Deephaven*). The community's cruelties and limitations are always visible. Even Almira falls short—even at the Bowden reunion!—when it comes to one of her husband's cousins and to Marie Harris (chap. 18). When Mrs. Caplin infamously remarks that Marie looks like "a Chinee," Almira's argument for tolerance of differences—in defense of the disappointed alcoholic, Santin Bowden—falters, because she dislikes Marie. Mrs. Blackett intervenes with her characteristic charity: "Mari' Harris was pretty as a child, I remember." But Almira clings to her resentment over Marie's mistreatment of Captain Littlepage. The narrator tries to change the subject, and Mrs. Blackett helps with an admonition to live and let live. These comments leave the implicit racism of Caplin's remark untouched, suggesting that even Mrs. Blackett and the narrator *may* not share twenty-first-century sensitivities to racial slurs. But Mrs. Blackett's comments also gently inquire into how the community has failed to make of Marie a more pleasant person, a question that gets a partial reply in the exclusionary gossip that Mrs. Caplin loves and in Almira's cultivation of resentment. Further explanation comes in "The Foreigner," in which Marie is one of the leaders in the local church's exclusion of Mrs. Tolland. Marie, it would seem, has learned exclusionary ways under the dominant Protestantism of the region.

What makes Dunnet Landing special despite its weaknesses is "the golden chain of love and dependence" the narrator finds in this imperfect circle of friends and family. The book lacks any assertion that such circles are exclusively rural or that they are passing out of existence. As Donovan suggests, Jewett's daily associations with the circle of friends she and Fields shared is a continuing, mainly urban, example of a "golden chain" (*Sarah Orne Jewett* 15–16). In both country and city, friendship is religious *work*; the work of friendship is not to acquire or control, and it is the opposite of domination. Insofar as the Dunnet Landing stories constitute a "devotional text," they critique and oppose the imperialist impulses Brodhead and others attribute to late-nineteenth-century public ideology.

Noticing the contrast between the exclusiveness of Harris and Caplin, in part a product of a narrow Protestantism, and Mrs. Blackett's more inclusive religion of friendship, suggests one of the ways in which Jewett's religious views offer an alternative to public culture. Presented mainly through positive examples in action rather than through polemic or the didactic fictional style of older contemporaries such as Stowe or Cooke, Jewett's religion of friendship may seem less radical than it is. The religion of friendship is an alternative to the patriarchal Protestantism that had in too many cases dithered on or supported slavery, typically opposed women's suffrage, and so often was held responsible for the manifold sufferings of women in regional fiction (see Carpenter and Kolmar). As Cooke's

Aunt Huldah sniffs, "Scripter [Scripture] has a good deal to answer for!" (Fetterley and Pryse 100; see also Roman 38, 89)

American Protestantism generally provides, in authoritative interpretation of Scripture, a detailed view of humanity's work within a cosmic history, along with related rules by which one seeks and maintains a sanctified state. Central to this transcendental narrative is a transcendental signified, Christ, whose scriptural story completes the cosmic drama of original sin and redemption. This Protestantism requires intense individualistic attention to one's personal salvation, supports a vigorous work ethic, and historically has justified institutions of social control. Jewett's religion undoes this Protestant ideology, with its reliance upon scriptural authority more than personal experience. Her alternative belief system does without the authoritative narrative of cosmic purpose that undergirds identity and authorizes hierarchical and exclusive churches. Shannon, for one, makes a good case that a function of Captain Littlepage's tale of "the waiting place" in *Pointed Firs* is to undercut the notion of grand, authoritative narratives. Littlepage begins his tale by asserting that when the authorities finally look into his evidence, they will find certainty about the existence of an afterlife, but he ends it with a bewildered look at a modern map of the northern polar regions, absent his waiting place and his chance at certainty. Opposed to this attempt at transcendental narrative is the visit to Green Island, which begins, when Mrs. Todd first points it out to the narrator, with images that connect it to "the waiting place": "The sunburst upon that outermost island made it seem like a sudden revelation of the world beyond this which some believe to be so near" (chap. 7). The series of epiphanies and communions of the Green Island visit show that all the world is a waiting place, and that any place or moment when a person experiences communion or vision is a moment of heaven. Not authoritative texts, but concrete experiences of intimacy reveal the spiritual dimensions of life.

There is ample evidence, in the work of Josephine Donovan, for example, that Jewett was influenced by Emmanuel Swedenborg through Theophilus Parsons. It is likely as well that she was influenced by Phillips Brooks (see Brastow). Though she often quotes the Bible, she almost never uses the Bible as an authority or appeals to any other external religious authority. She believes that the soul is immortal and that punishment is not part of the afterlife. This faith is based on the experience of friendship and supports an ethic of friendship that focuses on how to live fully rather than on how to please a judging divinity by fitting into "the one story." Except for being benevolent, the god of the religion of friendship is almost wholly unspecified. Jewett simply declines after the mid-1880s to say much at all about any divinity. In *A Country Doctor* (1884), when Nan Prince claims a divine sanction for her vocation as physician, she bases this not on a transcendent authority, but upon her personal self-knowledge and an appeal to the common sense of those she wishes to persuade: "God would not give us the same talents if what were right for men were wrong for women" (chap. 18). And her mentor, Dr. Leslie, confirms this view in his own thoughts (chap. 21).

The religion of friendship is egalitarian rather than hierarchical, spontaneous rather than institutional, communal rather than individualistic, and "everyday" rather than formal. In the Dunnet Landing works, groups of people, usually women, visit and tell stories, and then they open their souls to each other, making worship out of intimacy, without a pastor, a church organization, or a special building, without public ritual or pious formula. The religious impulse arises from within and is answered by a like impulse in another. Again and again, religious insight is formulated in words only after a story has made the idea concrete, as when Almira speaks about the reality of dreams in "The Queen's Twin." Even a quasi-formal "occasion" like the Bowden reunion reaches spiritual heights through visiting, not through the rituals of marching and speech making, though those formal activities help create the "space" of the event. In their introduction to *Haunting the House of Fiction*, Lynette Carpenter and Wendy Kolmar point out that one of the functions of ghost stories by American women was to erode "the boundaries between natural and supernatural, life and afterlife" (8). In Jewett's presentation of mind reading, transfiguration, and seeing the dead, we see her making these boundaries permeable. Insofar as it becomes possible in ordinary life to experience the spiritual in oneself, in nature, and in one's friends—and even to glimpse another, spiritual world—the authority of the traditional hierarchical religious institutions of the United States is undermined.

As Ann Romines shows, the meaningful rituals in Jewett that are appropriate for nurturing friendships are everyday work and the ordering of private domestic spaces. Such rituals contrast with the formal rituals of patriarchal Christianity that Jewett represents—acts of piety that are also acts of submission to authority: attending "meeting" in an appropriate bonnet, deferring to male spiritual leaders, and refraining from dancing. Generally, Jewett's Protestant ministers are poor "housekeepers." Though Jewett portrays spiritually supportive clerics—especially her Catholic priests—her Protestants are often self-absorbed and insensitive, like Parson Dimmick, who visits Joanna on Shell-heap Island and provokes Almira to stare "right at him" while he prays (chap. 14). Like the congregation that excludes Mrs. Tolland, churches often seem indifferent or even hostile to a religion of friendship. Mary Fleming of "An Every-Day Girl" experiences the supernatural when she communicates with Aunt Hannah or contemplates a natural setting, not when she participates in worship at church: "She never had liked sermons and prayer meetings." In the last part of "An Autumn Holiday" (1880), elderly Daniel Gunn, after a sunstroke, becomes "haunted" by his dead sister, and he cross-dresses and carries on her activities most afternoons. One way to read his actions under her influence is as disruptions of Protestant and patriarchal authority that push both church and family to be more domestic and inclusive.

Though woman-centered, Jewett's religion is inclusive. As Mrs. Blackett and Almira show in the Dunnet Landing stories, especially "The Foreigner," and as Judith Fetterley asserts about women's regionalism in general, Jewett's religion works "to dismantle and deconstruct hierarchies based on categories of gender, race, class, age, and region" ("Not in the Least American" 25–26). And as Helen Levy argues, the regionalists' "home place" depicted a localized family life that was superior to the bureaucratization and standardization of life at the national level. One purpose of this literature is "to restore the emotional force of the integrated community [. . .] under the leadership of the accepting wise woman" (17–18). This home welcomes all, including men like William or Captain Tilley, who eschew the morality and rewards of the social competition for individual dominance. Because of the cooperative and accepting setting, which does not favor the masculine as a superior destiny, women are spared the distortions of feminine identity that Nancy Chodorow characterizes as the "reproduction of mothering." One function of Jewett's religion is to help readers imaginatively construct this home place—a local, egalitarian, inclusive, woman-centered community—rooted in a specific place and offering self-possession to women and men (Levy 4–7).

Gently but firmly presented in a large body of fiction, poetry, essays, and letters, Jewett's religion of friendship contributes to a cultural project shared by many post–Civil War women regionalists to forward an alternative model that might replace the public culture that these writers saw as increasingly characterized by materialism, extreme individualism, impersonal patriarchal institutions, capitalist commercialism, and an appropriating colonialism. In her emphasis on a healing spiritual communion,

Jewett resembles Nathaniel Hawthorne, who, in *The Scarlet Letter* (1850) and most of his other works, affirms a need to participate mystically in "the great heart of mankind." It may not be too much of "a stretch" to see Jewett as like her heroine Nan Prince, "the teller of new truth, a revealer of laws" (*A Country Doctor* chap. 21), or as the sort of prophet for which Hawthorne's Hester Prynne hoped, a woman wise "not through dusky grief, but the ethereal medium of joy; and showing how sacred love should make us happy" (185–86).

NOTES

1. Except for Richard Cary's *Sarah Orne Jewett Letters,* all of Jewett's works to which I refer here are available at the Sarah Orne Jewett Text Project (SOJTP): http://www.public.coe.edu/~theller/soj/sj-index.htm. I quote from these Internet texts. And I would like to thank Lynnette Carpenter for helpful revision suggestions.

2. Laurie Shannon's essay is available in full text from OCLC FirstSearch; for this reason, I do not use page numbers to locate the passages that I have quoted.

WORKS CITED

Ammons, Elizabeth. "Jewett's Witches." in *Critical Essays on Sarah Orne Jewett.* Edited by Gwen Nagel, 165–84. Boston: G. K. Hall, 1984.

———. "Material Culture, Empire, and Jewett's *Country of the Pointed Firs.*" In *New Essays on The Country of the Pointed Firs.* Edited by June Howard, 81–99. New York: Cambridge University Press, 1994.

Baym, Nina. *Women's Fiction: A Guide to Novels by and about Women in America, 1820–1870.* Ithaca, N.Y.: Cornell University Press, 1978.

Blanchard, Paula. *Sarah Orne Jewett: Her World and Her Work.* New York: Addison-Wesley, 1994.

Brastow, Lewis O. "Phillips Brooks." In *Representative Modern Preachers.* New York: Hodder & Stoughton, 1904.

Braude, Ann. *Radical Spirits.* Boston: Beacon, 1989.

Brodhead, Richard. *Cultures of Letters.* Chicago: University of Chicago Press, 1993.

Carpenter, Lynette, and Wendy Kolmar. *Haunting the House of Fiction: Feminist Perspectives on Ghost Stories by American Women.* Knoxville: University of Tennessee Press, 1991.

Cary, Richard. "Jewett to Dresel: 33 Letters." *Colby Library Quarterly* 11:1 (Mar. 1975): 13–49.

Chodorow, Nancy. "Family Structure and Feminine Personality." In *Woman, Culture, and Society.* Edited by Michelle Rosaldo and Louise Lamphere. Stanford: Stanford University Press, 1974.

Donovan, Josephine. *Sarah Orne Jewett.* New York: Ungar, 1980.

———. "Sarah Orne Jewett's Critical Theory: Notes toward a Feminine Literary Mode." In *Critical Essays on Sarah Orne Jewett.* Edited by Gwen Nagel, 212–25. Boston: G. K. Hall, 1984.

————. "Jewett and Swedenborg." *American Literature* 65:4 (Dec. 1993): 731–50.

————. "A Woman's Vision of Transcendence: A New Interpretation of the Works of Sarah Orne Jewett." *Massachusetts Review* 21 (Summer 1980): 365–80.

Easton, Alison. "'How Clearly the Gradations of Society Were Defined': Negotiating Class in Sarah Orne Jewett." In *Jewett and Her Contemporaries: Reshaping the Canon.* Edited by Karen Kilcup and Thomas Edwards, 207–22. Gainesville: University Press of Florida, 1999.

Fetterley, Judith, "'Not in the Least American': Nineteenth-Century Literary Regionalism as UnAmerican Literature." In *Nineteenth-Century American Women Writers: A Critical Reader.* Edited by Karen Kilcup, 15–30. Oxford: Blackwell, 1998.

Fetterley, Judith, and Marjorie Pryse, eds. *American Women Regionalists: 1850–1910.* New York: Norton, 1992

Folsom, Marcia. "'Tact Is a Kind of Mind Reading': Empathic Style in Sarah Orne Jewett's *The Country of the Pointed Firs.*" In *Critical Essays on Sarah Orne Jewett.* Edited by Gwen Nagel, 76–89. Boston: G. K. Hall, 1984.

Hawthorne, Nathaniel. *The Scarlet Letter.* 1850. Reprint. New York: Norton, 1961.

Heller, Terry. "The Rhetoric of Communion in Jewett's 'A White Heron.'" *Colby Quarterly* 26:3 (Sept. 1990): 182–94.

Humma, John. "The Art and Meaning of Sarah Orne Jewett's 'The Courting of Sister Wisby.'" *Studies in Short Fiction* 10 (1973): 85–91.

Jewett, Sarah Orne. *Letters of Sarah Orne Jewett.* Edited by Annie Fields. Boston: Houghton Mifflin, 1911. http://www.public.coe.edu/~theller/soj/let/let-frm.htm

————. *Sarah Orne Jewett Letters.* Edited by Richard Cary. Waterville, Me.: Colby College Press, 1967.

————. *The Sarah Orne Jewett Text Project.* Edited by Terry Heller. 1997–2003. http://www.public.coe.edu/~theller/soj/sj-index.htm

————. *Verses.* Boston: privately printed, 1916. http://www.public.coe.edu/~theller/soj/poe/verses.htm

Kilcup, Karen, and Thomas Edwards, eds. *Jewett and Her Contemporaries: Reshaping the Canon.* Gainesville: University Press of Florida, 1999.

Levy, Helen F. *Fiction of the Home Place.* Oxford: University Press of Mississippi, 1992.

Mobley, Marilyn. *Folk Roots and Mythic Wings in Sarah Orne Jewett and Toni Morrison.* Baton Rouge: Louisiana State University Press, 1991.

Murphy, Jacqueline. "Replacing Regionalism: Abenaki Tales and 'Jewett's' Coastal Maine." *American Literary History* 10:4 (Winter 1998): 664–90.

Pryse, Marjorie. "Sex, Class, and 'Category Crisis': Reading Jewett's Transitivity." In *Jewett and Her Contemporaries: Reshaping the Canon.* Edited by Karen Kilcup and Thomas Edwards, 31–62. Gainesville: University Press of Florida, 1999.

Roman, Margaret. *Sarah Orne Jewett: Reconstructing Gender.* Tuscaloosa: University of Alabama Press, 1992.

Romines, Ann. *The Home Plot: Women, Writing and Domestic Ritual.* Amherst: University of Massachusetts Press, 1992.

Schrag, Mitzi. "'Whiteness' as Loss in Sarah Orne Jewett's 'The Foreigner.'" In *Jewett and Her Contemporaries: Reshaping the Canon.* Edited by Karen Kilcup and Thomas Edwards, 185–206. Gainesville: University Press of Florida, 1999.

Shannon, Laurie. "'The Country of Our Friendship': Jewett's Intimist Art." *American Literature* 71:2 (June 1999): 227–62. [OCLC]

Sherman, Sarah. *Sarah Orne Jewett: An American Persephone.* Hanover, N.H.: University Press of New England, 1989.

Silverthorne, Elizabeth. *Sarah Orne Jewett: A Writer's Life.* Woodstock N.Y.: Overlook Press, 1993.

Thoreau, Henry David. *Walden.* 1854. Reprint. New York: Norton, 1992.

Zagarell, Sandra. "*Country's* Portrayal of Community and the Exclusion of Difference." In *New Essays on The Country of the Pointed Firs.* Edited by June Howard, 39–60. New York: Cambridge University Press, 1994.

———. "Narrative of Community: The Identification of a Genre." *Signs* 13:1 (Spring 1988): 498–527.

———. "Troubling Regionalism: Rural Life and the Cosmopolitan Eye in Jewett's *Deephaven.*" *American Literary History* 10:4 (Winter 1998): 639–63.

The Politics of Heaven

The Ghost Dance, *The Gates Ajar,*
and *Captain Stormfield*

JOHN J. KUCICH

The spread of the Ghost Dance among the tribes of the Great Basin and Plains in 1890 precipitated a crisis not only in the United States' Indian policy, but in white representations of Native American religions as well. In the first accounts of the Ghost Dance to appear in the *New York Times* in late 1890, we see a metropolitan newspaper struggling to comprehend a visionary Indian theology by stretching the resonance of "heaven." The first report, "New Indian Messiah," published on November 16, describes the experience of the Arapaho medicine man Sitting Bull as a "vision, for such it appears to have been," in which Christ appeared, promised "the restoration of the old order of things," and fed him buffalo meat. The article doesn't use the term "heaven" to describe this distinctly Indian spirit world, a reluctance shared in "Weird Things in Dreams," published two weeks later, which summarized the proceedings of an American Folklore Society meeting devoted to the Ghost Dance. The anthropologists refer to the movement as a "craze" characterized by visions of a "spirit land" or "luminous place" full of dead Indians; a number draw links to other religious revivals among people safely removed from modern European American society. "There seems to be a strong impulse," notes one anonymous professor, "to excitements like this Indian craze among all oppressed races" ("Weird Things in Dreams"). Yet the effort to separate the Ghost Dance from a viable belief in heaven among turn-of-the-century whites did not succeed. The day after the article on the American Folklore Society appeared, the *Times* ran another article accurately citing Jack Wilson, or "Wo-vo-Kar," as the Ghost Dance prophet who tells his followers that "he has been to heaven and that the Messiah is coming to the earth again, and will put the Indians in possession of this country; that he has seen in heaven a heap of Indians, some of them dressed in white man's clothes" ("Messiah and His Prophet"). Heaven, in this account, at least, is broad enough to include the Ghost Dance, and whereas the spirit world in this context is not synonymous with the spirit world central to European American religion, the two share a signifier.

At least three versions of heaven took shape in the United States in the latter half of the nineteenth century. Though rooted in very different cultural contexts, both the Ghost Dance and the *Gates* novels (*The Gates Ajar, Beyond the Gates,* and *The Gates Between*) of Elizabeth Stuart Phelps, published between 1868 and 1888, offer elaborate, compelling, and strikingly similar portraits of heaven. Yet their visions of heaven bear the marks of the struggle for the very land under their authors' feet. A third text, Mark Twain's *Extracts from Captain Stormfield's Visit to Heaven,* had gone through forty years of revisions before it saw print in 1907; begun as a simple satire on *The Gates Ajar,* it eventually used its heavenly setting to grapple with some of the very questions raised by juxtaposing the *Gates* novels and the Ghost Dance. What do these heavenly portraits have to tell us about the meaning of culture, nationality, and identity in nineteenth-century America? These visions of heaven are, ultimately, visions of America; what unites and divides them to a large degree unites and divides the different cultures that share this land.

These detailed images of the afterlife appeared at the time when the United States had reached its continental limits, defeated the last independent Native American peoples, absorbed millions of immigrants, and confronted its place as an industrial world power. These transformations presented the country with a consequent question of cultural identity. Was the United States a white nation fulfilling its Anglo-Saxon heritage, or a nation that could assimilate the many cultures that had contributed to its history? As this question was worked out in military, economic, political, and social arenas, it was also negotiated in the realm of the supernatural, in the visions of heaven that these competing cultures presented to themselves and to each other. For both Native Americans and European Americans, the end of the nineteenth century was an era of profound cultural transformation, and these detailed portraits of heaven document strategies employed by these cultures to adapt to a changing world. The anthropologist A. F. C. Wallace first described how an intensely reimagined spiritual world can spark what he termed a "revitalization movement" in a threatened culture. By using this concept, which he first applied to the

Seneca at the end of the eighteenth century, to interrogate both Native and European American cultures at the end of the nineteenth century, we can better understand how representations of heaven shape both marginalized and dominant cultures. Heaven in both these contexts reified threatened norms, thereby helping endangered traditions adapt to new social conditions and transform the very terms of cultural identity. Heaven in this era helped reinvigorate and critique life on earth, shoring up marginalized cultures and unsettling dominant ones. In an era of sharp and lethal cultural divisions, heaven was a crucial means of mediating the differences among the peoples of the United States. By examining these visions of heaven, we can gain a far richer sense of how these cultures interacted in their efforts to reimagine the land that they shared.

I. The Ghost Dance:
Revitalization and Visionary Nostalgia

Despite the best efforts of the *New York Times* circa 1890, the term "heaven" applies imperfectly at best to Native American religions. Although the hundreds of traditional Indian cultures in the United States differ greatly in the tenor and terms of their religious beliefs, none share the Judeo-Christian duality of a perfect heaven defined against a fallen creation. Most Indian cultures instead share a conception of the world as fundamentally sacred, in which material and spiritual elements seamlessly coexist and communion between the living and the dead, the earthly and the spiritual, is a central fact of life. Spirits frequently linger among the living, who can, in trances, sojourn among the spirits. Most tribes that adopted the Ghost Dance share what Lee Irwin calls a "visionary episteme," a cosmology "based in religious world views that are enhanced and qualified according to individual visionary experiences, which are integrated into broadly shared repertoires of behaviors, attitudes and enactments that are found throughout the Plains area" (6). As a result, Native American religions proved tremendously adaptable, evolving over time to reflect various cultural influences and pressures. Thus, the Ghost Dance of 1890 was, in its innovation, very much in line with traditional Indian conceptions of the spirit world.[1]

Of course, the Ghost Dance itself was not entirely new in 1890. James Mooney's classic *The Ghost Dance Religion and Wounded Knee* (1896) is the first of many histories to treat the Ghost Dance not as one movement, but as many, beginning with the Pueblo Revolt of 1680 and continuing through a long series of traditional religious revivals that followed European expansion. Though medicine men often borrowed theological elements from Christian missionaries as warriors borrowed guns, their doctrines were firmly rooted in traditional beliefs and ceremonies. Most of these movements ended with military defeat, yet many left indelible marks on tribal memories. By 1890 the last of the Indian wars had been fought. All major tribes had been confined to reservations, and those reservations had long been carved up for white settlement. The Dawes Act of 1887, which sought to acculturate Native Americans by substituting individual allotments for tribal land ownership and establishing boarding schools for Indian children, tried to accomplish through reeducation what centuries of literary myth and military brutality had not: the vanishing of the American Indian.

Thus, when news began to spread among Indians of the Great Basin and Plains that a young Paiute named Wovoka had been to heaven and brought back the promise of a new millennium, tribal delegations flocked to hear the words from the prophet himself. Wovoka's message was clear and compelling: Follow the Ghost Dance and see your tribe return to its precontact glory.

> He fell asleep in the daytime and was taken up to the other world. Here he saw God, with all the people who had died long ago engaged in their old-time sports and occupations, all happy and forever young. It was a pleasant land and full of game. After showing him all, God told him he must go back and tell his people they must be good and love one another, have no quarreling, and live in peace with the whites; that they must work, and not lie or steal; that they must put away all the old practices that savored of war; that if they faithfully obeyed his instructions, they would at last be reunited with their friends in this other world, where there would be no more death or sickness or old age. He was there given the dance which he was commanded to bring back to his people. By performing this dance at intervals, for five consecutive days each time, they would secure this happiness to themselves and hasten the event. (Mooney 771–72)

The dance involved a circle of believers adorned with body paints and bearing sacred feathers singing special "ghost songs" for hours; dancers regularly collapsed and, while fellow dancers stepped around their fallen bodies, journeyed to a spirit world devoid of whites, where they were greeted by deceased relatives and friends and supplied with new songs for future dances.

The Paiute dancers were soon joined by members from the American West's many other tribes, from the northern Bannock to the southern Hopi to the Eastern Plains's Arapaho, Cheyenne, and Sioux. By the fall of 1890, Indian nations all over the West participated in the dance, visiting the spirit world in trances and hoping to hasten its coming. Most believed it would arrive with the green grass of spring in the following year, sliding atop the old world and burying both whites and Indian unbelievers under an avalanche or a wall of fire, even as the dancers themselves were carried to a new world teeming with game and filled by the vast ranks of Indians who had gone before. Whites who heard of the dance grew uneasy. In the late fall of 1890, the U.S. cavalry intercepted one band of Sioux at Wounded Knee Creek on December 29. As federal troops began disarming the warriors, a medicine man named Yellow Bird urged them to resist—the ghost shirts they wore, he said, would make them invulnerable to the white man's bullets. When one warrior did resist, the cavalry opened fire with light artillery and machine guns, killing about a hundred warriors and 120 women and children, many of whom were shot down as they sought refuge in the creek bed or fled as far as two miles from the scene. With the slaughter died most of the enthusiasm for the Ghost Dance, and the movement dwindled rapidly.[2]

Most whites and some Indians saw the Ghost Dance as the last gasp of a dying culture. American anthropologists had long worked from a model of cultural evolution most fully developed by Lewis Henry Morgan in the 1870s, in which primitive societies inevitably yielded before more developed civilizations. From this perspective, the Ghost Dance was doomed from the start, and most white observers who decried the massacre at Wounded Knee argued that it was poor policy toward a movement that should have been left to wither of its own accord. James Mooney's 1896 study of the Ghost Dance, still the standard text on the movement, marked a turning point in anthropology from efforts to chart the evolution of "civilization" to attempts to understand the workings of human culture in general.[3] Subsequent accounts, from Black Elk's to Alice Beck Kehoe's, have portrayed the Ghost Dance as an example of what A. F. C. Wallace termed a revitalization movement. Out of cultural disintegration, a prophet arises promising the return of a community's prestige and integrity if members adopt a new code of beliefs. The new code is nativistic in orientation but incorporates enough new elements to address the changes that led to the cultural distortions in the first place. Successful revitalization movements thus use spiritual beliefs to help a threatened culture adapt to a

changed world. The concept of revitalization provided a corrective to earlier ethnographies of such Indian spiritual movements, which portrayed
them as little more than the last gasps of cultures inevitably losing their
evolutionary struggle. The rituals of the Ghost Dance brought Indians
together within and across tribal lines, strengthening social ties and renew-
ing the participants' focus on the many elements of traditional religious
practice that the Ghost Dance preserved.

While contemporary white observers tended to read the Ghost Dance
as bastardized Christianity, the Ghost Dance was nevertheless fashioned
out of Native American materials. Of the 160 Ghost Dance songs that
Mooney recorded from almost a dozen tribes, almost fifty center on traditional religious elements. Some, like this example from the Arapaho, feature animal spirits and their totems. In this case, the crow is the traditional
messenger to the spirit world:

> The crow is circling above me,
> The crow is circling above me.
> He says he will give me a hawk feather,
> He says he will give me a hawk feather. (Mooney 991)

Others, like this one from the Cheyenne, involve ritual body paints: "The
crow—Ehe'e'e'ye'! / The grease paint—He'e'ye'! / He brings it to me"
(Mooney 1037). Still others rehearse the individual traditions of the tribes
who took up the Ghost Dance, like the Cheyenne's origins on the Turtle
River (Mooney 1029); cite particularly sacred animals and the dances devoted to them (Mooney 1033); illustrate traditional medicine (Mooney
1083); or reference myths whose meanings remain opaque even to as dili-
gent an outside observer as Mooney. The songs whose referents he can
trace, however, offer enough material for Mooney to recreate dense sum-
maries of the various tribal belief systems, and more than enough to show
that—for members of the tribes themselves—the Ghost Dance provided
a rich opportunity to preserve and rehearse their traditions.

Such traditions, of course, were preserved under dismaying conditions.
It is no surprise that studies of the Ghost Dance focus on the massacre at
Wounded Knee. Yet from that vantage point, the Ghost Dance appears
merely as warfare by other means. This was, of course, an important part
of the movement. Mooney collected, from six of the seven tribes that he
studied, songs featuring the coming apocalypse. While confined to their
reservation, Arapaho Ghost Dancers sang of triumph over whites: "I'yehe!

we have rendered them desolate—*Eye'de'yuhe'yu!* / The whites are crazy—
he'yuhe'yu!" (Mooney 972) and "*He'yoho'ho! He'yoho'ho!* / The yellow-hide,
the white-skin [man] / I have now put him aside!" (Mooney 978). The
Kiowa, in turn, sang, "The spirit army is approaching, / The whole world
is moving onward" (Mooney 1082), while one Sioux song promised to
confer military invincibility to earthly warriors: "The shirt will cause you
to live, / Says the father, says the father" (Mooney 1073). Such songs do
much to explain the appeal of the Ghost Dance at this nadir in the history
of the Plains tribes, especially to the Sioux band camped under the
Hotchkiss guns by Wounded Knee Creek. Yet such explicitly militaristic
elements make up a remarkably small portion of the Ghost Dance movement. Of the songs recorded by Mooney, only forty or so concern the
arrival of the new earth, and only two, both from the Arapaho, contain
references to the destruction of the whites. To be sure, Ghost Dancers,
especially among the Sioux, may have been reluctant to share their most
incendiary songs with a white anthropologist on the government payroll
in the early 1890s; Mooney's ability to collect two such songs from the
Arapaho, however, illustrates the depth of confidence Mooney had won
from his informants.

Yet the centrality of Wounded Knee skews our understanding of the
Ghost Dance toward its apocalyptic dimension, whereas the songs themselves indicate that the crucial affect of the movement lay in its vivid visions
of heaven. Of the 160 songs in Mooney's *Ghost Dance Religion*, almost sixty
contain representations of a spirit land identical to the world that Indians
remembered from before the era of white expansion. Another twenty-five
describe the meeting of deceased friends and relatives. Thus, over half of
the songs portray a heaven that is explicit, detailed, intimately familiar,
and close at hand—accessible to anyone willing to believe and able to participate in the rituals of the dance. A Sioux woman could visit the spirit
land and return to sing,

E'yaye'ye'! E'yaye'ye'!
It is my own child,
It is my own child. (Mooney 1069)

Other dancers woke from their trances to tell of seeing fathers and mothers and hosts of friends, all living according to ways of life that had van-
ished from the reservations. An Arapaho woman returned to sing of a camp
full of buffalo-skin teepees:

E'yehe'! they are new—
The bed coverings,
The bed coverings. (Mooney 963)

A Sioux woman, joining her spirit friends as they began to butcher buffalo, sang,

Give me my knife,
I shall hang up the meat to dry—*Ye'ye'!*
When it is dry I shall make pemmican. (Mooney 1066)

Still others sang of playing traditional games—a ball-and-stick game called "shinny," the "awl game," the "dice game," and games involving buttons and tops, or hoops and arrows. All this occurs in a verdant landscape abounding with each tribe's favorite traditional foods, from the *wai-va*, or wild millet, of the Paiute to the cottonwood of the Arapaho to the thunderberries of the Kiowa to the buffalo that fed, clothed, and housed the Plains tribes.

Such specific descriptions of the spirit land contrast sharply with the more traditional visionary experiences of the western Indian nations, in which contact with spirits was marked by strangeness. Among the Sioux, the spiritual was *wakan,* by definition beyond the bounds of daily experience. "Wakan was anything that was hard to understand," according to the Lakota Good Seat (Walker 70). Although spirits were a regular presence in the communal life of the Sioux and other tribes, the spirit land itself was far away "beyond the pines," in a mystical northern world that the living did not visit. Ordinary people seldom had visions, and when they did, it was usually in moments of great personal crisis, and even then only after elaborate preparation. And finally, visions came couched in a highly charged, richly symbolic language quite distinct from the idiom of daily life. Most depended on holy men and women for interpretation: "A wakan man knows things that the people do not know [. . .]. He can tell people what their visions mean" (Walker 69). One who received a vision might, like Black Elk, spend a lifetime trying to unravel its import or, like the Paiute Tävibo, who started a Ghost Dance movement in 1869, decide after some years that the vision was the work of evil spirits (Kehoe).

Such ambiguity and interpretive apparatus were strikingly absent from the Ghost Dance songs. Dancers instead had immediate and regular access to visions whose meanings were direct and clear. Indeed, the Ghost Dance inverted the traditional Indian cosmology. Whereas contact with the spirit world had previously given a numinous charge to the ordinary world, in the Ghost Dance, people turned from a physical world grown alien and strange to find, in the spirit world, the familiar environs of home. In the Ghost Dance, the visionary becomes nostalgic. Rather than mystify ordinary social relations, the visionary nostalgia of the Ghost Dance songs helped preserve threatened traditions. Ghost dancers journeyed to heaven to save the earth they once knew.

This heaven had no room for whites. The people who responded to Wovoka's message sought to reproduce through their religious rituals a communal, tribal subjectivity that was coming under increasing threat from a U.S. government promoting individual ownership of land and from Protestant missionaries working toward individual salvation. The oral channels through which the Ghost Dance spread—with Wovoka at one end of a chain of creation that linked tribal delegations, medicine men, and the dancers themselves—made it a communal creation. Individual visions were carefully contained within a communal framework, and the songs these worshipers made from their visions typically speak of the tribe or family rather than the individual. And while the Ghost Dance may have taken shape in response to U.S. imperialism, it hardly imagined a world of interracial harmony. Though Wovoka preached a gospel of peace, and though intertribal cooperation may have been his most powerful legacy, the Ghost Dance imagined, instead, a world of Indian autonomy and separatism.[4]

II. The *Gates* Novels: White Revitalization

While heaven was hardly a new concept in European America, it evolved considerably during the nineteenth century. Protestant religions had been tempering Calvinist visions of hellfire since the eighteenth century, gradually shifting from the threat of damnation to the promise of salvation in their efforts to attract believers. Yet, like the spirit land in most Native American religions, in most Christian denominations heaven remained a thinly sketched promise. With the advent of Spiritualism at mid-century, however, heaven became a more central category of religious experience. Once spirits had established their otherworldly credentials at a typical séance, they were peppered with questions about their surroundings. Some described an afterlife that conformed to the Swedenborgian idea of successive spiritual spheres; others sketched an idealized American landscape drawn from the iconography of the Hudson River School. The effort to domesticate heaven, to chart its pleasures in terms immediately recognizable to a still-rural nation, increased and indeed still persists in the form of lush garden cemeteries that began appearing across the country in the years before the Civil War.[5] By the time Elizabeth Stuart Phelps began sketching her own version of heaven, white Americans had long been accustomed to contemplating the pleasures of the afterlife.

Growing up in Andover, Massachusetts, during the Civil War, Phelps had seen young men march off to Southern battlefields and had been engaged to one who didn't come back. Like the Native American peoples devastated by war, Phelps's mind was focused on those left on the battlefields. "The Grand Review passed through Washington," she wrote, looking back on the years following the war; "four hundred thousand ghosts of murdered men kept invisible march to the drumbeats" (*Chapters* 96). Such metaphors came naturally to Phelps. Though never an avowed Spiritualist, she happily advertised her works in the Spiritualist press and invariably spoke kindly of the movement, a stance she traced to her affection for her grandfather, the Reverend Eliakim Phelps, whose home was the scene of the widely reported Stratford Rappings in 1850 (*Chapters* 6–9). Phelps's relative openness to new theological ideas was typical of mainstream white reactions to Spiritualism. Harriet Beecher Stowe, who was a neighbor and friend of the Phelps family in the late 1850s, also proved a cautious proponent of Spiritualism, publishing her own investigations of the planchette alongside Austin Phelps's earnest account of the Stratford Rappings in Charles Beecher's *Spiritual Manifestations* (1879). Thus, as Phelps began drafting her version of heaven in the years after the Civil War, she had before her models of the afterlife that clothed the vivid details drawn from the séance in the more familiar trappings of Protestant Christianity.

The Gates Ajar (1867), published some twenty-five years before Wovoka's vision spread across the West, consists of diary entries written by a young woman, Mary, whose brother dies in battle. Sunk deep into grief, she finds consolation not in the stern doctrines of the deacon or minister, whose sermon on heaven follows the abstract syllogisms of classic Puritan theology, but in the vivid images of heaven lovingly offered by her aunt, Winifred, who promises a heaven full of friends and loved ones and cozy homes surrounded by gardens. While Phelps rigorously documents her ideas with references to biblical and scholarly texts, her model for heaven is clearly the idealized Andover of her childhood, close-knit, genteel, intellectual, and homogeneous. Although the deceased do not spend their time communicating with the living through rappings and Ouija boards, Winifred "cannot doubt that our absent dead are very present with us" (60). When not haunting the earth, the spirits of the dead pursue their earthly interests in heaven, from writing poetry to playing piano to, in one case, making improvements to carpet sweepers.

The specificity with which she imagined heaven was novel indeed, and when *The Gates Ajar* was published in 1868, the response was overwhelming. The first printing of four thousand copies sold out in a few weeks; over two hundred thousand were sold in the United States and abroad by the century's end. The book was also subject to one of the first mass-marketing campaigns of modern times, infiltrating every corner of American popular culture through the medium of *Gates Ajar* clothing, cigars, funeral wreaths, and patent medicines (Smith vi). Having become a literary celebrity, Phelps quickly embraced a variety of social causes, writing a series of novels, including *The Silent Partner* (1871), *The Story of Avis* (1877), and *Doctor Zay* (1882), strongly advocating women's rights, temperance, and reforms to protect the working class.

Her modest contemporary reputation as an early feminist and social realist rests largely on these works, but they were poorly received by her contemporaries, and Phelps later returned to the heavenly fictions upon which her career was built.[6] She wrote two sequels to *The Gates Ajar*. *Beyond the Gates* (1883) is narrated by another Mary, an unmarried schoolteacher active in the variety of social causes near and dear to the author's heart. She lives in a Massachusetts factory town with her mother until stricken with a brain fever; one night her long-dead father appears at her bedside to lead her to a heavenly sphere far above the earth. After being greeted by the lost waifs and wounded soldiers she had helped on earth, and by Christ himself, and following a quick return to visit her funeral, she takes up the business of heaven. She moves into her father's neatly appointed cottage, located in the suburbs of a city complete with schools (for both men and women), museums, parks, a hospital (for those sick in their souls), and a concert hall, in which Beethoven and Mendelssohn premier their latest works. Just as she begins to settle in, she wakes to find her vision the result of a fevered dream.

No such device frames the third novel of heaven, *The Gates Between* (1887). Esmereld Thorne, a gruff and successful doctor, finds himself utterly bewildered after being thrown from his horse and killed; unable to accept his death, he wanders miserably around the city for days until a former patient, a pious invalid happily named Mrs. Faith, points the way to heaven. He finds his scientific and worldly knowledge a handicap in a world in which sensitive and spiritual matriarchs have the upper hand; his redemption comes only when he learns to humble himself before his child and long-abused wife. Like Wovoka, who highlighted the spirit land's domestic pleasures, Phelps centered the promise of heaven on the hearth.

This most striking feature of the *Gates* novels also sets them apart from earlier European American representations of the afterlife. The earthly texture of Phelps's heaven made it more compelling than the visionary, highly figurative, and relentlessly allegorical descriptions of heaven that appeared regularly in séances and that reached their spiritualist apogee in the work of Andrew Jackson Davis. Phelps insists on what I term visionary realism. "The Father's house are [*sic*] many mansions," says Winifred in *The Gates Ajar*. "Sometimes I fancy those words have a literal meaning which the simple men who heard them may have understood better than we, and that Christ is truly 'preparing' my home for me" (94). Like the ghost dancers, Phelps's heaven is a mimesis of earthly reality. Previous representations, from biblical prophecy to Dantean allegory to Swedenborgian mysticism, gained power by stressing heaven's otherness—its distance from the mundane minutiae and the petty and profound pains that characterize earthly life. However, the visionary realism in the *Gates* novels works by refracting earthly reality through an idealized lens.

Heaven, for Phelps as for the ghost dancers, is a utopia, a prosperous and harmonious society that has proven elusive on earth. Phelps formulates a particularly vivid heaven not to transcend intractable earthly problems, but rather to resolve them. *The Gates Ajar* offers a new setting for sentimental love and family fractured by the Civil War, whereas Phelps builds her vision of the heavenly city in *The Gates Between* from fragments of the wreckage of an industrial-reform movement that she had worked on for more than a decade.

These utopian retreats, like the Ghost Dance, may be read as strategic withdrawals. Wallace's concept of revitalization, discussed above in relation to the Ghost Dance, applies equally well to Phelps's work. Phelps, like Wovoka, is a spiritual prophet offering a new code of beliefs to a society under severe stress; by adopting her beliefs, European American culture might better adapt to a changed social, political, and economic context. Her *Gates* novels neatly follow Wallace's model. After adapting to a social and economic milieu (exemplified in Phelps's case by her mother's 1851 idyll, *Sunnyside*), European American culture underwent the wrenching distortions of civil war and industrialization. To the extent that *The Gates Ajar* offered a "reformulation of a cultural pattern" to meet the disruption of middle-class mourning rituals, as Lisa Long argues, or that *The Gates Between* and *Beyond the Gates* reimagine reform movements disrupted by political corruption, industrialization, and economic panic, Phelps's novels contribute to a postbellum revitalization of European American bourgeois culture. The *Gates* novels are one more example of how a utopian spiritual movement can refashion a culture under duress.

Phelps revitalizes a European American society in crisis by weaving together ideologies that were increasingly at odds in postbellum culture. Upon a traditional Protestant Christian tradition, Phelps grafted a radical spiritualist sensibility and used the result to reimagine modernity. The heavenly utopias hinted at in *The Gates Ajar* and more fully developed in *Beyond the Gates* and *The Gates Between* portray an America revitalized through pious modernity, a society that balances spirituality with the material abundance of capitalism. The vague promise in *The Gates Ajar* of "organized society" evolves in *The Gates Between* into a description of a heavenly city that reads more like the travel report of an urban planner than the raptures of a visionary: "The width and shining cleanliness of the streets, the beauty and glittering material of the houses, the frequent presence of libraries, museums, public gardens, signs of attention to the wants of animals, and places of shelter for travelers such as I had never seen in the most advanced and benevolent of cities below [. . .]" (118). Mary continues on to the suburbs and stops before "a small and quiet house built of curiously inlaid wood," perfectly set in a picturesque landscape of trees and flowers. She enters, admires "certain useful articles [. . .] and works of art," and finds that the house belongs to her father. "Heaven itself seemed to have been ransacked to bring together the daintiest, the most delicate, the purest thoughts and fancies that celestial skill or art could create" (128–29). Phelps's description of heaven as a bourgeois fantasy sprung from the pages of a home-and-garden magazine, though frequently mocked, nevertheless bespeaks her effort to imagine a modern, capitalist, consumerist society that remained profoundly spiritual at its core. Indeed, Phelps's work anticipated the Christian undercurrents of the Progressive movement that put so many of her ideas into practice. Though the Progressives may not have recreated Phelps's heavenly city on earth, they did manage

to achieve the final stage of Wallace's revitalization: a satisfactory adaptation to a changed world.

While Phelps's heaven bore striking similarities to the Ghost Dance,
it also marked the cultural chasm separating these two movements. The
changed world was, after all, structured by imperialist capitalism. In contrast to the oral media of the Ghost Dance, the *Gates* novels were products
of the newly emerging mass-publishing industry. In contrast to the communal subjectivity of tribal culture, Phelps crafts a heaven structured
around bourgeois individualism. Mary's greatest horror in *The Gates Ajar*
is the possibility that her thoughts in heaven will not be private: "I would
rather be annihilated than spend eternity with heart laid bare,—the inner
temple thrown open to be trampled on by every passing stranger!" (55).
Aunt Winifred assures her that in contrast to "this promiscuous theory
of refraction," bourgeois notions of privacy will prevail in heaven. Finally,
her heaven, described by David S. Reynolds as "a place combining the
bucolic beauty of Kansas with the cultured domesticity of Boston" (67),
fashions an ideal America that has no place for the people it has displaced.
A work published a year after Wounded Knee carries Phelps's heavenly
imperialism to its logical conclusion: In *The Heresy of Mehetable Clark*
(1892), Annie T. Slossum describes a heaven in which God and Jesus live
in an exact replica (or prototype?) of the White House. Heaven in both
the *Gates* novels and the Ghost Dance may have played a crucial role in
revitalizing white and Indian cultures at the end of the nineteenth century,
but they did nothing to bring them together.

III. *Captain Stormfield:*
HEAVEN AND DEVITALIZATION

Not every representation of heaven was so culturally monolithic. One,
indeed, placed a "heap of Indians" in a heaven patterned explicitly after
Phelps's. Published in 1907 in *Harper's Magazine*, Mark Twain began
Extract from Captain Stormfield's Visit to Heaven as early as 1868 as a re-
joinder to *The Gates Ajar* and its "mean little ten-cent heaven about the
size of Rhode Island" (*Autobiography* 277).[7] By weaving an Indian presence into his version of heaven, Twain not only unsettles imperialist
ideology, but also undercuts the cultural certainties (both white and
Indian) that shaped the afterlife in the *Gates* novels and the Ghost Dance.
The Ghost Dancers and Phelps use heaven as a mechanism to revitalize

a threatened culture. Twain, on the other hand, uses heaven to threaten a dominant culture grown dangerously self-assured. *Captain Stormfield* devitalizes Anglo-Saxon hegemony on earth with its radically multicultural vision of the afterlife.

The published text begins long after Stormfield's death. After some thirty years of interstellar travel, interrupted only by passages through the odd star and a brief race with a comet, Stormfield arrives in heaven, though at the wrong gate—the clerks are familiar with the sky-blue, seven-headed, one-legged creatures who duly arrive, but have never heard of Earth, much less San Francisco, and they send him on his way only after much confusion. A quick ride on a magic carpet brings Stormfield to the gates of the earthly heaven, where he is greeted by "a Pi Ute Injun I used to know in Tulare County; mighty good fellow—I remembered being at his funeral" (156). Stormfield soon receives his regulation wings, halo, and harp, only to find that neither his nor the myriad other angels' harp playing and singing have improved since death. He quickly abandons his angelic accouterments along with all his other preconceptions of the afterlife. Guided by an old, bald-headed angel named Sandy McWilliams, Stormfield learns that spirits of the dead live as they wish, studying or visiting or farming or gossiping as they please. Babies who arrive in heaven grow and change, much to the horror of bereaved mothers who expect to cuddle their infants when they themselves arrive in heaven. Stormfield is startled to learn that unhappiness is an integral part of heaven, a necessary contrast for happiness and a crucial spur to a soul's continued development. The excerpt ends with a grand welcoming ceremony for a reformed barkeep, which provides a rare chance to glimpse some of the biblical patriarchs.

Although *Captain Stormfield* has long been read as a spoof of what Barton Levi St. Armand called "Phelps's Biedermeier paradise" (139), Twain includes none of the posthumous house-and-garden raptures that appear in *The Gates Ajar* and *Beyond the Gates*. He more directly targets one of the principal appeals of both consolation literature and the Ghost Dance. Twain ends the first published section of *Captain Stormfield* with the devastating story of a long-dead baby girl who, grown into a serious scholar in heaven, has little interest in seeing her uneducated mother. The story drives a deep wedge between the sentimental ideology that fueled the popular success of the *Gates* novels and the feminist undercurrent that provided much of their critical force. Yet the story of the thwarted mother-child reunion nevertheless illustrates how much Twain borrowed from Phelps. Both writers reject a conventional heaven full of harp-playing angels in favor of one more analogous to earth, in which people continue their education and activities according to their temperaments, free from the barriers of class and gender.[8]

Such borrowings, however, serve primarily to underscore the utterly different cultural functions of these two works. Phelps turned to heaven to shore up an ideology of white American triumphalism threatened by the carnage of civil war and the turmoil of industrialization; Twain, instead, turned to heaven to fracture that ideology. One element in this process of devitalization has long been noted—the use of astronomical speeds and distances to dwarf any familiar human norms of scale. Twain is less concerned with the accuracy of the numbers than he is with their sheer immensity; he moves easily from millions to billions, and when he really wants to impress he simply invents new measurements. A comet bound for hell, for example, carries a load of passengers weighing "eighteen hundred thousand billion quintillions of kazarks," a figure that grows more daunting when Stormfield learns that a kazark "is exactly the bulk of *a hundred and sixty-nine worlds like ours!*" (150). The captain's ego is dealt a crushing blow when he arrives at the wrong gate to find his familiar geography utterly insignificant. "San Francisco," "California," and the "United States" are meaningless terms to the clerk at the gate, who consults a map "as big as Rhode Island" to find the earth:

> [H]e kept on doing this for a day or two, and finally came down and said he thought he had found that solar system, but it might be fly-specks. So he got a microscope and went back. It turned out better than he feared. He had rousted out our system, sure enough. He got me to describe our planet and its distance from our sun, and then he says to his chief—"Oh, I know the one he means, now, sir. It is on the map. It is called the Wart." (153)

The result of Twain's effort to represent accurately the earth's place in the heavens is a realism that mocks any human sense of reality, especially of the sort that Phelps portrayed in the *Gates* novels and that the Ghost Dancers described in their songs. Whereas those demarcated a heaven based on the scale of the parlor or teepee, *Captain Stormfield* presents a heaven on a superhuman scale. The homely elements sprinkled throughout the text, such as Sandy McWilliams's cranberry farm, thus appear not as ordinary, naturalized elements of heaven that reify life on earth, but as mere devices, as self-evident props that demystify their earthly counterparts.

This radically unsettling sense of scale also drastically alters the meaning of ethnic identity. Most jarring is the depiction of the status of whites, for the American corner of heaven is populated almost completely by the spirits of Indians. Tourists from other, more populous parts of heaven, Sandy tells Stormfield, "say this wilderness is populated with a scattering of a few hundred thousand billions of red angels, with now and then a curiously complected diseased one. You see, they think we whites, and the occasional nigger, are Injuns that have been bleached out or blackened by some leprous disease or other—for some peculiarly rascally *sin*, mind you. It is a mighty sour pill for us all" (175). Much of Twain's satire is directed against the implicit whiteness of heavens like Phelps's—his accommodates not only blacks, Indians (American and Asian), Mexicans, Arabs, and Jews, but seven-headed, blue-skinned, one-legged extraterrestrials as well. Such a polyglot mixture deals a heavy blow to the ideology of Anglo-Saxon superiority that imagined the heavenly mansion as the White House.

As Twain puts earth in a universal perspective, he places whites in their proper global perspective, as a minority race that has no inherent title over its neighbors. Nor, indeed, can it claim the exceptional cultural heritage claimed in the ideology of Anglo-Saxon superiority. England, says Sandy, "is not so very much better than this [American] end of the heavenly domain. As long as you run across Englishmen born this side of three hundred years ago, you are all right, but the minute you get back of Elizabeth's time the language begins to fog up, and the further back you go the foggier it gets. [. . .] Back of [that] time the English are simply foreigners, nothing more, nothing less" (176). The white privilege that drenches Phelps's version of heaven begins to evaporate in Twain's, and we are left not with a sense of a deeply rooted civilization overwhelmed by hordes of dark foreigners, as the rhetoric of white supremacy would have imagined, but instead with a sense that the roots of European American civilization are not so deep after all.

The cosmic scale and radical multiculturalism of *Captain Stormfield* build on a strategy that Twain had been developing throughout his late writings. Susan Gillman has connected such works as *Following the Equator*, "Three Thousand Years among the Microbes," and *The Mysterious Stranger* through what she terms the "racial occult," in which Twain, like his contemporaries Pauline Hopkins and W. E. B. DuBois, applied the New Psychology idea of divided consciousness to the question of race. Twain's late writings, argues Gillman, "invoke and adapt the notion of spirit communication and disembodied space-and-time travel, made newly respectable at this time by the investigation of psychical researchers, as a means of revisiting the old terrain of U.S. slavery and linking it to the newer global imperialism, the worldwide nationalism, nativism, and racism of the late 1890s" (194). By using race as an occult presence in such work, Twain opens a window on "the cultural unconscious of the late nineteenth-century world of empire" (208). Though Gillman does not cite *Captain Stormfield* as an example, the text clearly deploys spiritualist categories in order to explore race; the length of time it took Twain to complete the work also indicates that the racial occult was an important category for Twain long before the 1890s. And while "occult" might at first glance seem an odd term to apply to such a vigorous burlesque, it nevertheless captures the unease—or, better, dis-ease—surrounding whiteness in the text. White Americans are not simply minority inhabitants of heaven in *Captain Stormfield;* they are themselves made to partake of the malignant otherness that white supremacy consigned to people of color on earth. They are, in the eyes of extraterrestrial tourists, merely "curiously complected, diseased" Indians, former inhabitants of a world that, when finally distinguished from a fly speck, is known as "the Wart." The anxieties of whiteness, stabilized in such purified imaginary utopias as Phelps's *Gates* novels, won't be displaced in *Captain Stormfield's* heaven. There, the limits of racial identity are everywhere apparent.

Twain submits the category of "Indian" to almost as much scrutiny as the category of "white." There is no direct evidence that *Captain Stormfield* emerged in reaction to the Ghost Dance in the same manner that it grew from *The Gates Ajar.* Yet the extent to which the text represents an important development in Twain's attitude toward Native Americans, and especially their role in European American ideology, has been largely ignored by critics.[9] In fact, the Indian presence in heaven marks how far Twain had come from his days as a reporter in the Nevada Territory, when he happily participated in the general maligning of the Paiute and Ute peoples who had proven remarkably cooperative during white settlement. Some Indian-hating rhetoric survives in Sandy McWilliams's words to Stormfield. When advising the captain on where to settle in heaven, he says, "You see what the Jersey district of heaven is for whites; well, the California district is a thousand times worse. It swarms with a mean kind of leather-headed mud-colored angels—Digger Injuns, mainly—and your nearest neighbor is likely to be a million miles away" (175). But Sandy's account is countered to some degree by Stormfield's fond reunion at heaven's gate with the "Pai ute" he knew from his own California days, a "mighty good fellow" and a member of the tribe to which the so-called Diggers also belonged. Stormfield himself remembers the Paiute's funeral, "which consisted of him being burnt and the other Injuns gauming their faces with his ashes and howling like wild-cats" (156).

Unremarked by Twain is that among these Diggers and Paiutes the Ghost Dance of 1890 began—nor does he mention the earlier Ghost Dance of 1870, which proved especially durable among the California tribes. Twain left no record of his reactions to either of these movements, yet *Captain Stormfield* bears striking similarities to both. Indians do, in fact, reassemble in heaven in all their strength and glory to resume their rightful place in an American landscape; although whites are neither burned, buried, nor forced across the ocean, they scarcely need to be, so small and scattered are their number. Twain, moreover, pays the red angels the unusual respect of privacy. Indians, in heaven, are left alone to live as they wish. Yet while the great majority of Indians live in heaven as if whites never existed, Twain presents an alternative, for as in the *New York Times*'s account of Wovoka's vision, cited at the beginning of this essay, among the "heap of Indians" in heaven is one "dressed in white man's clothes" ("Messiah and His Prophet"). The Paiute clerk, like Wovoka himself, sends his heavenly message to people of all races, a symbol of the cross-cultural promise of heaven. Although *Captain Stormfield* is almost unique in turn-of-the-century European American fiction in imagining a world in which Indian culture remains untouched by whites, it is nonetheless careful to offer, in the person of the Paiute clerk, a counter to the monolithic cultural traditionalism of the Ghost Dance.

In addition to undermining conventional racial identities, Twain is intent on fracturing the formal harmonies so important in work like Phelps's. *Captain Stormfield*, in fact, might be read as an example of aesthetic devitalization. Many readers of the text have commented on its fragmented nature, and most have traced the story's rough form to Twain's difficulty in completing the text to his satisfaction. Twain's decision to publish *Captain Stormfield* as a fragmentary extract has been seen by at least one critic as a far better solution than attempting to finish it.[10] The story remains, in the words of another critic, "outlandish," full of the disruptive wildness that lurks beneath the surface of even Twain's most conventional work and that, in his late works, emerges as an "anti-story configuration" (Michelson 220–22). The formal disruptions of *Captain Stormfield*, the abrupt beginning, repeated inversions, outlandish inventions, absurd realism, and unlocatable premise (who, after all, is telling the tale?) do more than chart and resolve Twain's personal "metaphysical dislocations" (Michelson 222). If, as Richard Ohmann has argued, the formal structures of the fiction that appeared in popular magazines like *Harper's* at the turn of the century played an important role in iterating bourgeois ideology, then Twain's antistory works against that goal, exposing and widening the ideological fissures that Phelps's heaven (and Wovoka's spirit land) sought to close. *Captain Stormfield*, with its hybridity, inversions, and playful deformulation of conventional aesthetics, shares with postcolonial fiction everything but cultural marginality. Located at the very center of metropolitan literary production, the text illustrates how an aesthetic of devitalization can work to subvert a dominant culture from within.

Twain's heaven, then, not only defamiliarizes dominant images of heaven, but also demonstrates the varying political purposes that heaven can serve. Rooted in the same cultural matrix as Phelps's novels, Twain's heaven assaults the domestic and ethnic certainties central to the appeal of the *Gates* novels. And while his image of a heavenly America in which red angels live unchallenged by white contact bears an uncanny resemblance to visions recorded by the ghost dancers themselves, his heaven offers a model of cultural integration that is very different from that which fueled Wovoka's message. In struggling to adapt to the often-brutal economic and social conditions of a changed world, Phelps and Wovoka used their heavens to integrate elements of the new (commodity capitalism for Phelps; the abandonment of warfare for Wovoka) with key features of the old. The results were visions of heaven that were deeply rooted in their respective monocultural traditions, even as they took shape in a society charged with cross-cultural tension. While the *Gates* novels and the Ghost Dance both structure similar versions of heaven from the two margins of America's continental empire—heavens fashioned out of idealized simulacra of an earthly reality—*Captain Stormfield*'s heaven resists such cultural navel-gazing. By borrowing from both representations, Twain constructs a heaven that foregrounds its own determination and revels in the free play to be found in the discursive spaces between Wovoka's and Phelps's visions of the afterlife. In this play lies the radical politics of heaven, not as a place that reifies the deep cultural divisions of America at the turn of the twentieth century, but as a place that challenges cultural norms and ethnic identity. This spectral America is one place, at least, where the norms, biases, categories, and assumptions that structured the injustices of the era could be challenged and, crucially, reimagined. Twain, marked by the biases inherent in his location at an imperial metropole, may not fully comprehend the cultural positions of a Paiute prophet or, for that matter, a spiritual feminist. Nevertheless, *Captain Stormfield* illustrates that although these heavens and the cultures that gave them birth may seem, at times, light years apart, they can reside in the pages of a single book.

NOTES

1. I begin with the Ghost Dance for several reasons. Although it is generally understood as a singular movement in the early 1890s, there were in fact numerous Ghost Dance movements throughout the history of European colonization. Thus, while the Ghost Dance of 1890 occurred a generation after Phelps published *The Gates Ajar,* its immediate predecessor, the Ghost Dance of 1870, was contemporaneous with Phelps's first novel. More importantly, I want to prioritize what has traditionally been marginalized, and hence use the Ghost Dance to frame my discussion of Phelps. Whites have long sought to understand Indian spirituality from a European American perspective; much can be gained by reversing the process.

2. It did not, however, entirely die out. The Ghost Dance remained a powerful presence among a number of tribes long after Wounded Knee, and Wovoka is still revered as a powerful holy man among the Paiutes and among the broader population of Native Americans. Alice Beck Kehoe describes a community in Saskatchewan that still adhered to his teachings in the 1960s.

3. Mooney's *The Ghost Dance Religion and Wounded Knee* (1896) is one of the first scholarly accounts of the Ghost Dance, and remains the most authoritative. Recent studies have been content either to update Mooney for a contemporary audience, like Alice Kehoe's *The Ghost Dance: Ethnohistory and Revitalization* (1986), or situate Mooney's account among the ideological battles of turn-of-the-century America, like Michael Elliot's "Ethnography and the Problem of the Real: James Mooney's *Ghost Dance Religion*" (1998). More accounts of the Ghost Dance have focused on specific tribes, such as William McLoughlin's *The Cherokee Ghost Dance.* My summary of the Ghost Dance draws largely on Mooney. For an account that places Mooney in the context of contemporary anthropology, see L. G. Moses's *The Indian Man: A Biography of James Mooney.*

4. The totalizing undercurrent of Ghost Dance ideology attracted the attention of at least one contemporary writer. Sherman Alexie's short story "Distances," in *The Lone Ranger and Tonto Fistfight in Heaven,* imagines the Ghost Dance as a dystopia of Indian traditionalism run amok.

5. Stanley French provides a good introduction to the rural-cemetery movement in "The Cemetery as Cultural Institution," in *Death in America.* Barton Levi St. Armand discusses the broader cultural context of the "Mount Auburn School" in *Emily Dickinson and Her Culture.*

6. The *Gates* novels have attracted modest critical attention. David Reynolds's *Faith in Fiction* and Barton St. Armand Levi's *Emily Dickinson and Her Culture* typify the view of Phelps as liberal Christian writer. Feminist assessments of the *Gates* novels

roughly track efforts to recuperate sentimental writing in general. Ann Douglas, writing in 1974, damns Phelps as "always a sentimental, often a sloppy writer" (66–67) with an undercurrent of assertiveness. Carol Kessler, writing in the 1980s, argues that the *Gates* novels should be read as a proto-feminist utopia. Lisa Long, in a more recent article, argues that *The Gates Ajar* is best read not as one example of feminine consolation literature, but as an integral part of Civil War literature that attempts to reimagine a fractured European American ontology through the prism of female sensibility.

7. For a detailed discussion of the composition of *Captain Stormfield*, see Howard Baetzhold's and Joseph B. McCullough's introduction in *The Bible According to Mark Twain.*

8. Robert Rees traces Twain's borrowings from Phelps in "*Captain Stormfield's Visit to Heaven* and *The Gates Ajar.*"

9. David L. Newquist makes no mention of *Captain Stormfield* in "Mark Twain among the Indians." Louis J. Budd, in *Mark Twain: Social Philosopher,* briefly mentions *Captain Stormfield* in noting Twain's gradual drift away from racism (189).

10. Everett Emerson, *The Authentic Mark Twain,* 113.

WORKS CITED

Alexie, Sherman. "Distances." In *The Lone Ranger and Tonto Fistfight in Heaven.* New York: Atlantic Monthly Press, 1993. 104–9.

Baetzhold, Howard G., and Joseph B. McCullough, eds. "Introduction." In *The Bible According to Mark Twain.* Athens: University of Georgia Press, 1995.

Beecher, Charles. *Spiritual Manifestations.* Boston: Lee & Shephard, 1879.

Budd, Louis J. *Mark Twain, Social Philosopher.* Bloomington: University of Indiana Press, 1962.

Douglass, Ann. "Heaven Our Home." In *Death in America.* Edited by David Stannard, 49–68. Philadelphia: University of Pennsylvania Press, 1975.

Elliot, Michael. "Ethnography and the Problem of the Real: James Mooney's *Ghost Dance Religion.*" *American Quarterly* 50:2 (June 1998): 201–33.

Emerson, Everett. *The Authentic Mark Twain: A Literary Biography of Samuel L. Clemens.* Philadelphia: University of Pennsylvania Press, 1984.

French, Stanley. "The Cemetery as Cultural Institution." In *Death in America.* Edited by David Stannard, 69–91. Philadelphia: University of Pennsylvania Press, 1975.

Gillman, Susan. "Mark Twain's Travels in the Racial Occult: Following the Equator and the Dream Tales." In *The Cambridge Companion to Mark Twain.* Edited by Forrest G. Robinson, 193–219. New York: Cambridge University Press, 1995.

Irwin, Lee. *The Dream Seekers: Native American Visionary Traditions of the Great Plains.* Norman: University of Oklahoma Press, 1994.

Kehoe, Alice Beck. *The Ghost Dance: Ethnohistory and Revitalization.* Fort Worth: Holt, Rinehart & Winston, 1989.

Kessler, Carol Farley. "The Heavenly Utopia of Elizabeth Stuart Phelps." In *Women and Utopia: Critical Interpretations.* Edited by Marleen Barr and Nicholas D. Smith, 85–95. Latham, Md.: University Press of America, 1983.

Long, Lisa. "'The Corporeity of Heaven': Rehabilitating the Civil War Body in *The Gates Ajar.*" *American Literature* 69:4 (Dec. 1997): 781–811.

McLoughlin, William, Walter H. Conser, and Virginia Duffey McLoughlin. *The Cherokee Ghost Dance: Essays on the Southeastern Indians, 1789–1861.* Macon, Ga.: Mercer University Press, 1984.

"The Messiah and His Prophet." *New York Times,* Nov. 30, 1890, p. 9.

Michelson, Bruce. *Mark Twain on the Loose: A Comic Writer and the American Self.* Amherst: University of Massachusetts Press, 1995.

Mooney, James. *The Ghost Dance Religion and Wounded Knee.* Washington, 1896.

Moses, L. G. *The Indian Man: A Biography of James Mooney.* Urbana: University of Illinois Press, 1984.

"The New Indian Messiah," *New York Times,* Nov. 16, 1890, p. 11.

Newquist, David L. "Mark Twain among the Indians." *Midamerica* 21 (1994): 59–72.

Ohmann, Richard. *Selling Culture: Magazines, Markets and Class at the Turn of the Century.* New York: Verso, 1996.

Phelps, Elizabeth. *The Sunnyside, or The Country Minister's Wife.* Boston, 1851.

Phelps, Elizabeth Stuart. *Beyond the Gates.* Boston, 1883.

———. *Chapters from a Life.* Boston, 1896.

———. *Doctor Zay.* Boston, 1882.

———. *The Gates Ajar.* 1867. Reprint. Cambridge: The Belknap Press, 1964.

———. *The Gates Between.* Boston, 1887.

———. *The Silent Partner.* Boston, 1871.

———. *The Story of Avis.* Boston, 1877.

Rees, Robert A. "*Captain Stormfield's Visit to Heaven* and *The Gates Ajar.*" *English Language Notes* 7 (Mar. 7, 1970): 197–202.

Reynolds, David S. *Faith in Fiction: The Emergence of Religious Literature in America.* Cambridge: Harvard University Press, 1981.

St. Armand, Barton Levi. "Dickinson, Phelps and the Image of Heaven." In *Emily Dickinson and Her Culture.* Cambridge: Cambridge University Press, 1984.

Slossum, Annie T. *The Heresy of Mehetable Clark.* New York, 1892.

Smith, Helen Hootin. "Introduction." In *The Gates Ajar,* by Elizabeth Stuart Phelps. Cambridge, Ma.: Belknap Press, 1964.

Twain, Mark. *The Autobiography of Mark Twain.* Edited by Charles Neider. New York: Harper, 1959.

———. *Captain Stormfield's Visit to Heaven: The Bible According to Mark Twain.* Edited by Howard G. Baetzhold and Joseph B. McCullough. Athens: University of Georgia Press, 1995.

———. *Following the Equator: A Journey around the World.* Hartford, Ct.: American, 1897.

———. *The Mysterious Stranger.* New York: Prometheus Books, 1995.

———. "Three Thousand Years among the Microbes." In *Collected Tales, Sketches, Speeches and Essays by Mark Twain.* New York: Library of America, 1992.

Walker, James R. *Lakota Belief and Ritual.* Edited by Raymond J. Demaille and Elaine A. Janer. Lincoln: University of Nebraska Press, 1991.

Wallace, A. F. C. "Revitalization Movements: Some Theoretical Considerations for Their Comparative Study." *American Anthropologist* 58 (1956): 264–81.

"Weird Things in Dreams," *New York Times,* Nov. 29, 1890, p. 8.

Technologies of Vision

Spiritualism and Science in Nineteenth-Century America

SHERI WEINSTEIN

In March of 1848, two adolescent sisters named Katie and Margaret Fox played a ventriloquistic trick from their attic bedroom in Hydesville, New York. Rapping their finger and toe joints against a bed post and claiming that the sounds emanated from the ghost of a murdered peddler, the girls created an apparent reanimation that garnered them immediate and sensational local attention. As Western New York residents flocked to the Fox home to witness the phenomenal contact powers of the sisters, the girls were sequestered in their older sister Leah's home in Rochester, New York. But it wasn't long before their rapping communications resumed and Kate and Margaret became the center of a newfound spiritualist movement. The eminent *New York Tribune* editor Horace Greeley even brought the girls to New York City in 1850 to give rapping séances to a rapt public at Barnum's Hotel. And upstate, "the house was besieged by eager seekers after spiritual truth. An excellent living—far more than they could hope for in another way—was to be made by charging a dollar a head for participation in their spirit circles. They were surrounded by enthusiastic supporters; and they resigned themselves, not too unwillingly, to their fate" (Brandon 23).

Throughout their reign, the Foxes had no involvement with the political ideologies and social platforms espoused by well-known spiritualists such as Andrew Jackson Davis, Victoria Woodhull, and Emma Hardinge Britten.[1] They were performance artists. As such, they were investigated on a number of occasions by academic scientists eager to prove that spiritualist rappings were a product of performative duplicity and not scientific authenticity. The most infamous investigation took place at the University of Buffalo medical school, where doctors concluded that the girls were producing the rapping sounds, which Margaret called a "spiritual telegraph," through their finger and toe joints (Issacs 94). Yet despite, or perhaps because of, this report, which was reprinted in major newspapers throughout the Northeast and Midwest, the public remained fascinated with the Foxes, and their careers continued to flourish. Kate toured England throughout the 1870s, drinking her way through her financial profits, while Margaret eventually denounced spiritualists and blamed the popular spiritualist movement for her sister's alcoholism (cf. Issacs).

Then, in 1888, Margaret appeared at the Boston Music Hall to expose her and Kate's fraudulence.[2] With Kate in the audience, in a demonstration that became known as the "death blow to spiritualism," Margaret confessed to the rapping technique and proved the Buffalo doctors correct in their original assessment (Issacs 93–96). But this was not in fact the death blow to Modern Spiritualism. America was hungry for more, if not from the Fox sisters, then from other séances with other spiritualists. After all, the Foxes' act had never really been about the Foxes; they "were in the right place at the right time, with the right message, at the right time; they introduced spirit rappings to a world that was hungry for spirit rappings" (Pimple 81).[3]

The American public's rapid and widespread attraction to mediumship, the omnipresence of private parlor and public auditorium séances, and the dozens of spiritualist periodicals spawned between the 1850s and the turn of the century speak to paradigms of human communication and desire that render spiritualism a movement that reinvented American spiritual culture. Even further, these paradigms represented a movement that was also deeply engaged with secular and material culture. Modern Spiritualism was hugely popular throughout the latter decades of the nineteenth century and was predominant in the American Northeast and Midwest. In 1859 one and a half million Americans claimed to have spiritualist affiliations (Cross 349). In his *Mesmerism and the American Cure of Souls*, Robert Fuller estimates that by the 1870s, spiritualism could claim as many as eleven million believers (95). At the very least, as Barbara Goldsmith writes, there were at least two million followers of American spiritualism by 1870, their numbers largely due to the death and devastation of the Civil War (78).

As a means of reproducing and reanimating the dead, spiritualism fostered new types of vision, new terms for vision and, overall, new conceptions of visuality. Because spiritualists believe in the communicative and emotional power of the spirits of the dead, which they cannot see but *can* "witness" through a spiritualist medium's channeling, spiritualism problematized a rampant "we know it when we see it" understanding of knowledge as scopic, derived from "the open study of what can be viewed, hence valid[ated] (Jordanova 94). In place of a trajectory that validated things through viewing them, spiritualism offered an economy of human relationships and knowledge that was deliberately oriented toward intuition, invisibility, and perspective.[4]

A belief in life after death is certainly not something invented by the nineteenth century. However, what I argue is especially "modern" about Modern Spiritualism is that the movement was part and parcel of particularly scientific and empiricist discourses. Spiritualism aimed to authenticate the immaterial presence of spirits of the dead through "objective," observable, and repeated experiences and through a rationalist discourse of "factual" evidence. As an 1884 editorial in Brittan's *Journal of Spiritual Science* asked, "*Do the facts of Spiritualism* demonstrate the continued existence of man after the destruction of his physical body?" (Buchanan)

At the same time, though, spiritualists were caught in a bind. They lived in an extraordinarily scientific age, yet many spiritualists viewed empiricism as an insufficient method of understanding the relationship between vision and experience, sensory impressions and "fact." An advertisement for "The Writing Planchette" in an 1884 issue of the spiritualist journal *Banner of Light* read: "Science is unable to explain the mystery of this wonderful little instrument, which writes intelligent answers to questions either asked or thought mentally" (*Banner*). Thus, spiritualism maintained that observation and experience themselves could not alone completely explain irrational, supernatural, and invisible phenomena; there exist, said spiritualists, decisively nonempirical forms of vision that may be procured *through* objects and human bodies but are not dependent for their existence *on* them. In his 1863 *Plain Guide to Spiritualism*, Uriah Clark references this notion of "invisible vision" when he writes, "If one sees with the eyes closed, he demonstrates the existence of a *spiritual* sense of sight" (93, emphasis added).

Most spirit communication occurred through human spirit-mediums and trance speakers, many of whom deployed material media such as Ouija boards, materialization cabinets, and automatic-writing tools as aids. There were and still are two basic threads of spiritualism. One is religious and serious in tone, engaged in the social analyses engendered through spirit revelations. The second is more secular and spectacular in nature, concerned

with the performative aspects of séances. Typically, these threads inter-
twine, and in both aspects of spiritualism, the central debate is not about
whether or not there is life after death. The debate, rather, is about whether
or not rappings, writings, trance speaking, and mediumistic materializa-
tions constitute authentic and credible *proof* of such spirit life (cf. Pimple
83–84).

From P. T. Barnum's exposé *Humbugs of the World* to his best-selling
1855 autobiography of showmanship, *Struggles and Triumphs*; from Harry
Houdini's love for optical illusion and contempt for spiritualist trickery to
Arthur Conan Doyle's passionate lectures to packed auditoriums on spiritualism's authenticity, the nineteenth century considered the relationships
between spirituality and spectacle, intuition and vision, paramount. Indeed,
by the 1870s, the séance table was seen as much more than a medium of
spiritual contact and an emblem of extrasensory communication; it was
already part of a larger, American carnival of vision. For instance, at one
annual spiritualist meeting, there were "a carousel, a singing midget, a
Mrs. Suydam, who held fire in her hands, and a so-called Spiritualist who
painted flowers while blindfolded" (Goldsmith 425). Spiritualism produced
"a spectacle of human beings intimately connected to one another by invisible influences [. . .]. [T]he human and the mechanical were not exactly
the same thing, but disturbingly interchangeable. And the human psyche
itself was shown to be elastic and progressive" (Winter 117).

Spiritualism was popular and important because it offered Americans
an alternative version of scopic authority and ocular abilities. In arguing
that the boundaries between heaven and earth and between life and death
are permeable, spiritualism dramatized a general and pervasive American
spirit of boundless expansion, a "manifest destiny" ideology motivating
the nation, and especially its technological innovations and sociopolitical
agendas, in both the antebellum and postbellum years. We might even say
that spiritualism constructed its own manifest destiny inside the psyche.[5]

Spiritualist practice had much in common with scientific investigations, but spiritualism looked to dining-room tables instead of operating
tables, planchettes instead of microscopes, and the spirit-medium instead
of the medical doctor as the force that can cause spectacular reactions and
changes in human bodies and the environs, "much as a catalyst allows a
chemical reaction to take place between two substances without actually
entering into the reaction itself" (Pimple 79). Many scientists, in an effort
to garner public interest in and support for science, resorted to sensation,
magic, and glamour. For example, scientists capitalized on the marvelous

entertainment value of engineered spectacles of human progress such as human automatons, "electric girls"—female mannequins decorated with electric lights—and various other electrical media (Marvin 131–39).

Scientists called on spiritualistic media and rhetoric to enlarge the boundaries and significance of their pursuits: Scientist Robert Hare "understood electricity as the mechanism of cosmic mediumship, and advanced spirits as 'electrical conductors'" (Carroll 68). A newspaper reported in 1888 that Thomas Edison owned a clock that said, "It's midnight. Prepare to die." While this was likely a joke, it certainly points us to a nineteenth-century sense that technological communication could have potentially infinite, spiritual, and even apocalyptic powers (cf. Marvin 54). Nevertheless, spiritualism used the ideologies and rhetoric of science when it was convenient. In an 1864 article entitled, "Disembodied Spirits May Surround Us," published in the spiritualist *Herald of Progress*, a spiritualist believer named W. T. H. writes,

> I have often wondered that the advocated of Spiritualism [*sic*] have never pointed out to those more positive skeptics who maintain that spirits cannot exist because they are not seen, the very obvious destruction of that fallacy by the merest glance at the wonders revealed by the microscope [. . .]. I think it quite possible that in some future time, optical instruments may be invented sufficiently powerful to enable men as clearly to see the present "viewless tenants" of the atmosphere as they can now see myriads of microscopic organisms in a glass of water [. . .] to see disembodied spirits peopling what we now consider the "empty air." (9)

Spiritualists aimed to demystify spiritualism in large part by differentiating themselves from occultists and their penchant for perpetual enigmas and unrecoverable spiritual conundrums; spiritualists argued, "[T]his is not a superstitious age, but one of THOUGHT—it is not an age of religious culture and illumination, but one of materiality and SCIENCE." The spiritual is subjugated to the material," wrote one of spiritualism's most famous and ardent believers (Davis 9). Spiritualists found that reconciling the tensions between the material and the ethereal was not at all simple. On the one hand, spiritualists opposed the presumption of philosophical materialism, which holds that nothing exists beyond matter and the empirically knowable; on the other hand, spiritualists wanted to *prove*— empirically and beyond question—the definitive existence of spirit life. To authorize their movement, many spiritualists deployed empiricist language calling for evidence of psychic phenomena and arguing that, paradoxical as this may seem, *spirits* provided such evidence. For example, in 1870, the prolific and famous spiritualist medium and speaker Emma Hardinge Britten wrote,

> The philosophy of spiritualism, however beautiful in theory or true in principle, grows out of its facts, for if spirits are not the authors of the communications received in their names, the whole theory of a hereafter [. . .] crumbles [. . .] unless we have facts and basic fundamental principles. To demonstrate these [. . .] spirits have come to earth [. . .] in short, the entire intercommunion between the two worlds must be based on the impregnable rock of truth. (3)

And in 1873 John Buchanan wrote, "But the vital question is not, how do the Spirits talk, and have that measure of intelligence they are able, under the circumstances, to display. The far more important question [is] *do the facts of Spiritualism demonstrate the continued existence of man after the destruction of his physical body?*" (554).

What *are* the "facts of spiritualism," a movement that prized immaterial, protean, and perspectival truth as much as it did certainty and objectivity? And how does an epistemology that is about the hypersensory and the metavisual render itself *evidential?* To address the apparent breach between the idea that human beings exist after their deaths in communicative, immaterial forms and the idea that such existence must be palpably, tangibly, or at least somehow empirically sensed and demonstrated, many spiritualists resorted to technology and machinery. N. Zwaan invented the "Super-Ray" in the early 1850s, claiming that the machine could produce its own psychical phenomena such as levitation; Zwaan also founded an organization called "The Spirit Electronic Communication Society" (McHargue 50).

John Murray Spear, an American Universalist church preacher, converted to spiritualism in 1851 and became a trance medium. In 1853 he became involved with the spiritualist Association of Electrizers, which led Spear to construct the infamous New Motor. This machine supposedly generated spirits through a more credible and objective means than could the spirit-medium, a "human machine" of spirit (re)production that was potentially fallible and duplicitous. Also called the "wonderful infant" and thought by many to be propelled by feminine energy (Goldsmith 34), the New Motor was a perpetual-motion device that was also supposedly a living organism in its own right; the machine was expected to self-generate an endless supply of electric power (McHargue 53–54). Of course, it couldn't do so, and it was ultimately destroyed in Lynn, Massachusetts, by an angry mob unconvinced of its efficacy, a mob that feared and loathed the idea that a machine could "replace" God in its infinite generation of energy and animation (Moore 94). But the intrigue Spear's device attracted signifies to us that the public was searching for some medium *between* visibility and invisibility, some evidential realization of the line between materiality and ethereality.

Many other spiritualists did not go so far as to try to construct scientific objects with spiritualist capabilities, but instead used scientific discourse and rhetoric to supplement their intuition with what they considered hard evidence. They maintained that the spirit-medium is a "machine, a body which produces influences and effects" (Lowe 10). Human mediums, like machines, are productive but, even more importantly, like machines, they are deceptive. Both possess appearances and surfaces that neither reflect nor reveal their inner workings; both human and mechanistic mediums reject mimesis and transparency. Of course, from the inception of mesmerism, before spiritualism's boom, "electrical psychology" was considered a spiritual phenomenon based on chemical reactions within and between bodies. What makes spiritualist interest in scientific discourse innovative, though, is that many believers adopted a particularly materialist vocabulary to validate ethereality. Arguing that energy travels in a variety of ways, many spiritualists countered skeptics' opposition by asserting that electricity, too, is simultaneously invisible and real, and that intelligent and productive agents of light/enlightenment can operate unseen but still be actual and authentic.

While individuals and machines had not yet been completely amalgamated in mid-nineteenth-century America into one concept, they nonetheless were being thought of as less and less distinct from one another. The trope worked in both ways: As science became more and more sophisticated, human beings began to embody a biomechanics whereby persons took on the values and abilities of inanimate machines; likewise both physiologists and engineers began to speak of machines as possessing a vital, human nature. In 1873 physician, physiologist, and photographic pioneer Etienne-Jules Marey wrote in *Animal Mechanism: A Treatise on Terrestrial and Aerial Locomotion*, "Modern engineers have created machines which are much more legitimately to be compared to animate motors" (quoted in Rabinbach 90).

Indeed, by 1820, scientists worldwide began to observe that electrical currents have magnetizing effects on human beings, and by the 1830s magnetism first as medical cure and then as mesmeric performance was widespread throughout Europe and the United States. For both spiritualists and electricians, the latter of which formed a burgeoning profession in the nineteenth century, electricity "was the transformative agent of social possibility" (Moore 7). Electrical impulses and energy were never merely science, but were creators of "social miracles." Historians of Modern Spiritualism are incorrect to argue that spiritualism tried to borrow from the vocabulary and prestige of nineteenth-century science (Moore 7). The relationship was more mutual than this, and not nearly so diachronic.

The problem for many people was not that spiritualism was insufficiently scientific, but that science had become overly spiritualistic.[6] Both spiritualism and science shared an overriding system of beliefs yet remained skeptical about the competency of the other's specialized discourse in relation to that belief system. Spiritualists were not the quacks in counterpart to the rational, educated men of science in the late nineteenth century. It is crucial to realize that scientific and spiritualist discourses about the infinite possibilities of human vision and communication emerged in conjunction with one another; it is not accurate to say that psychical research "preferred to borrow the techniques of science" (Briggs 54). Neither scientists nor the public at large necessarily found electricity less mystifying or more explicable than spiritualism. Both electrical and spiritualist illuminations were invisible, magical apprehensions, and if scientists could explain such phenomena through investigation and evidence, said spiritualists, then they could as well.

Furthermore, if spiritualists did take their point of departure from science, then they argued that spiritualism begins precisely where science hits its inherent limitations and essential fallibilities. S. B. Brittan's *Journal of Spiritual Science*, whose motto was "Reverent in Spirit, but Independent in Thought," was one of the premier spiritualist periodicals to engage seriously with science and to argue for the cultural equation of physical and psychical forms of matter. In an 1874 editorial entitled, "The Wings of Science," a writer argued,

> [T]hose who are finely organized can use their intuitive powers to detect in the apparently dead materials of a manuscript a latent spiritual energy before unknown and[,] by coming into contact with this new psychic element, float out into a realm of investigation and discovery which, if we are

not greatly mistaken, will prove to be that vast ocean, on the borders of which Newton wandered as a child and sighed for the ability to cross its trackless depths. (199–200)

Science was not primary and spirituality secondary in Modern Spiritualism, and the relatively new field of electricity was not necessarily more reliable, understandable, or accessible for individuals than were phenomena of spirit communication. Realizing the electrical nature of human bodies and their technological abilities did not completely clarify the status of human life and death, nor did it undermine the spiritual nature of these. Furthermore, scientific methodologies may have enhanced the credibility of spiritualism for believers and nonbelievers alike, but scientific matter was only the *means* through which a higher order of knowledge could materialize and manifest itself, only a medium through which "communicative magic" could transpire. Science was mere matter, but spiritualists argued that "spirit matter" could invariably alter the very constitutions of personal and social identity. As William James wrote in 1889, "Of course, the great *theoretic* interest of these automatic performances, whether speech or writing, consists in the questions they awaken as to the boundaries of our individuality" (45).

A spiritualism/science paradigm about the nature of evidence was largely responsible for the 1882 founding of the Society for Psychical Research (SPR) in England.[7] The SPR was composed of both spiritualists and nonspiritualists. It was a society that embraced the study of psychical manifestations but did not embrace the more religious or political tenets of spiritualism per se. Henry Sedgwick was the society's first president; well-known intellectuals such as Frank Podmore (*Studies in Psychical Research,* 1897; *Modern Spiritualism, a History and a Criticism,* 1902), Edmund Gurney (*Phantasms of the Living,* 1886), and William James were among the society's active membership. The SPR claimed to be devoted to the empirical investigations of psychical phenomena and the authentication of supposed "spiritual realities" such as clairvoyance and telepathy. Its first annual proceedings state that the SPR was formed

> for the purpose of making an organized and systematic attempt to investigate that large group of debatable phenomena designated by such terms as "mesmeric," "psychical" and "spiritualistic." From the recorded testimony of many competent witnesses, past and present, including observations recently made by scientific men of eminence in various countries, there appears

to be, amidst much illusion and deception, an important body of remarkable phenomena [. . .]. The aim of the Society is to approach these various problems without prejudice or prepossession of any kind, and in the same spirit of exact and unimpassioned inquiry which has enabled science to solve so many problems. (Circulars of the SPR 6–7)

The language of these proceedings is quite revealing. Empiricist language such as "investigate" and "systematic," "observation" and "testimony," implies a sort of organized objectivity, a faith in the senses' impartiality. But by disavowing prejudice and bias and glorifying science as an exact and "unimpassioned" form of inquiry, this statement in fact tells us that testimony and observation are always possibly fallible and unreliable. The SPR courts the idea that its conclusions could be based on illusion and deception. In other words, we must trust the society as we must trust science: with faith in its mission but skepticism about its efficacy and its purported empirical truth. Put another way, if the society was empiricist, then its empiricism did not preclude relativity and provisionality. As William James wrote, "We all, scientists and non-scientists, live on some inclined plane of credulity" (41).

Nineteenth-century America's fascination with technological models of psychical travel was particularly manifest in mid-century scientific innovations such as the railroad, the telegraph, and the daguerreotype. The advent and rapid proliferation of all three of these communicative media spoke in important ways to the individual's increasingly spiritualist ability to project herself or himself into "foreign" and illegible territories. American spiritualism's inception thereby coincided with a larger cultural and industrial moment calling for and enabling human beings to be transported in mystifying, immeasurable, and excitingly infinite ways.

In 1838 the Morse Telegraph was invented; its public use began in 1844. The first telegraphic network began in the summer of 1846; lines stretched north from Washington, D.C., south from Buffalo, and west from Boston and met in New York; all points could now receive a single message instantly, simultaneously, and by a single transmission (Blondheim 190). The daguerreotype industry began gaining ground in the United States with the popularity of portraiture in the 1830s and did not wane until photography began to displace it in the late 1850s. Photography was an especially handy medium for spiritualists: From the 1860s through the turn of the century, the photographic production of "spirits" under controlled test conditions was considered by both spiritualist believers and skeptics to be

credible proof of the authenticity of those spirits. Indeed, spirit photography was an authenticating and fashionable tool. "Everywhere, spirit 'extras'
began to appear in photographs. Shadowy figures, readily identifiable as
dead relatives, hovered behind live sitters. [These figures] almost certainly
strongly resembled the face in an existing photograph" (Brandon 222–23).

If spirit photography allowed the visual transportation of the dead back
to earth, then the railroad industry inaugurated new tropes and language
for human beings' own transportational abilities. The railroad industry
boomed throughout the 1840s, soon laying tracks cross-country and neces-
sitating a national standardization of time and new, fluid conceptions of
human mobility and physicality. Telegraphy and the railroad jointly coor-
dinated new versions of time, making long distances seem shorter than
they used to and removing the obstacle of distance from communication.
Spiritualist mediumship attempted the same feat in its communication
with the dead.

These technologies of vision and communication were not distinct
from one another. Railroad companies were prime users of telegraphy as a
means of managing the safety and speed of their vast transportation and
communication networks. The opening of the Atlantic Telegraph Cable,
which the railroad industry both precipitated and capitalized on, occurred
in 1865. All three media—telegraphs, trains, and spirit-mediums—signified a new space-time continuum for Americans. In response, perhaps, to
the inherent chaos of disembodied and panoramic communication and
transportation that these media offer, the United States followed Britain's
lead and began to standardize time. In 1884 Greenwich Time became the
official, global standard for time's measurement, and in 1889 the United
States was divided into the local time zones that we still observe today (cf.
Schivelbush).

The ethos of spirit mediumship functioned in very similar ways to the
industrial ethos of the period. Much like the railroad, spirit mediumship
aimed to transcend boundaries. The human medium reaches toward a
"higher plane" of spirit life. The medium yearns simultaneously to reach
beyond the materiality of the body and its hermetic nature and to bring
the transcendent world of spirit bodies down to the level of her or his
own, earthly body and its communication with other vital, material bodies. In spiritualist mediumship, the animation of the spirit of the person
with the spirit of the dead occurs not on a vertical axis (as toward a Christian heaven), but on a social, horizontal axis. The paradigm is not one of
transcending the limitations of human, sensory powers in a hierarchical

sense, but of realizing the inherently transportative powers of the human senses in a lateral way, from person to person, much as the railroad does. "'Annihilation of time and space' was the topos that the early nineteenth century used to describe the new situation into which the railroad placed natural space after depriving it of its hitherto absolute powers. Motion was no longer dependent on the conditions of natural space, but on a mechanical power that created its own new spatiality" (Schivelbush 10).

It is remarkable that much nineteenth-century rhetoric of railroad travel is a rhetoric of transcendence in which the body encounters levels of knowledge and access that it never before knew possible—the passenger literally moves across land toward new horizons. On the one hand, the railroad signifies the individual's triumph over natural obstacles—the person's infinite mobility and mutability—much as spiritualism does. On the other hand, though, the railroad is perpetually confined, like the medium in her natural body, limited "by its iron rails to a pre-determined path." Thus, like the spirit-medium, the railroad marks a newly ambivalent concept of mobility and "suggests a new sort of fate" (Marx 19) in which the very circumscription of an energy source actually enables the expansion of that source into new, uncharted realms. Science thereby encounters the spirit through these newly technological ways of seeing and knowing.

The nineteenth century's theorization—of which spiritualism is a huge marker, but only one of many—of the links between the electricities of the central nervous system and electrical technology outside the body hypothesizes that all electronic technology is organic. "Electricity in particular became for Spiritualists a crucial metaphorical concept in comprehending the operation of the spiritual universe" (Carroll 68). According to spiritualists, technology illuminates and provides access to the spiritual world not in spite of the human mediums but because of the magnetism present in them; individuals are the co-creators of sensory productions, not merely the consumers of them. As the medium and orator Andrew Jackson Davis wrote,

The young ladies of the Fox family, and hundreds of other individuals, through whom the spirits communicate, are mediums, because the electrical atmosphere which emanates from their systems contains but little gross electricity. The spirits sustaining a positive relation to us, are enabled through these mediums, or conductors, to attract and move articles of furniture, vibrate the wires of a musical instrument, and, by discharging the power of their wills, currents of magnetism, they can and do produce rappings. (27)

There are two primary consequences to this premise that certain human bodies not only contain biological, electrical impulses but can also function as utilities, as "conductors" of energy and forces of illumination in their own right. First, it means that definitions of "technology" must be enlarged so that they include, and don't merely reference, human beings. Second, individuals become types of machines that "work," as well as being users of fantastic machinery. Alison Winter's comments about mesmerism are even more relevant when applied to spiritualism: "[A] human being could be made or shown to be mechanical even in those most human of characteristics, thought and social interaction" (63).

As the human body's, and especially the human eye's, ability to perceive and receive sensory input became "automized" in the nineteenth century, there occurred a breach between tangibility and visuality (Crary 19). Especially as the field of psychology emerged, scientific and aesthetic discourses were increasingly interwoven, which allowed individuals to arrive at a modern definition of visual production whereby science and art, objectivity and subjectivity, were not diametrically opposed.

On the one hand, new spectacular discourses resulted *from* technological innovations in American culture. On the other hand, fortified *by* the material objects of spiritualism and science, such spectacular discourses also posed consequential shifts in the very lives of things, in the material components of vision. Recognizing the mutual influence of language and its referents and of objects and ideologies offers us an optimal lens into the nineteenth century's captivation with the visual order of things. The new modalities of vision in nineteenth-century America were fraught with complicated questions about sensory reality. Perhaps the troubled governess in Henry James's *The Turn of the Screw* puts it best: "Our *not* seeing it is the strongest of proofs" (emphasis added).

"Seeing" the invisible means that sight as well as presence needed to be revised and rethought. In 1870 Emma Hardinge Britten wrote, "Invisible armies marched to the rescue of America's freedom through mediumistic warriors" (507). The popular representations of visual recognition were increasingly shifting from an idea that vision is absolute, monocular, and fixed to a conviction that vision is relative and binocular. According to Jonathan Crary, a new visual technology such as the stereoscope hurried this cultural process along by challenging users to make two views appear as one (118–20). The popular uses of vision, in other words, were undergoing transformation in late-nineteenth-century America. The human spirit-medium performed a similar task, uniting the "vision" of the ghost of the dead with the ability of the séance sitter to see that ghost, and re-animating the dead through the voice of the living so that two previously separate entities—the dead and the living, the invisible and the visible, the medium and the message—became one.

Spiritualism and especially the human spiritualist medium emerged in an age of technological innovations and functioned, in the words of Robert Dale Owen in his 1860 *Footfalls on the Boundary of Another World*, as a "cerebral battery" (360). In an age of extraordinary visual and communicative capacities, spiritualism provided yet another way to view the conversion of power and energy from one form to another. Put bluntly, Modern Spiritualism assuaged individuals' fears of losing their humanity to the opaque technologies of telegraphs, railroads, and photography by making the human body itself into a type of penetrative and communicative "technology," a machine of communication, transport, and vision.

Modern Spiritualism is fascinating not because spiritualist believers were ingenuous and refreshingly innocent kooks, but because spiritualists were savvy and decisive members of mainstream America. Spiritualism's longing for communion with lost, invisible souls, its traversing of uncharted realms in order to reanimate the dead, spoke to a bereaved and racially conflicted country after the Civil War, and drastically altered conceptions of communication and representation in a land undergoing rapid expansion and industrialization. Spiritualism is important not because it was fantastically spiritual and ethereal, but because it wasn't. It was a movement about the natures of reality and materiality that worked to redefine what it means not to see, to know without seeing, to see in new ways whereby vision does not mandate presence and presence does not necessarily confer knowledge.

Spirit mediumship is a nineteenth-century technology of vision that clearly dramatizes the problematics of the representation and credibility of the human body in an increasingly mechanistic world. It explores how the animate and inanimate can be understood together, how the strange and familiar, the local and the foreign, relate to one another. Nineteenth-century America took pleasure in such exploration and welcomed the blurred vision of things that could not be seen and the effects that could not be foreseen. Modern Spiritualism emerged from and marked an America based not on order and homogeneity, but on the protean, unpredictable natures of vision and embodiment.

NOTES

1. There is no scholarly consensus as to the standardization of capitalization for the term "spiritualism." If one links all spiritualists and spiritualism directly to the nineteenth-century movement, then spiritualism should invariably read "Spiritualism." However, if one interprets spiritualism, as I do, as a more generic epistemology, a way of seeing the world, a rhetoric, discourse, and purview, then it does not warrant capitalization. I only capitalize the words "spiritualism," "spiritualist," and so forth in a direct quotation or when I refer in particular to the Modern Spiritualism movement that began in the United States in 1848.

2. The Boston Music Hall was frequently the site of spiritualist performances. Henry James has memorialized the space in *The Bostonians,* his novel of spiritualist influence and inspiration and their manifestations. *The Bostonians* was serialized in *Century* magazine in 1885 and published in 1886, not long before Margaret's appearance at the hall in 1888. The question of his heroine Verena's spiritualist authenticity is central to James's text, and the novel culminates with Verena locking herself in her dressing room and refusing to come out and enter into a spiritualist trance, thus implying the fraudulence of her mediumship.

3. See Frank Podmore, *Mediums of the 19th Century,* for a highly comprehensive, if somewhat dated, history of the Fox sisters phenomenon.

4. From the start, Modern Spiritualism was taken with the notion that communication with the souls of the dead constituted empirical proof of life after death, and that the authenticity of such communication was actual and verifiable. Spiritualists have always adhered to the seven principles of spiritualism. Those principles were "channeled" through the mediumship of Emma Hardinge Britten by Robert Owen in 1871, were originally published in the spiritualist magazine *Two Worlds,* and were adopted by the Spiritualists' National Union soon thereafter. They are concerned with universal "brotherhood," the continuous existence of the human soul, personal responsibility, and "communion of spirits and the ministry of angels" (Britten 39).

5. I am grateful to Carrie Tirado Bramen for this notion of a psychical manifest destiny.

6. For example, in 1842, Congress responded to Samuel Morse's funding request for electrical and telegraphic experimentation with the sarcastic comment that if Congress were to fund such research, then it might as well directly fund mesmerists (Braude 4).

7. The American Society for Psychical Research (ASPR) was founded in Boston and later moved to New York. Although the British and American societies were formally affiliated, the ASPR was never as large and powerful as the SPR and, by 1906, it was defunct.

WORKS CITED

Banner of Light. Jan. 3, 1864, p. 6.

Blondheim, Mehahem. *News over the Wires: The Telegraph and the Flow of Public Information in America, 1844–1897.* Cambridge: Harvard University Press, 1994.

Brandon, Ruth. *The Spiritualists: The Passion for the Occult in the Nineteenth and Twentieth Centuries.* Buffalo: Prometheus, 1983.

Braude, Ann. *Radical Spirits: Spiritualism and Women's Rights in Nineteenth-Century America*. Boston: Beacon Press, 1989.

Britten, Emma Hardinge. *Nineteenth-Century Miracles; or, Spirits and Their Work in Every Country of the Earth*. New York: William Britten, 1884.

Briggs, Julia. *Night Visitors: The Rise and Fall of the English Ghost Story*. London: Faber, 1977.

Buchanan, John. Untitled. *Brittan's Journal of Spiritual Science*. Vol. 2 (1874): 553–54.

Carroll, Bret E. *Spiritualism in Antebellum America*. Bloomington: Indiana University Press, 1997.

Circulars of the Society for Psychical Research. *Essays in Psychical Research*. Cambridge: Harvard University Press, 1986. 6–10.

Clark, Uriah. *Plain Guide to Spiritualism*. Boston: William White, 1863.

Crary, Jonathan. *Techniques of the Observer: On Vision and Modernity in the Nineteenth Century*. Cambridge: MIT Press, 1990.

Cross, Whitney. *Burned Over District: The Social and Intellectual History of Enthusiastic Religion in Western New York, 1800–1850*. Ithaca, N.Y.: Cornell University Press, 1950.

Davis, Andrew Jackson. *The Philosophy of Spiritual Intercourse, being an explanation of modern mysteries*. New York: Fowler & Wells, 1851.

Fuller, Robert. *Mesmerism and the American Cure of Souls*. Philadelphia: University of Pennsylvania Press, 1982.

Goldsmith, Barbara. *Other Powers: The Age of Suffrage, Spiritualism, and the Scandalous Victoria Woodhull*. New York: Knopf, 1998.

Issacs, Ernest. "The Fox Sisters and American Spiritualism." In *The Occult in America: New Historical Perspectives*. Edited by Howard Kerr and Charles L. Crow, 79–110. Chicago: University of Illinois Press, 1983.

James, Henry. *The Turn of the Screw and Other Short Novels*. New York: Penguin, 1980.

James, William. "Notes on Automatic Writing." 1889. In *Essays in Psychical Research*. Cambridge: Harvard University Press, 1986. 37–55.

Jordanova, Ludmilla. *Sexual Visions: Images of Gender in Science and Medicine between the Eighteenth and Twentieth Centuries*. Madison: University of Wisconsin Press, 1989.

Lowe, Louisa. *Rifts in the Veil*. London: W. H. Harrison, 1878.

Marvin, Caroline. *When Old Technologies Were New*. New York: Oxford University Press, 1988.

Marx, Leo. *The Machine in the Garden: Technology and the Pastoral Ideal in America*. New York: Oxford University Press, 1964.

McHargue, Georgess. *Facts, Frauds, and Phantasms: A Survey of the Spiritualist Movement*. Garden City, N.Y.: Doubleday, 1972.

Moore, Laurence R. *In Search of White Crows: Spiritualism, Parapsychology and American Culture*. New York: Oxford University Press, 1977.

Owen, Robert Dale. *Footfalls on the Boundary of Another World*. Philadelphia: Lippincott, 1860.

Pimple, Kenneth D. "Ghosts, Spirits and Scholars: The Origins of Modern Spiritualism." In *Out of the Ordinary: Folklore and the Supernatural*. Edited by Barbara Walker, 75–89. Logan: Utah State Press, 1995.

Podmore, Frank. *Mediums of the 19th Century.* Vol 1. New Hyde Park, N.Y.: University Books, 1963.

Rabinbach, Anson. *The Human Motor: Energy, Fatigue, and the Origins of Modernity.* Berkeley: University of California Press, 1992.

Schivelbush, Wolfgang. *The Railway Journey: The Industrialization of Time and Space in the 19th Century.* 1977. Reprint. Berkeley: University of California Press, 1986.

Winter, Alison. *Mesmerized: Powers of Mind in Victorian Britain.* Chicago: University of Chicago Press, 1998.

"Wings of Science." *Britain's Journal of Spiritual Science* 2 (1874): 199–200.

W. T. H. "Disembodied Spirits May Surround Us." *Herald of Progress.* (Feb. 20, 1864): 9–10.

Flight from Haunting

Psychogenic Fugue and Nineteenth-Century American Imagination

JESSICA CATHERINE LIEBERMAN

On January 17, 1887, the Reverend Ansel Bourne left his home in Greene, Rhode Island, to run errands in Providence. He was not heard from again until discovered on March 14, living as a shopkeeper in Norristown, Pennsylvania. Bourne had no recollection of his missing eight weeks and no idea how he had arrived in his circumstances: He simply woke up at 5 A.M. on a Monday morning unaware of the date and his surroundings and unable to recognize anyone he came across. However, his neighbors recognized him. They identified the disoriented Bourne as A. J. Brown, a quiet and responsible businessman who had arrived in town six weeks before. He cooked his meals, attended church, and went to Philadelphia to place orders and stock his confectionery shop at 252 East Main Street. None of these details had any meaning to Ansel Bourne, whose last memory was of standing at the corner of Dorrance and Broad Streets in Providence while on his way to visit his sister. Local doctors made inquiries into the possible truth of Bourne's account. Discovering Bourne's anxious family, they sent for his nephew in hopes of solving the mystery. Indeed, the man they knew as Brown was a Rhode Island farmer and itinerant preacher who had no prior shop-keeping experience and no connections in Pennsylvania. Bourne returned to Rhode Island, completely baffled in his amnesia (James; Hodgson; Kenny).

Early in 1890 William James, a professor of psychology at Harvard University, heard of the "singular case" of Ansel Bourne and proposed to hypnotize Bourne and recover his lost memories. James believed he could regain Bourne's history and prevent future recurrences by means of post-hypnotic suggestion. Bourne agreed to the experiment and began treatment with James and renowned spiritualist Richard Hodgson in May 1890. Under hypnosis, Bourne immediately reverted to his identity as Brown and, over a period of many sessions, delivered a history of his missing movements as well as details of Brown's personal history, birth place, and so on. The results of the sessions were published by James in volume 1 of *The Principles of Psychology* (1890) and detailed by Hodgson in "A Case of Double Consciousness" in the 1891 *Proceedings of the Society for Psychical Research.*[1] Hodgson provides a full account of Bourne's hypnotic recollections and of his own subsequent research into the verifiability of the statements made by "A. J. Brown."

In *The Principles*, James uses Bourne as an example in an exploration of self-consciousness. Arguing that the "same brain may subserve many conscious selves, either alternate or coexisting" (401), James casts Bourne's case as representative of "disturbances" in the continuity that holds the self together: "The sense of our own personal identity, then, is exactly like any one of our other perceptions of sameness among phenomena. It is a conclusion grounded either on the resemblance in a fundamental respect, or on the continuity before the mind, of the phenomena compared" (334). Identifying three possible forms of psychic disturbance as insane delusions, alternative selves, and possession by ghosts, James saw Bourne's disturbance as a bridge between "alternating personality" and "possession." James ultimately failed in his more specific scientific goal, "to run the two personalities [of Bourne and Brown] into one, and make the memories continuous." Despite many sessions of hypnosis, "no artifice would avail to accomplish this, and Mr. Bourne's skull to-day still covers two distinct personal selves" (392).

James's treatment of the Bourne case reveals a great deal about the cultural milieu in America in the second half of the nineteenth century, particularly when compared to other contemporaneous attempts to comprehend and explain a group of related phenomena. The phenomena in question were instances of flight: sudden uprooting and hasty departure, whether physical, psychological, or both. Manifest in a variety of contexts in America and throughout Europe, flight captured the interest and fueled the diagnostic tendencies of thinkers in government, law, medicine, and science. Within a few years, most cases of flight had been packaged to fit a short list of explanatory causes, two of which I will focus on here: a new psychological malady christened "fugue," and possession by spirits—reported both as paranormal events by Spiritualists and as possession by the devil or by God by Christians.

A comparison of the explanations in the Bourne case with other explanations for unexpected travel highlights the way each interpretation of these radical transformations deals with similar questions about the past. Does the past disappear? Does it persist? And, if so, in what form? How might we regain that past, and to what end? As I will show, in Bourne's America, answers came framed in the language of ghosts and haunting. I will begin with a brief but crucial overview of the European psychology of fugue in an atmosphere of vagabondage and military desertion and of the American Protestant interpretation of fugue in a time of popular Spiritualism. My main focus here is on a particular understanding of the American experience of flight: Rather than dismiss the phenomena as criminal or insane behavior, Spiritualists embraced the opportunity to invoke the past, wrestle with its spirits, and find the voices that might inform and expand an understanding of their world.

I. Fugue and American Ghosts

The French "alienists" had been hailing a "new science" since 1847, when France bore witness to a curious malady—a plague of individuals who had more than one identity.[2] Otherwise upstanding citizens, fugue patients took flight from their homes and military camps and headed off on voyages to the unknown territories, foreign lands, and exotic places romanced in Thomas Cook and Son brochures. These men (and men they were, although women would play a rather crucial role in the development of this diagnosis) came to be understood as cases for doctors rather than police, for diagnosis rather than court marshal. In the hands of, first, French alienists and, eventually, psychiatrists throughout the western hemisphere, these "travelers" shed the stigma of desertion and assumed a less stigmatized identity: They were *fugueurs,* men motivated to escape and travel by a distinct psychic disorder, a heretofore unrecognized insanity. In 1872 Jean-Martin Charcot responded to these cases of "multiplicity" at his famed Tuesday Lectures on hysteria at the Salpêtrière. He argued for a theory of "split consciousness" whereby a hysteric's stream of consciousness might break into fragments. With this "discovery" came a flurry of activity in the medical community in and around Paris. The first official diagnoses of "multiple personality" and "fugue" followed in 1885 and 1887 and, on January 31, 1888, Charcot christened an "epidemic" of fugue with the title *automatisme ambulatoire.*[3] This period of rampant fugue marked the adolescence of a new science: a psychology of memory, consciousness, and trauma.[4] With new interest in mental trauma and the unconscious, the French alienists embraced the crucial diagnosis of "travelling insanity" (by Achille Foville in 1875) as a means for them to intervene in the worlds of science as well as popular politics. Pierre Janet's pivotal work on fugue and amnesia in 1889 further developed the idea of the fugue patient's desire to run away, into our modern concept of psychic dissociation.[5]

Indeed, fugue means *flight*: flight from the self, from memory, from home.[6] Modern psychiatry identifies the primary symptom of fugue as sudden, unexpected travel away from home or work, usually accompanied by confusion about personal identity or even the assumption of a new identity and the inability to recall one's past (DSM-IV Task Force, 484). Though forgetful of his past, the patient does not wander but travels with perseverance, remaining alert and oriented within the identity of the fugue. He exhibits sophisticated social adaptation (such as seeking employment and making new friends), good coordination, and a capability for highly complex behavior. The onset can be traced to a single severe stressor or trauma, often linked to war, violence, marital discord, financial difficulty, or suicidal ideation. Fugue occurs in times of great stress and is reported "in a variety of traumatized populations, including soldiers exposed to combat [. . .] concentration camp survivors [. . .] victims of torture [. . .] victims of rape [. . .] sexually and physically abused children and adolescents [. . .] and adult survivors of sexual abuse" (Loewenstein).[7]

In the late nineteenth century, the ambulatory personality disturbance was not only prevalent in France but was also at the center of controversy in Austria, Germany, England, Italy, and Russia. Because it was characterized by identity confusion and sudden disappearance, the unexplained flight patterns of fugue provoked the interest not only of the "new" psychology but also of materialist science, arbiters of social propriety, and the military and criminal justice systems. Hosting prolific debates over fugue's dissociative psychology, France was facing what it viewed as "epidemic" numbers of military deserters and vagabonds in the form of Eastern European refugees, primarily Jews. From these populations, great numbers of fugue cases emerged, and the interest of famed scientists such as Charcot, Janet, and Philippe Tissié were deeply influenced by the anger of the public and the sanctions of the government. Thus, when fugue originated as a medical concept in Tissié's thesis of 1887 in Bordeaux, it was indicative of the French enthusiasm for psychiatric nosology and social change.

Ansel Bourne's fugue in New England occurred in the same year as that of Tissié's patient, Albert Dadas, whose diagnosis was groundbreaking.

Yet the 1887 fugue in America provoked a very different interpretation from the 1887 fugue in France. In order to highlight the difference between the trajectories of the American and French models (and that of their European counterparts who followed the French), I must make clear how similar their starting points were. For all these scientists, the study of fugue seemed an ideal vantage point from which to witness the dialectical relationship between individual and society. Michael Kenny explains that the "vital French cases occurred in an intellectual milieu agitated by philosophical criticism of the Christian/Cartesian notion of a unitary responsible self[. . . . A]ll the world came to France in search of answers to the riddles of the mind" (4, 85). In much the same way, American scientists began to rethink their own more orthodox science, which had been predominantly materialist. They learned to embrace new "socio-centric psychologies" that "subverted the view that selfhood must be viewed in terms of a unitary ego" (Kenny 95). William James, on the lookout for some ordering principle that might explain the chaos of identity, had described consciousness as "a system of relations that sometimes binds impressions together in relation to a self that has them, but sometimes merely assigns them to the outside world without any clear reference to a self at all" (82). With the introduction of the French *fugueurs,* James found an opportunity to assess disruptions in the normal flows of consciousness and to witness the power of cultural factors in the formation of the self. For James, fugue episodes provided an ideal combination of social, spiritual, and psychic indicators: an alternate personality attributable to both the psychic (as dissociation) and spiritual (as possession) realms and having a pointedly contemporary compulsion to flight, either as escape or travel. Upon hearing of Ansel Bourne's American fugue in 1890, James realized his opportunity to disturb the long-standing Christian narratives of godly conversion or satanic possession with a new theory of the social influence on psychic constitution.

The America that embraced Bourne's fugue experience was one steeped in the culture of modern Spiritualism. The Spiritualists were scholars and laypersons who believed that the spirits of the dead communicate with the living (Brandon; Braude; Carroll; Moore). It was a time when "very few American cities, towns, and villages lacked a resident medium, and when every class and every occupation held people who were interested in Spiritualism" (Goldfarb 26). R. Laurence Moore explains that "[s]carcely another cultural phenomenon affected as many people or stimulated as much interest as did spiritualism in the ten years before the Civil War and,

for that matter, through the subsequent decades of the nineteenth century" (4). As a cultural phenomenon Spiritualism is said to have had millions of followers in the United States and Great Britain, in part because
it was "aggressive and modern" and "saw no contradiction between science
and religion" (Goldfarb 11). Though the spiritualist focus on communication with the dead did not figure in the European discussion of fugue
and its pathology, fugue cases provided groups such as the Society for Psychical Research (SPR) with more evidence for their cause. The SPR was
flourishing in post–Civil War Boston where James, Hodgson, and Morton
Prince established their practices. Boston of the 1890s was hungry for evidence of spiritual phenomena and enthusiastically embraced the psychological developments overseas to further their pursuits. Turning the study
of fugue toward their own purposes, these Bostonian Spiritualists imagined that the alternate state or secondary consciousness of fugue patients
might be manifest spirits. As Ian Hacking notes, Bostonians "loved [fugue]
as an option because the alter personality might be a dead soul speaking
from another place" (*Mad Travelers* 100). At the same time, they recognized an opportunity to challenge the Christian church's stronghold on all
things spiritual. Ansel Bourne was ideal for the cause: Not only was he a
local *fugueur* in need of help, but he had experienced a number of previous psychic disturbances, the most profound of which had been famously
co-opted by the Christian church as a triumphant conversion. In 1857,
thirty years before his fugue, Bourne had suffered a dramatic loss of consciousness followed by a complete loss of speech, sight, and hearing. Upon
their restoration, Bourne accepted the embrace of the predominant Christian community and took to the (notably travel-oriented) calling of an
itinerant preacher.

In retelling the story of Bourne's earlier "singular" experiences, Hodgson
is careful to give a full account of the dissonance surrounding the divine
interpretation. Noting the objection of Bourne's doctor, William Torrey
Thurston, to evidence of supernatural events, Hodgson offers a physical
assessment of cause. He suggests that Bourne may have suffered from
"some form of epilepsy" (237). But Thurston's objection is shot down by
a united front of witnesses: Reverend A. G. Comings, the congregation of
the Christian Chapel, and, notably, Bourne himself. Dr. Thurston's opin-
ion is easily overwhelmed by the evangelical motives of the large, Christian community that has rallied around its confused neighbor.

A widely circulated pamphlet written by Comings and overseen by
Bourne tells the story of his conversion: a man "who, in the midst of

opposition to the Christian religion, was suddenly struck blind, dumb, and deaf; and after eighteen days was suddenly and completely restored, in the presence of hundreds of persons, in the Christian Chapel, at Westerly, on the 15th of November, 1857." Entitled "Wonderful Works of God," the pamphlet hails Bourne's religious awakening and his visitation by spirits. While mute, deaf, and blind, Bourne was witness to a vision and felt as if he were "among the moving dead" (19). He describes his fantastic experience as a miraculous journey into death and then rebirth in God's glory. The eighteen-day silence was "as though the soul had been cast into a deep, bottomless and shoreless sepulchre, where dismal silence was to reign eternally" (14). The month of November 1857 saw a number of letters published in the Providence *Journal* that argued the spiritual merits of the "Singular Case." Thurston's letters, which insist on the "legitimate result of the treatment" and appeal to the "sober-minded and rational portion of the community," are relegated, in Hodgson's definitive account, to footnotes. The "Singular Case" of Ansel Bourne is appropriated by the prevailing evangelical Protestantism: He had been chosen as a medium between God and the people of Westerly, Rhode Island. But in 1890, the sixty-one-year-old Bourne found himself surrounded not by traditional Puritan fervor but by representatives of early modern psychology, post-Darwinian science, and fin-de-siècle Spiritualism. Bourne's situation could now be seen in a new light. As Kenny argues, rather than see Bourne as passively submitting to the "wonderful works of God," we can now read his experience as the construction of a more emphatic and social persona, one that is strongly defined and admired by the local community.

In the second half of the nineteenth century, then, we find that psychologists both in Europe and America were attempting to comprehend and explain this phenomenon of sudden flight. In Europe, the fugue state was analyzed in terms of the dissociating interior of identity as tied, along with hysteria and epilepsy, to the growing family of identity disorders and their requisite social and legal implications. The Americans, meanwhile, identified fugue as a plausible reaction of the self when faced with foreign invasion; they took the idea of the human "world" and expanded it to include an elusive, spiritual arena that might also act upon humanity with forces of its own. "[C]oncerned with how the buzzing flux of experience becomes structured into a generally orderly inner and outer world" (94), James concluded that "insane delusions, mediumistic possessions, and alternating personalities have the common feature that personified external or quasi-external forces intrude into the self's domain" (88). In the

American context, fugue and haunting possession were two nearly interchangeable examples of the apparent permeability of the self.

This historical moment of contact between American Spiritualist culture
and the scientific classification of dissociative fugue illuminates the important role of *ghosts* in late nineteenth-century America's unique attempts to
understand identity. The distinctly American aspects of the popular movements of mesmerism and Spiritualism influenced the psychology of the
unconscious as powerfully as the more recognized forces of Empiricist
philosophy, Romanticism, neurobiology, and evolutionary theory. American Spiritualism extended the spiritual quest of Puritan forefathers into a
more modern era of séances, mediums, and ghostly possessions. The popularity of fugue in America can be readily accounted for by its location
at a crossroads in belief: one, a Puritan heritage from which demonic
possession and exorcism were lauded as plausible scientific explanations for
unusual behavior; and two, a new sociological interest in cultural phenomena and biological science. The fugue of Ansel Bourne and the responses
of his doctors and biographers highlight America's transition from Puritan
Protestant spirituality and its enthusiasm for spiritual conversions and
toward a post-Darwinian science. Bourne's case—not only the 1857 and
1887 events, but also a number of blackouts, headaches, depressions, mini-
fugues, and an earlier conversion—long interpreted by friends, family,
and church members as a repentant religious conversion on the part of a
wayward sinner, was soon shown to have secular, scientific implications.

Spiritualism and determinist psychology feuded over their readings of
subversive psychic phenomena but not over their importance. At this cultural flash point between interpretive models, the possessing ghost itself
remains oddly unscathed: In question is the origin and treatment of the
invader, but not the invasion itself. James himself equivocated between
Spiritualism and materialism, taking the view that "the apparent existence
of the 'spirits' is largely induced by social factors: by a predisposition
to believe in them activated during ritual occasions such as the séance"
(Kenny 20). Such a socio-centric psychology would soon come into vogue
as arguments such as those of Dr. George Miller Beard moved to center
stage. In 1881 Beard had claimed that nervous afflictions were directly
related to the sociological conditions of the age. He went on to insist that
nineteenth-century societies, particularly that of the United States, were
exhibiting the disordered effects of modernity itself. "The chief and primary cause of this development and very rapid increase of nervousness
is *modern civilization*, which," Beard reveals, "is distinguished from the

ancient by these five characteristics: steam-power, the periodical press, the telegraph, the sciences, and the mental activity of women" (9). With such arguments, socio-centric psychology allowed for sweeping explanations of victimization and identity confusion in the modern age. Nevertheless, despite pronouncements of cause for universal affliction, Americans maintained a distinct interest in the ghostly incarnations of their angst. Whether orthodox members of the Christian church or loyal followers of the SPR, Americans found the presence of ghosts a more compelling explanation for psychic crisis and identity confusion than the European fascination with insanity.

II. Fugue Goes West

Three days after Ansel Bourne disappeared from his home, the Providence *Bulletin* printed an article entitled "A Missing Preacher." This missing-persons announcement proposed that Bourne "may have started for the West." The possibility is posed without indictment: The piece does not read as a criticism of a man who appears to have abandoned his wife and children. All inference is left to the reader's understanding of the phrase "started for the West." The year 1887 was a time of great change in conceptions of the Western "frontier." The era of American isolationism, an internally focused time fueled by the settlement of the West, was confronted with the exigencies of the Civil War and postwar depression.[8] Modernization needed new markets. Industrial production exceeded domestic market capacity, and America would not acquire the needed "colony" markets of Cuba, Samoa, and the Philippines until the Spanish-American War a decade later. As Frederick Jackson Turner explains in his famous "The Significance of the Frontier in American History" (1893),

> [E]ach frontier did indeed furnish a new field of opportunity, a gate of escape from the bondage of the past; and freshness, and confidence, and scorn of older society, impatience of its restraints and its ideas, and indifference to its lessons accompanied the frontier. What the Mediterranean Sea was to the Greeks, breaking the bond of custom, offering new experiences, calling out new institutions and activities, that, and more, the ever retreating frontier has been to the United States. [. . .] And now, four centuries from the discovery of America, at the end of a hundred years of life under the Constitution, the frontier has gone, and with its going has closed the first period of American history. (38)

Thus was the character of American frontierism—a combination of bombastic hope and impending loss. Bourne's friends and neighbors still subscribed to the great mythology of Manifest Destiny, westward migration, and upward mobility: Like most late-nineteenth-century Americans, they viewed economic opportunity as fundamental to their self-definition and attributed poverty and failure to the shortcomings of the individual.

In this context, Bourne's own words under hypnosis are illuminating: "Didn't know where [I] was going . . . Wanted to get away somewhere . . . Passed through great deal of trouble . . . losses of friends, losses of property . . . Trouble away back yonder . . . Don't like to think of it . . . All disagreeable remembrance . . . Got into a spot—don't know how I come there—both ends are blank" (May 28, 1890). The following day he announced, "I'm hedged in either way, can't get back and go-ahead." On May 30 he stated that his trouble was the following: "Something I have been trying to get out for a long time—where I am and where I am going to" (Hodgson 242–46). Bourne continued on for several days with confused articulations of feeling trapped, needing to get away, fleeing troubles, and seeking escape. His expressions of desire reflect precisely the anxiety and promise of the frontier. The theory that the missing Bourne may have gone West is justified by the claims of his recovered memory. His fugue was indeed "a gate of escape from the bondage of the past."

In the mid-1850s, Bourne was able to shape an understanding of his otherwise inexplicable experience using the force of evangelical Protestantism. His explanation fit into a prevailing conversion narrative: The conflicts of the soul find peace when the self is surrendered to God. But in the last years of the century, the pious imagination of New England Protestantism was insufficient to explain his amnestic transformation. There was no holy calling. Bourne had abandoned his family, abandoned his service as a preacher, and it appears—though Hodgson and James are careful to cover any shady dealings—had misbehaved.[9] What remained unchanged thirty years later was the atmosphere of inquiry into the "problem of the self as such—of a distinctly American self, a self perfectible through striving—the inheritance of a rapidly changing society still greatly influenced by its Puritan roots" (Kenny 8). But the notions of striving and of perfectibility through hard work and perseverance were growing increasingly complicated for men like Ansel Bourne, men who found themselves hemmed in by circumstance and desperate for escape. Bourne's fugue was an extreme form of self-liberty; it was the great escape: going West, finding a new life unfettered by the chains of the past—even if that past included personal identity and its constitutive memories.

In 1890 James was arguing for a new understanding of identity, one not so immutable, ineluctable, and irreducible. Personal identity, he explained, is constituted of "*as many social selves as there are individuals who recognize him*" (294). The fragile balancing act among these selves, one performed by "continuity" and "resemblance," is easily disturbed and can, in extreme cases, result in a "take-over" by a "foreign control." James's use of imperialist rhetoric in characterizing personal identity—"take-over" by "foreign control"—deserves attention for it hints at the prevailing cultural pathos of a young nation in the throws of modernization. James notes that when the subject is possessed, or in a state of "secondary consciousness," he "speaks, writes, or acts as if animated by a foreign person" (393). Dismissing the long-held Christian belief that foreign control was the work of the devil, he suggests that the visiting personality is usually the "harmless" spirit of a dead person casually communicating with the living world. The harmless ghosts on which James focuses, however, are not the varied spirits encountered in the hauntings and possessions of ghostly lore the world over. Instead, James betrays his decidedly Americanist, sociological, and racist interests as he engages the ghosts of the contemporary New England unconscious. Specifically, James's spirits are Native Americans: "'[C]ontrol' here in America is [often] a grotesque, slangy, and flippant personage ('Indian' controls, calling the ladies 'squaws,' the men 'braves,' the house a 'wigwam,' etc., etc., are excessively common)" (394), and "With us he [the possessed] gives himself out at the worst for an Indian or other grotesquely speaking but harmless personage" (393). In one simple move, James has recast the Christian schema—man is possessed by mischievous demons sent by the devil to disarm the faithful—and dismissed the stigma that lent terror to ghostly encounters. "At worst" the spirit represents the "grotesque" Indian of Puritan nightmares. But, just as the white man once conquered this primitive native, so too will he now find the "foreign" foe to be a "harmless personage."

Even when the ghost is not so decidedly a figure of American history and lore, the foreign control can still influence its host in an *American way*, as in the case of Ansel Bourne's possession by an alternate personality: Frontierism's pioneering hope of conquering new territories is translated to fit the longings of modern men—the new frontier was the individual and his consciousness. To "Go West" in this new context, then, would be to escape the limits of individualism, to contest the boundaries of singular consciousness, to conquer the divide between life and death. Specifically, James made of Bourne an example of a man possessed, not simply by an alternate personality, but by the spirit of the age. Bourne's experience is an extreme reaction. Unable to cope with his own world, he takes flight into the alternative reality of another man.

Spontaneous travel may have been less disturbing to frontier-happy Americans for whom *flight* was already connected to notions of personal and national liberty. In the 1840s and 1850s, prominent journalist Horace Greeley helped popularize the phrase "Go West, young man" as he advised struggling New Yorkers to flee for the frontier: "[T]urn your face to The Great West and there build up your home and fortune" (Greeley in Parton, 414).[10] The sentiment was a popular one and it fit neatly into a culture that preferred to move onto new territories rather than delve too deeply into the problems of the old. So, while the fin-de-siècle scientists— and their latter-day critics—labored to understand the causes, symptomology, and veracity of fugue's fragmented identity, they lent little weight to the subjective experience of the fugue patient himself. The sensibility of the patient may have been important for diagnostic purposes, but did not play into the theoretical models derived from dissociation. Indeed, psychology's diagnosis of fugue reveals more about the society that attends it than it does about the patient who suffers from it. In marked contrast to the localized and plentiful discussion of Ansel Bourne's views on his spiritual conversion, Bourne's own opinions are remarkably absent from the series of debates surrounding his late-life fugue. The arbiters of Bourne's story were no longer a regional congregation of American folk. Bourne had quite literally fled the boundaries of personal experience and run right into a larger national (and international) phenomenon of flight.

Presented with an American cultural milieu of budding socio-centric psychology, enthusiastic Spiritualism, and the waning promise of frontierism, I have argued here for the introduction of *fugue*, and its operative metaphor of *flight from haunting*, into our lexicon of terms for the discussion of American subjectivity. Ansel Bourne was America's first documented fugue patient: a plaything of the scientific avant garde and a man desperately crying for help on behalf of the less fortunate working class of polite society. Frontierism's pioneering hope of conquering new territories translated to fit the longings of modern men—the new frontier was the individual and his consciousness. To "Go West" in this new context, then, was to escape the limits of individualism, to contest the boundaries of singular consciousness, to conquer the divide between life and death.

Such a return to nineteenth-century ghosts is a necessary, historical resurrection when the traumatic contexts of such haunted and haunting figures are so easily dismissed along with their ghostly manifestations. The American Spiritualists made of Bourne an example of a man possessed, not simply by an alternate personality, but by the spirit of the age.

NOTES

1. James and Hodgson (along with Morton Prince and F. W. H. Myers) labored primarily to prove evidence of spiritual phenomena for their Society for Psychical Research and its avid American constituency of Spiritualists.

2. "Alienist" was a designation for doctors in the nineteenth century who treated mental diseases. Also referred to as "mad doctors," alienists were so dubbed because they sought out the causes of alienation in the mad individual.

3. Ian Hacking argues extensively, in a number of books and articles, that fugue "is exemplary for, even a caricature of, late nineteenth-century madness. It is also a "distorting mirror of one of the middle-class obsessions of the modern world, the world of Thomas Cook and Son, the world of the comfortable traveller" ("Automatisme" 31). He goes on to explain: "People have gone on strange unmotivated trips forever, but at the time when fugue became a medical entity, we had truly become modern" (32). The victims of ambulatory automatism, *dromomanie, poriomanie, Wandertrieb, determinismo ambulatorio*, and psychogenic fugue in the heyday of "travelling insanity" are now represented in the *Diagnostic and Statistical Manual of Mental Disorders* as individuals with "various culturally defined 'running' syndromes (e.g., *pibloktoq* among native peoples of the Arctic, *grisi siknis* among the Miskito of Honduras and Nicaragua, Navajo 'frenzy' witchcraft, and some forms of *amok* in Western Pacifica cultures) [which] may have symptoms that meet diagnostic criteria for Dissociative Fugue" (482).

4. In *Rewriting the Soul*, Hacking argues that the inclusion of trauma in psychological study is noteworthy. Until this time, the idea of trauma was applicable only to physical wounds or lesions. Its expansion into the connotative realm of psychic damage was an effect of this new discourse.

5. For current diagnostic criteria for fugue and dissociation see the *DSM-IV* of the American Psychiatric Association or the *ICD-10* of the World Health Organization (WHO). The theory of dissociation is an attempt to understand the encounter of the self with the "real world" in greater detail. Specifically, dissociation brings about resolution to a trap or impasse, defending the ego against what it perceives as dangerous or crisis-provoking material in its world and experience (Freedman 342). In its milder or more banal manifestations, it is an adaptive function—one of the mind's protective mechanisms for dealing with information that is, for whatever reason, too much for it to cope with "normally." Dissociative disorders manifest "loss of the normal integration between memories of the past, awareness of identity and immediate sensations, and control of bodily movements" (WHO 151). The theory posits the ego as permeable, alterable by "traumatic, stressful, or overwhelming life events" (*DSM-IV* 482). Indeed, it was this flexibility on the part of subjectivity—variability highlighted

by the possibility of dissociation—that intrigued scientists at the end of the century. A major attraction for these scholars was their belief that "[p]sychopathology, through showing how consciousness disintegrates [. . .] show[s] in reverse how it is constituted" (Kenny 85). It was the constitution of consciousness and, within the next few years, the unconscious that motivated much psycho-scientific discovery. Modern theorists such as Kenny and Hacking now attribute Bourne's fugue to another kind of dissociative disorder, manic depressive disorder.

6. The *Oxford English Dictionary*'s entry for fugue reads: "French *fugue*; Italian *fuga* literally 'flight'; from the Latin *fuga,* related to *fugere* to flee [. . .] 2) Psychiatry: A flight from one's own identity, often involving travel to some unconsciously desired locality." It is a dissociative reaction to shock or emotional stress in a neurotic, during which all awareness of personal identity is lost though the person's outward behavior may appear rational. On recovery, memory of events during the state is totally repressed but may become conscious under hypnosis or psychoanalysis. A fugue may also be part of an epileptic or hysterical seizure.

7. Indeed it was the connection between fugue and war that brought it to the attention of the world at the end of the century: "The psychiatric community, eager to extend its area of expertise, quickly perceived the relevance of this newly recognized variety of pathology to contemporary issues [such as] military desertion" (Goldstein 538). Because *fugueurs* were often army deserters, efficacy of the new diagnosis became a matter for social and judicial, as well as medical, concern. If the soldier were insane, then he could not be a criminal, or so the logic went. Doctors viewed such cases of fugue as a kind of safety valve or circuit breaker that prevented the witness to wartime violence from self-destruction, while popular sentiment presumed "malingering or a wish to escape danger or responsibility" (Loewenstein).

Actually, Goldstein continues on to argue that military desertion was not the most pressing of the concerns that fugue spoke to: "Far more pressing and timely than military desertion was, however, the issue of vagabondage [. . . and] bourgeois anxiety about the situation" (538). He goes on to offer a remarkable study of the figure of the "wandering Jew" as a psychopathological type. He argues that France, faced with the Jewish "invasion" after the Russian pogroms of 1881, was primed for a peculiarly psychiatric rendition of the old legend. Building on Charcot's account of Jewish nervousness in the 1880s, diagnoses of fugue were readily linked to anti-Semitic panic.

Growing out of Charcot's work on hysteria, fugue went on to be attributed to a great number of causes. Linked with hysteria, epilepsy, sleepwalking, neurosis, and psychosis throughout the last century, fugue has recently come to rest as an extreme form of dissociative behavior. The diagnostic manuals of the American Psychiatric Association and the World Health Organization have, as of this decade, reclassified "psychogenic fugue" as "dissociative fugue," bringing it back, interestingly enough, to Pierre Janet's pioneering work on fugue and dissociation over one hundred years before.

8. See Nell Irvin Painter's *Standing at Armageddon: The United States, 1877–1919* for a history of the economic and political climate of America at the turn of the century.

9. Bourne left Rhode Island having withdrawn a sum of money. When Hodgson and James attempted to account for Bourne's activities, they discovered an "unexplained deficiency of about $150.00." At some point, the "circumstances" under which

the money was spent were determined and Hodgson will only say of them that they "involve matters which we do not feel justified in publishing" (235).

10. An interesting note: Horace Greeley also promoted the veracity of the spiritualist séances performed by the Fox sisters in the 1850s. He endorsed their activities publicly in the pages of the *Tribune*.

WORKS CITED

"A Missing Preacher." *Bulletin of Providence*, Jan. 20, 1887.

Beard, George Miller. *American Nervousness, Its Causes and Consequences: A Supplement to Nervous Exhaustion (Neurasthenia)*. New York: G. P. Putnam's Sons, 1881.

Brandon, Ruth. *The Spiritualists: The Passion for the Occult in the Nineteenth and Twentieth Centuries*. New York: Knopf, 1983.

Braude, Ann. *Radical Spirits: Spiritualism and Women's Rights in Nineteenth-Century America*. Boston: Beacon Press, 1989.

Carroll, Bret E. *Spiritualism in Antebellum America*. Bloomington: Indiana University Press, 1997.

Charcot, Jean-Martin. "Ambulatory Automatism." *Medical News* 52 (1888): 309–12.

Comings, A. G. *Wonderful Works of God*. 1858. Reprint. Fall River, Ma.: W. S. Robertson, 1877.

DSM-IV Task Force. *Diagnostic and Statistical Manual of Mental Disorders*. 4th ed. Washington, D.C.: American Psychiatric Association, 1994.

Freedman, Alfred M., Harold I. Kaplan, and Benjamin J. Sadock, eds. *Modern Synopsis of Comprehensive Textbook of Psychiatry*. Baltimore: Williams & Wilkins, 1972.

Goldfarb, Russell M. and Clare R. *Spiritualism and Nineteenth-Century Letters*. London: Associated University Presses, 1978.

Goldstein, Jan. "The Wandering Jew and the Problem of Psychiatric Anti-Semitism in Fin-de-Siècle France." *Journal of Contemporary History* 20 (Oct. 1985): 531–32.

Hacking, Ian. "Automatisme Ambulatoire: Fugue, Hysteria, and Gender at the Turn of the Century." *Modernism/Modernity* 3.2 (1996): 31–43.

———. *Mad Travelers: Reflections on the Reality of Transient Mental Illnesses*. Charlottesville: University Press of Virginia, 1998.

———. *Rewriting the Soul: Multiple Personality and the Sciences of Memory*. Princeton: Princeton University Press, 1995.

Hodgson, Richard. "A Case of Double Consciousness (Ansel Bourne)." In *Proceedings of the Society for Psychical Research*. Vol. 7. London: Society for Psychical Research, 1892. 221–57.

James, William. *The Principles of Psychology*. New York: Henry Holt, 1890.

Janet, Pierre. *The Major Symptoms of Hysteria*. London: Macmillan, 1907.

Kenny, Michael. *The Passion of Ansel Bourne: Multiple Personality in American Culture*. Washington, D.C.: Smithsonian Institution Press, 1986.

Loewenstein, Richard. "Psychogenic Amnesia and Psychogenic Fugue: A Comprehensive Review." *Review of Psychiatry* 10 (1991): 189–222.

Moore, R. Laurence. *In Search of White Crows: Spiritualism, Parapsychology, and American Culture*. New York: Oxford University Press, 1977.

Painter, Nell Irvin. *Standing at Armageddon: The United States, 1877–1919*. New York: W. W. Norton, 1987.

Parton, James. *The Life of Horace Greeley*. New York: Mason Brothers, 1855.

Turner, Frederick Jackson. *The Frontier in American History*. Malabar, Fl.: Robert E. Krieger, 1920.

World Health Organization. *The ICD-10 Classification of Mental and Behavioural Disorders*. Geneva: World Health Organization, 1992.

The Girl in the Library

Edith Wharton's "The Eyes" and American Gothic Traditions

CHARLES L. CROW

In the preface to her collected ghost stories, written in the last year of her life, Edith Wharton implied that such tales were mere "dabbling" for a serious author, a technical exercise in producing the expected "thermometrical quality," the "cold shiver down one's spine" for an increasingly dimwitted mass audience (*Ghost Stories* 4). Yet Wharton was no stranger to the "thermometrical quality" herself. In childhood she was the victim of many fears and phobias: of certain houses, of open spaces, of crossing her own threshold (Benstock 25–26). Ghost stories added their own terrors to this childhood. Wharton confessed that, as late as age twenty-seven, she could not sleep if she knew a volume of ghost stories was in the house and, though a lifelong book lover, sometimes burned them to exorcise their threat. Indeed, perhaps Wharton became a writer of ghost stories in order to conquer these fears; as Shari Benstock suggests: "She could call up ghosts at will, rather than being surprised by them at the doorstep" (27). Only a hint of this emotional connection to her material is offered in Wharton's preface, when she states that in an effective ghostly tale "the teller should be well-frightened in the telling" (*Ghost Stories* 4).

Though a small portion of the mighty shelf of Wharton's writing,[1] her ghost stories have a reputation that has grown steadily since Margaret McDowell's pioneering article in 1970. Most Wharton scholars now concur with McDowell's assessment that the ghost stories "go beyond her initial aim and reveal extraordinary psychological and moral insight" (134). Following R. W. B. Lewis's *Edith Wharton: A Biography* (1975), scholars have been able to trace the biographical details of these tales with greater accuracy. Recently the ghost stories were the sole subject of a book by

Jenni Dyman (1996) and were discussed by Kathy Fedorko in the larger context of Wharton's Gothic fiction (1995).

This study focuses on "The Eyes" (1910), considered by many one of her finest ghost stories; and indeed, for some readers, it is simply "one of Wharton's most brilliant short stories" (Wolff 155). Like Fedorko, I view this tale as a Gothic work, and I agree with many critics since Ellen Moers's *Literary Women* (1977) that there are different traditions of male and female Gothic writing.

I will argue that "The Eyes" is a covert biography of Edith Wharton's creative life, her life as an artist. The story reveals her Läocoön-like struggle with inherited genre conventions, and a keen understanding of their gender significance. "The Eyes," indeed, is a story about storytelling. Authors, books, libraries, and the narrative act are everywhere in front of us. I suggest, moreover, that "The Eyes" parodies and discredits an aspect of the dominant literary tradition, which is characterized by its clubby, masculine atmosphere and avuncular confidential voice, a tradition Wharton associates with Washington Irving, who was a key figure in her own development as a storyteller. A familiar, conventional-seeming, safe tale is exploded before us, its conventions discredited, as Wharton replaces a patriarchal with a female Gothic form.

I. Gothic Narrators

Little of this may be apparent from a casual reading of what seems, indeed, a somewhat predictable and bland ghost story. In "The Eyes," an unnamed narrator is in a comfortable private library among a group of men who have been telling ghost stories. The story begins late in the evening, after all the guests have told their tales. Then, unexpectedly, the host, a degenerate older man named Culwin, is moved to tell the group of the most uncanny episodes of his life: the appearances of leering red eyes, as he was about to fall asleep, at two moments of moral failure. Their first appearance preceded his abandonment of a loving young woman, his cousin Alice, whom he had met and promised to marry in the "Gothic library" of a "Gothic mansion" on the Hudson River. The second preceded his humiliation of a young, enthusiastic, but apparently clueless writer, Gilbert Noyes, a cousin of the abandoned Alice, who had been sent to him in Europe for encouragement, with her letter of introduction. As he concludes his narrative, Culwin chances to look into a mirror and with horror realizes that the leering red eyes of his visions are now his own.

Thus summarized, the story seems a somewhat predictable variation on Wilde's "Picture of Dorian Gray," with strong overtones of Henry James as well. Yet anyone casually familiar with Wharton's biography and the major novels will recognize something familiar about Culwin. Of course he resembles a common Jamesean character, the man of sensibility who discovers that he has wasted his life in sterile inaction (as, for example, John Marcher in "The Beast in the Jungle"). But he also resembles a similar recurring character in Wharton's fiction, whom David Holbrook has labeled "the unsatisfactory man," a man of apparent strength or charm who ultimately fails the heroine. We recognize such men in Laurence Seldon of *The House of Mirth*, in Lucius Harney of *Summer*, in Ethan Frome (in a harsh reading perhaps), and, indeed, in a series of men who bumble their way through most of her narratives. Critics trace this character variously to the real-life Walter Berry, to Teddy Wharton, to Morton Fullerton, and, in the thinking of some, to her father, George F. Jones (though in Holbrook's view, these characters are unsatisfactory because they fail to match her idealized vision of her father).

In "The Eyes," Wharton presents the "unsatisfactory man" as a Gothic villain, with strong elements of the vampire. Culwin's flight from Alice can be seen as a typical male escape from domesticity. But there are also several hints that Culwin is bisexual or homosexual. He is indifferent to the physical appearance of Alice but praises the beauty of Gilbert, comparing him to Antinous, the boy consort of the emperor Hadrian (38). Thus, his escape may represent, as several critics have suggested, a form of homosexual panic, though it is by no means clear how well Culwin understands his own motives. In the narrative present (the frame), Culwin's current young faun, Phil Frenham, is on display in the paneled library in which the stories are told. Even before the final mirror scene, in which everyone else (Culwin, the narrator, the reader) experiences a revelation, Frenham seems to understand the implications of Culwin's story: He is the last in a series of young victims to be sucked dry by the aging lecher. Though Culwin is like an old stick, the narrator tells us, he "liked 'em juicy" (29).

While Culwin is everywhere in the story, as a character or a narrative voice, his first victim, Alice, is present in only a single scene, in her romantic encounter with Culwin in the Gothic library, and then indirectly in the letter she writes to introduce Gilbert to Culwin. She has received little attention from critics. Yet she is the key figure in "The Eyes," its Gothic heroine, and an obvious self-portrait of Wharton as a young woman.

II. Gothic Heroines and Libraries

Edith Wharton's early life was that of a Gothic heroine. She was, as Kathy Fedorko summarizes, "trapped in suffocating interiors, suppressed by patriarchal restraints embodied by her mother, isolated by her writing and tortured by her acute sensibilities, but at the same time pleasurably, even erotically charged by those sensibilities" (1). Insecure, made to feel freakish for her red hair and her intellect, her only refuge, from age ten, was her father's library. At the same time, as Wharton recalled, she was constructing within herself "a secret retreat where I wished no one to intrude, or at least no one whom I had yet encountered" (*Glance* 70). The inner refuge in her spirit corresponded to her physical sanctuary in the library. As Fedorko convincingly argues, both the inner and the outer spaces reflected "patriarchal restraints." The library was, after all, her father's, a masculine place dominated by carved mantle figures of visored knights; and her mother, clearly the strongest voice in the family and representing a patriarchal culture, asserted the right to determine what Wharton read there. Thus, though Wharton could "enter the kingdom of my father's library" (*Glance* 43) in a spatial sense, she could never "come into" the kingdom in the sense of possessing it as a rightful inheritance. She could never make it a room of her own. Likewise, the secret room in her own mind, her place of ultimate identity, where she wrote the narrative of her life, was not quite her own either: not yet. Like the typically trapped and imperiled heroine in the masculine tradition of Gothic romance, she awaited deliverance.

Since libraries were, for Wharton, sites of contested identity, it is not surprising that they appear repeatedly in her fiction. One of her heroines, Charity Royall, is even a librarian. So many scenes of erotic peril occur in Wharton's libraries that they have encouraged speculation that the young author may have suffered some sort of incestuous abuse there. This theory, advanced separately by Barbara White, David Holbrook, and Gloria Erlich in the early 1990s, seems to have lost favor and is not mentioned by either of Wharton's most recent biographers, Shari Benstock and Eleanor Dwight. I am also skeptical about the specific claim of incest abuse, though this is often the uncanny secret within Gothic narratives; and all Gothic plots, as Anne Williams reminds us, are family plots (22). While Erlich is right in seeing the library in Wharton's fiction as "a place of secret initiation" (43), the adored father is usually absent from this kingdom. As a guide, protector, deliverer, and king, he is desired, but never arrives. He is, indeed, the first of Wharton's inadequate men. Alice has no father in "The Eyes."

III. House Made of Hair

Thus, we see the intensely personal referencing in the brief appearance of Alice Nowell, the Gothic heroine of "The Eyes." Like young Edith Jones, Alice lives in a library. She hopes for a friend who will share her interests and lead her into maturity and the greater world outside. Like the young author, her opportunities for expression are constrained by the roles forced upon her. Culwin has come to the Gothic library hoping to write a book. Alice is assigned to Culwin by their mutual aunt (a patriarchal woman) as a copyist: a handmaiden in the service of his art. Even her attempt to free herself is constrained by literary convention and conventional gender roles. She tries, "like any artless heroine," to ambush Culwin romantically in the library, pretending to have mislaid a book there (32). When Culwin, amused by the transparent fiction-inspired ploy, tells her he is leaving for Europe, she boldly kisses him—an action Culwin describes as more "fresh and shy and brave" (33) than anything he has ever felt—and she wins his offer of marriage. Nonetheless, she is abandoned after Culwin sees the leering red eyes for the first time.

The implications of Alice's and Wharton's libraries are clarified if the apparently casual details of the setting and its owner are noted:

> I had [. . .] settled down for the winter near New York with an old aunt who had known Washington Irving and N. P. Willis. She lived, not far from Irvington, in a damp Gothic villa overhung by Norway spruces and look-ing exactly like a memorial emblem done in hair. Her personal appearance was in keeping with this image, and her own hair—of which there was little left—might have been sacrificed to the manufacture of the emblem. (32)

This is a remarkably rich though little-discussed passage. The house on the Hudson is clearly based on Rinebeck, the estate of Wharton's aunt Elizabeth Jones. As a girl, Wharton had found the Gothic mansion both ugly and frightening, and there she once was terrified by the conviction that there was a wolf (the wolf from the story of Red Riding Hood) under her bed (*Glance* 28). Wharton transfers this childhood terror to Culwin, as he lies in bed after proposing to Alice and first sees the leering red eyes. But the connections to biography here are less interesting than the descriptive language and literary allusions. A house made of a woman's hair: the image is disturbing, both funereal and vaguely erotic. When Culwin has his romantic library encounter with Alice, there flashes through his mind the thought that her hair, "though it was fairly thick and pretty, would look exactly like my aunt's when she grew older" (32). This strange and disruptive image, the emblem done in hair, uniting the villa and Alice and her aunt, is the first strong appearance of the uncanny in the tale. It combines death, Eros, and female power; it not only reveals Culwin's fear of women but anticipates the reversal with which the story will end. The apparently masculine library, in which Culwin seems so at home, is contained within a building owned by a woman and is symbolically woven out of her hair. In all of Wharton's canon, this passage is one of the clearest illustrations of a pattern that critics have noted repeatedly: the house equated with the female body (see Fedorko 18). Though the women have surrendered their space, their houses, their bodies to Culwin, they may reclaim them.

But why are the Gothic villa, its owner, and its library linked to Washington Irving? The aunt was a correspondent of Irving and Willis (the latter seems, for our purposes, a cipher). Irvington was nearby, we are told. It appears that none of this has the least relevance to the story's plot. The search for the implications of these allusions was my point of entry into this project; it leads us to some of the crucial issues in Wharton's development as a writer, and to the meaning of Alice as a Gothic heroine.

IV. IRVING AND GOTHIC TRADITIONS

Washington Irving was a member of the old New York social set that included the tribes of the Joneses and the Rhinelanders (Wharton's mother's family). He was considered one of the few writers who were socially acceptable in New York society, and he was acquainted with George F. Jones, the author's father. George Jones loved Irving's works, and when he took his family to Europe, early in Wharton's girlhood, they traveled in Spain, visiting the sights mentioned in Irving's *The Alhambra*. Irving was a part of Wharton's family history and literary heritage and even helped form Wharton's lifelong love of Europe and travel.

Moreover, there is a deeper, more intimate connection between Irving and Wharton's art. As she recalls in *A Backward Glance*, her creative life began when she was six years old, during a period when her parents lived in a hotel in Paris. She began "making up" stories while she walked around the living room of their suite, holding a book in her hands, pretending to be reading aloud (though she could not yet read). Her favorite book to use for "making up" stories was her father's copy of Irving's *The Alhambra*:

> Well—the "Alhambra" once in hand, making up was ecstasy. At any moment the impulse might seize me; and then, if the book was in reach, I had only to walk the floor, turning the pages as I walked, to be swept off full sail into the sea of dreams. The fact that I could not read added to the completeness of the illusion, for from those mysterious pages I could evoke whatever my fancy chose. (*Glance* 34)

The pretended reading was intended, evidently, to conceal what she was doing from her mother, who disapproved of creativity and imagination as unladylike. Thus, Irving was present at the ur-moment of Wharton's artistry, her "birth of Apollo," as her storytelling was masked and sheltered by his authority. Irving was thus a kind of literary father or bachelor uncle to the author of "The Eyes."

And Irving would exert a real, if secondary (and generally unremarked), influence on Wharton throughout her career. It can be seen, for example, in the novellas *Summer* and *Ethan Frome*, behind the more obvious and insistent influence of Hawthorne. Consider the Mountain of *Summer*, brooding over the village of North Dormer, eventually leading the heroine, Charity, to journey up it to meet the fabled people who live there—following the pattern of Rip Van Winkle's adventure in the Kaatskills, with gender roles reversed. One might read *Ethan Frome*, likewise, as a nightmare version of "Rip Van Winkle," with Dame Van Winkle turned from a mere termagant wife into a vengeful witch, and doubled.

Yet it was a complex and confining patrimony that Irving left later American writers, especially female writers. What is the reading experience of the girl or woman reading Irving's most popular story? According to Judith Fetterley, she "finds herself excluded from the experience of the story [. . .]. She is asked to identify with Rip and against herself, to scorn the amiable sex and act just like it, to laugh at Dame Van Winkle and accept that she represents 'woman,' to be at once both repressor and repressed, and ultimately to realize that she is neither" (*Resisting Reader* 10–11). Yet this story, so troubling for girls and women, set a basic pattern of American literature, the masculine escape from domesticity through a redemptive journey into nature.

Irving also contributed a certain stance, attitude, or tone of voice that also is troubling for female writers and readers. Irving's career had qualities of the dilettante and connoisseur; he was a tourist, an observer, a well-connected gentleman, a bachelor, a host. His fiction projects these values of masculinity and privilege and distance. We are addressed, in reading Irving, as if by a convivial uncle; we are invited into the role of comfortable observer. Unthreatened ourselves, the world is there to amuse us. This stance is embodied in the quotation from Robert Burton's *The Anatomy of Melancholy* that Irving chose as an epigraph for *The Sketch Book*: "I have no wife nor children, good or bad, to provide for. A mere spectator of other men's fortunes and adventures, and how they play their parts; which methinks are diversely presented to me, as from a common theatre or scene" (Irving 735). Later nineteenth-century American writers would invoke this world of clubby privilege as the standard frame for the ghost story: It is there in James's *The Turn of the Screw*, and in W. D. Howells's Turkish Room stories. And it is this fictional space we are in throughout "The Eyes": It is the private clubroom of the narrative frame; and if the Gothic library is not quite the same space (in a house woven of women's hair), Culwin at first tries to view it, and use it, as such.

What I am suggesting, then, is that the eponymous eyes of the story are the eyes of all storytellers in this tradition, subjecting the world, and women especially, to their masculine gaze. Compare Irving's quotation from Burton, the artist as mere spectator, with the first appearance of the eyes to Culwin. He is in bed, a situation that we should now understand as the first in a series of ironic gender-role reversals:

> What turned me sick was their expression of vicious security. I don't know how else to describe the fact that they seemed to belong to a man who had done a lot of harm in his life, but had always kept just inside the danger lines. They were not the eyes of a coward, but of someone much too clever to take risks; and my gorge rose at their look of base astuteness. Yet even that wasn't the worst; for as we continued to scan each other I saw in them a tinge of derision, and felt myself to be its object. (34)

As he tells the story, Culwin cannot realize that the eyes represent the very tradition of which he and his narrative are a product. But Wharton understands them, and these eyes in fact burn through much of her fiction, though the person most often stared at, of course, is a woman. For example, the passage in all of Wharton's work that has possibly been most discussed by recent critics is the *tableau vivant* in *The House of Mirth*, in which Lily Bart offers herself up to the male gaze in a filmy costume, representing Sir Joshua Reynolds's portrait of Mrs. Lloyd, and the men of the novel comment on her elegant shape. This scene is a perfect embodiment of Lily Bart's situation in the novel, and that of other women in our society who must make themselves into visual commodities—works of art—for sale on the marriage market. On another level, the tableau mimics the situation of the female artist, who offers her work up to public display—a particular psychological barrier for writers of Wharton's time and class, who were taught that authorhood was unladylike. Thus, as Susan Wolstenholme has argued, *The House of Mirth* can be read as "an extended meditation, first of all, on the significance of art generally for women—how art represents women, their bodies, their desires, their lives—and, more particularly, on the problem of writing for a woman" (130). The same purpose informs "The Eyes."

As brave as Alice Nowell may be in kissing Culwin in the Gothic library, she cannot be rescued by him, for he represents exactly the forces that hold her prisoner. Indeed, in Gothic narratives written by men, "plot and narrative conventions also focus on female suffering, positioning the audience as voyeurs who, though sympathetic, may take pleasure in female victimization" (Williams 104). Allegorically, Alice's embrace of Culwin represents the compromised position assumed by the female writer entering patriarchal discourse conventions, as represented here by the tradition of Irving.

While Wharton's exposure of this tradition will reach its climax back in the clubroom of the narrative frame, we should note that Alice, the author's double, does continue to play a role offstage, though she is no longer visible to us. In the second year of Culwin's residence in Europe after fleeing Alice, he receives a letter from her introducing Gilbert Noyes, another cousin, and asking him to assist the young man in becoming an author. "I had always wanted to do her some service, to justify myself in my own eyes" (38), Culwin recalls, and he agrees. (Culwin is apparently not a cousin to Gilbert Noyes, though both are cousins of Alice Nowell in the strange and undefined kinship patterns of this story.) Alice's motives are difficult to fathom. Culwin, and probably most readers, see this as simply another example of the nice young woman's unassuming, self-sacrificing helpfulness. Or is she still trying to embrace art vicariously, by assisting another male who wants to write? Or is she saying, in effect, if you don't like girls, I'll send you a boy? The letter offers Culwin another victim and leads to the second apparition of the leering eyes. But in identifying

Gilbert as another juicy dish for the vampire, we might miss an obvious point: The two cousins of Alice are very much alike. Both are artists-*manqué*, indecisive no-yes (Noyes) men lacking self-awareness and incapable of helping her. The final sight of a dissipated Gilbert bears some resemblance to Culwin. So perhaps we should note this narrative fact: When the first cousin-knight presents himself in Alice's library, she kisses him; when the second arrives, she sends him away.

V. GOTHIC MIRROR

When Culwin tells his story of the two appearances of the leering eyes, he is unable to interpret their meaning. "Put two and two together if you can," says Culwin at the end of his tale. "I haven't found the link" (45).

His protégé Phil Frenham, however, has found it. As Culwin approaches him, meeting his eyes for a moment, Frenham "flung his arms across the table behind him, and dropped his face upon them" (46). The melodramatic pose—suggesting a woman in a Victorian play or painting—is taken by Culwin as evidence that Frenham's nerves have been unstrung by the ghost story: "My dear boy—my dear fellow—I never had such a tribute to my literary ability, never!" (46). Moving forward, the narrator behind him, Culwin approaches Frenham and the mirror, on which his eyes fix: "He paused, his face level with the mirror, as if scarcely recognizing the countenance in it as his own. But as he looked his expression gradually changed, and for an appreciable space of time he and the image in the glass confronted each other with a glare of slowly gathering hate" (46). The tableau fuses the themes of the tale. Culwin believes that he has achieved a literary triumph (at last), a narrative act that is a consummation of the tradition represented by the library. The tale depends upon the detached tone—the "vicious security"—of the storyteller. But the mirror destroys the distance between subject and object, makes Culwin himself the object of the leering male gaze, and destroys the safe distance between self and other. His story collapses upon itself. The tableau indicts not only Culwin but also the framing narrator (this is why he also looks into the mirror), and the form of storytelling practiced in Culwin's library, and even the reader's participation in its voyeuristic pleasures. The promised safe story has been exploded, leaving instead a female Gothic tale, "a meditation on the issue of writing as a woman" (Wolstenholme xi).

"The Eyes" reveals Wharton's mature awareness of the tradition of storytelling that she had inherited from Irving and other male predecessors.

When she was a young writer, the tradition sheltered her and nourished her growth as an artist. Later, however, it came to seem enslaving and perverse. While Wharton may not have seen herself as a feminist author, "The Eyes" is a complex response to the dilemma of a woman's writing within gender-coded literary conventions. Wharton holds a mirror up to that dominant tradition, here represented by Culwin's eyes, and exposes its leering impotence and smug self-congratulation. Thus, the story documents the author's own imaginative liberation, the triumphant escape of the heroine from the Gothic library.

NOTE

1. There were eleven stories in the 1937 Appleton-Century edition of *Ghosts.* The 1973 Scribner's collection, *The Ghost Stories of Edith Wharton,* replaces one of the original stories, "A Bottle of Perrier," with "The Looking Glass." The 1975 Constable edition from which I quote follows the Scribner's edition.

WORKS CITED

Benstock, Shari. *No Gifts from Chance: A Biography of Edith Wharton.* New York: Scribner's, 1994.

Dwight, Eleanor. *Edith Wharton: An Extraordinary Life.* New York: Harry N. Abrams, 1994.

Dyman, Jenni. *Lurking Feminism: The Ghost Stories of Edith Wharton.* New York: Peter Lang, 1996.

Erlich, Gloria C. *The Sexual Education of Edith Wharton.* Berkeley: University of California Press, 1992.

Fedorko, Kathy. *Gender and the Gothic in the Fiction of Edith Wharton.* Tuscaloosa: The University of Alabama Press, 1995.

Fetterley, Judith. *The Resisting Reader: A Feminist Approach to American Fiction.* Bloomington: Indiana University Press, 1978.

Holbrook, David. *Edith Wharton and the Unsatisfactory Man.* New York: St. Martin's Press, 1991.

Irving, Washington. *Washington Irving: History, Tales and Sketches.* New York: The Library of America, 1983.

Lewis, R. W. B. *Edith Wharton: A Biography.* New York: Harper & Row, 1975.

McDowell, Margaret. "Edith Wharton's Ghost Stories." *Criticism* 12 (1970): 133–52.

Moers, Ellen. *Literary Women: The Great Writers.* New York: Anchor, 1977.

Wharton, Edith. *A Backward Glance.* New York: D. Appleton-Century, 1934.

———. *The Ghost Stories of Edith Wharton.* London: Constable, 1975.

White, Barbara A. *Edith Wharton: A Study of the Short Fiction.* New York: Twayne, 1991.

Williams, Anne. *The Art of Darkness: A Poetics of Gothic.* Chicago: University of Chicago Press, 1995.

Wolstenholme, Susan. *Gothic (Re)Visions: Writing Women as Readers.* Albany: State University of New York Press, 1993.

Wolff, Cynthia Griffin. *A Feast of Words: The Triumph of Edith Wharton, 2nd Edition.* Reading, Ma.: Addison-Wesley, 1995.

"Commitment to Doubleness"

U.S. Literary Magic Realism
and the Postmodern

ELIZABETH T. HAYES

In their introduction to *A Postmodern Reader,* Joseph Natoli and Linda Hutcheon call attention to postmodernism's characteristic "commitment to doubleness [. . . and] to the juxtaposition and equal weighing of [. . .] seeming contraries" (xi). Such "doubleness" is, of course, the hallmark of magic realism, the literary mode in which the supernatural and the material are the equally weighted contraries simultaneously inscribed in the text as experienced reality. Similarities between postmodernist and magic realist narratives have been noted by such literary critics as Hutcheon, Brian McHale, Wendy B. Faris, Lois Parkinson Zamora, and Theo D'haen, who share my view of magic realism as one important room in the postmodernist house of fiction. While contemporary magic realism as a literary mode originated in Latin American fiction, it has by now become an international phenomenon, with a distinctive—and distinguished—presence in contemporary fiction written in the United States. U.S. magic realist narratives are postmodernist texts that destabilize, that question, that challenge ideological assumptions, that refuse closure, unity, totality; and they do so through their juxtaposition of seeming contraries. That the magical and the realistic are equally weighted and equally valued is neatly manifested in the oxymoronic double-noun phrase "magic realism" that names the mode (for which reason I prefer the double-noun phrase to the adjective-noun phrase "magical realism," where the weight is placed on the noun "realism").

U.S. magic realism is notable for such postmodernist characteristics as multiplicity and polyvocality; the critique and subversion of rationalist ontologies; the rejection of "the imperial center" (Slemon 408) in favor of "ex-centric" discourse; and liminality, or the blurring of boundaries between worlds. While these characteristics have certainly appeared in American literary texts prior to the late twentieth century, the postmodernist insistence upon challenging any and all metanarratives has created an exceptionally conducive climate for the development of this new avatar of U.S. supernatural literature, and it has also facilitated the acceptance of magic realism into the contemporary intellectual and literary mainstream. Jeffrey A. Weinstock is no doubt correct in his speculation in the introduction to this volume that "the current fascination with ghosts," including those populating magic realist texts, "arises out of a general postmodern suspicion of metanarratives accentuated by millennial anxiety" (5).

As noted above, an important characteristic of magic realism is liminality, particularly the liminality of the borderline between the worlds of the living and the dead; thus, ghosts are relatively common in magic realist fiction. Of course, scholarly works like *Spectral America;* Carpenter and Kolmar's *Haunting the House of Fiction;* Ringe's *American Gothic;* and Kerr, Crowley, and Crow's *The Haunted Dusk: American Supernatural Fiction*, attest to the significance of ghosts and the Gothic to U.S. literature, particularly in the nineteenth century. Such eminent authors as Henry James, Edith Wharton, and Ellen Glasgow carried spectral fiction into early twentieth-century American literature, where it occupied a position outside the mainstream for half a century or more. With the advent of postmodernist magic realist texts like Toni Morrison's *Beloved* and August Wilson's *The Piano Lesson*, spectrality entered (or reentered) both the intellectual *and* popular literary mainstream in the United States simultaneously.

The postmodernist characteristics of magic realism destabilize readers in many ways, deliberately undermining readers' certainty in the validity of their reading of the text and forcing them to question their own ontological and epistemological presuppositions. In U.S. magic realist texts, "seeming contraries" abound: Ghosts appear as corporeal characters, characters know the future or remember or relive their past incarnations, and rationally inexplicable (i.e., "magical") events are normal, ordinary occurrences, part of the weave of the otherwise realist narrative. (It is here that magic realism differs from other genres encompassing the supernatural. In American Gothic and ghost-story literature, past and present—the acceptance of supernatural occurrences as quotidian, part of the warp and woof of everyday life—was not and is not the defining characteristic of the genre, as is the case with magic realism.) As Lois Parkinson Zamora observes, ghosts—liminal, nonrational, subversive, and destabilizing—are particularly useful to magic realist writers because by "mak[ing] absence present" the living dead "foreground magical realism's most basic concern—the nature and limits of the knowable" ("Ghosts" 498).

The multiplicity of valorized ontologies is perhaps the most striking postmodern feature of magic realism. Brian McHale's argument in *Postmodern Fiction* that the ontological is "the dominant of postmodernist fiction" (10) is richly borne out in contemporary U.S. magic realism, where the question "What is real?" and its corollary "How can I *know* what is real?" are explored—directly by the characters and indirectly by the reader—in every text. (A second corollary of particular interest in U.S. magic realist texts—"Who is sane?"—interrogates the connection between rationalism and "sanity," the latter being largely defined in Western cultures as knowing and responding only to what is "real.") The realism in magic realism, predicated as it is on a rationalist/empiricist view of the nature of being and reality, traditionally excludes the intuited, the supernatural, the magical, the occult—in other words, the nonrational—from the ranks of "the real," yet the matter-of-fact presence in magic realist texts of the supernatural, carefully authenticated through empirical evidence, constitutes a postmodernist challenge to the rationalist metanarrative of realism. That the nonrational should be considered just as ontologically valid as the rational demonstrates magic realism's radical doubleness.

In "Magic Realism and Postmodernism," Theo D'haen cites ex-centric discourse, "speaking from the margin," as an essential feature marking magic realism as a strain of postmodernism (194). The forceful challenge to, and deliberate subversion of, privileged discourses—rationalist, colonialist, logocentrist, patriarchalist—that we see in both modes is achieved in magic realism through the centering of the discourse of the heretofore marginalized: non-European ethnic and indigenous Americans, women, those from predominantly oral cultures, and others. The shift from margin to center not only gives voice to the silenced, but it effectively removes these formerly ex-centric speakers from the position of being the object that they have occupied in centrist writers' texts and places them in a position of being the subject in their own texts.

In a discussion of the postcolonial thrust of many postmodernist texts, D'haen observes that "magic realism [. . .] reveals itself as a *ruse* to invade and take over dominant discourse(s)" (195). Gabriel García Márquez, in an interview with Plínio Apuleyo Mendoza, goes further than D'haen by criticizing his own *One Hundred Years of Solitude* as "superficial" because "it was written with all the tricks and artifices under the sun" (156). While magic realism may be a ruse or a trick for many Latin American or Canadian postmodernist writers, I argue that it is not so for U.S. magic realist writers. In fact, D'haen's observation calls attention to a significant difference between U.S. magic realist writers and other American magic realist writers: Most of the Latin American and Canadian writers of magic realist texts are, by virtue of their race, class, and/or gender, much closer to the "privileged center" than to the margins of their own societies, while most—in fact, almost all—writers of magical realist texts in the U.S. are members of historically marginalized races, classes, and/or genders.[1] Thus, for Gabriel García Márquez, Carlos Fuentes, Robert Kroetsch, or even Isabel Allende, magic realist discourse might be a deliberately adopted ruse through which they are able to distance themselves from the discourse of the center to write ex-centrically, to speak from the margins for the marginalized with authority, originality, and power.[2]

In contrast, for United States writers of magic realist discourse—Toni Morrison, Gloria Naylor, Toni Cade Bambara, August Wilson, Alice Walker, Phyllis Perry, Tina Ansa, Louise Erdrich, Amy Tan, Maxine Hong Kingston, and others—to write from the margins is to write their own stories in their own voices, and to write magic realist narratives is to valorize and recuperate the history, mythology, folk beliefs, and ways of knowing and being of their own people. Most U.S. magic realist narratives, in fact, have a clear postcolonial subtext. They critique, subvert, destabilize, and displace the discourse of the center, correcting it with their own cultural and historical realities. As postcolonialist writers, U.S. magic realists are strongly committed to the "doubleness" of ex-centricity, multiplicity, and polyvocality so fundamental to postmodernism.

A typical postmodernist question, Brian McHale contends, is "What happens [. . .] when boundaries between worlds are violated?" (10). The answer to this question is worked out afresh in text after text in the U.S. magic realist canon. In such works as Bambara's *The Salt Eaters*, Morrison's *Beloved*, Naylor's *Mama Day*, Walker's *The Temple of My Familiar*, Erdrich's *The Bingo Palace*, Tan's *The Hundred Secret Senses*, Wilson's *Joe Turner's Come and Gone*, Ansa's *Baby of the Family*, and Perry's *Stigmata*, the boundaries between worlds—especially the worlds of the living and the dead, the past and the present—are permeable, accepted as such by the protagonists if not by many or all of the characters in the text. For example, when Sutter's ghost appears to Berneice early in August Wilson's *The Piano Lesson*, the discussion among the characters concerns *why* the ghost has appeared and why it is calling Boy Willie's name, not *whether* ghosts exist. All the characters accept the ontological validity of ghosts, including Boy Willie, even as he argues that Berneice has not seen Sutter's ghost. In ethnic American cultures, where resistance to the rationalist binaries of Eurocentric culture has traditionally been high, "the real" embraces the magical, the otherworldly, and the supernatural.

U.S. literary magic realism as postmodernism is strikingly illustrated in Gloria Naylor's novel *Mama Day*. Miranda ("Mama") Day, the matriarch of the African American island community of Willow Springs, is a conjure woman of nearly archetypal stature who has developed extraordinary intuitive abilities—"connected knowing" of the highest degree—over the course of her long lifetime. As verified in the text, Miranda speaks to and takes counsel from the dead, knows the future, reads minds, causes (or, more accurately, assists) lightning not only to strike but also to strike the same place twice, and performs other highly unusual, "magical" feats. Other women in the text have what appear to be supernatural abilities as well, particularly Miranda's African-born great-grandmother Sapphira, avatar of the archetypal Mother, the founder (through conjuring) of the Willow Springs community of free, landowning African Americans (an astonishing achievement in 1823 in the slaveholding South). Thus, the supernatural has always been an organic part of everyday reality for the Willow Springs community, and it continues to be so even at the end of the twentieth century, the setting for the novel. In this text, postmodern multiplicity takes the form of an ancient African, non-Cartesian system of belief existing side by side and on equal footing with twentieth-century Western rationalism. The coexistence of these two ontological positions is embodied in Mama Day herself, for in addition to her extraordinary intuitive powers, she is also a largely self-taught empiricist of the highest order, as her medical and pharmacological skills demonstrate. (Though Miranda had Sapphira's medicine pots and garden—until the garden was destroyed by a hurricane when Miranda was twenty-three—Sapphira herself had died or disappeared from Willow Springs seventy years before Miranda was born, leaving only sons and grandsons, none of whom became a root doctor. Surely Miranda learned some lore and midwifery from older people on the island, but much of what she knows, she intuited or learned on her own by observing nature and experimenting.)

The nonrationalist beliefs of the Willow Springs community are set sharply against the rationalist ideology of U.S. society in general through Miranda's clash with George, the husband of her great-niece (and foster daughter) Cocoa. An African American orphan from New York City, George is the embodiment of rationalism in the text. Largely because of his upbringing in a boys' shelter run according to strict utilitarian principles, George learned early in life to accept as real only what he can verify through observation or deduce through logical thinking. Until he falls in love with Cocoa, he has virtually no connection to his own African American heritage, living his life in European American culture, a mechanical engineer with a white business partner, white clients, and a white significant other. As his first meeting with Cocoa demonstrates, George finds the nonrational not just inexplicable but "terrifying" (28), and like many rationalists he keeps the nonrational firmly "in its place" by relegating it to the lowest rung of his Cartesian hierarchical ladder. Even when he is in Willow Springs, where he is literally the only person in that world who does *not* accept the ontological validity of the nonrational, George demonstrates the imperialist patriarchalism of the Western rationalist by persistently perceiving his own views as central and superior, and those of the Willow Springs community as "other" and inferior.

When Cocoa falls victim to a mysterious, hex-induced illness and is near death, rationalist George collides head-on with the supernatural, represented by Mama Day, who, like George, is desperately trying to save Cocoa's life. Miranda, however, is also trying to save George's life, which she can do only if George will cooperate with her to find a cure for Cocoa's illness using primarily nonrational means. Ontological questions arise repeatedly as George struggles to identify and "hold on to what [is] real" (291) while he frantically works toward rational solutions to Cocoa's health problems, but he can never move outside the rationalist paradigm to which he is wholly committed, as his delineation of the real illustrates: "ten more feet added on to the bridge—that was real. And the sun coming up [. . .]—that was real also" (291). He sees only empirically observable facts and "either/or" binaries with their implicit hierarchicalism: Rationalism to George is logical, fact-based, and correct, while nonrationalism (including lore, which he classifies as nonrational) is "mumbo jumbo" (295), "acute madness" (286), "pathetic" (286), "beyond ridiculous" (210)—and certainly not "real."

In contrast, Mama Day, like a true postmodernist, endorses multiplicity rather than unity. Her nonrationalism is not an exclusionary system, as is George's rationalism. As she explains to George, "There are two ways anybody can go when they come to certain roads in life—ain't about a right way or a wrong way—just two ways" (295). In this case, Miranda's way is to seek out, communicate with, and receive guidance from the dead. She returns to her ancestral home ("the other place"), the sacred space of Willow Springs, and receives nurturance from the person she refers to as "the great, grand, mother" (49), her long-dead great-grandmother Sapphira, who tells Miranda to uncover the old well in the garden of the other place and to "look past the pain" (283). When Miranda does as instructed, she is "almost knock[ed . . .] on her knees" (284) by the piercing screams of ghostly Day women: Sapphira, begging her slave owner Bascombe Wade for freedom; Miranda's baby sister Peace, who drowned in the well; and Miranda's mother Ophelia, distraught to the point of madness and suicide after Peace's death. In communicating with these spectral women, Miranda learns how to save Cocoa through "connected knowing."

That George's violent rejection of nonrationalism results in his death embodies a strong postmodernist critique of the epistemology and ontology of the center. George cannot even accept the validity of Miranda's knowledge that is based in empirically tested African lore, dismissing both her knowledge and African lore as superstitious mumbo jumbo. Although he is the one to offer the reader the scientific explanation of how metal could be used to cause lightning to strike the same place twice, he in fact does not know that Miranda sprinkled a metallic powder around Ruby's house before lightning struck the house twice, nor has he ever seen Miranda's medical expertise in action; he can thus be partially excused (but only partially) for his condescending conclusion that "no one was running around Willow Springs with that kind of [scientific] knowledge" (286).

George dies because he insists upon maintaining rigid boundaries between worlds, while Cocoa lives because Mama Day erases them. Furthermore, Miranda teaches Cocoa to erase boundaries and communicate with "the other side." After George's death, Cocoa returns frequently to Willow Springs expressly to "talk" to George: two-thirds of the narrative in *Mama Day* is presented as a conversation between Cocoa and George, the latter of whom has been dead for fourteen years by the time this conversation takes place. At the end of the novel, knowing that she will soon die, Mama Day confidently turns the leadership of the Willow Springs community over to Cocoa knowing that Cocoa is well versed in gaining support and assistance from the other side.

To represent the multiplicity of ontologies and voices in contemporary African America, Naylor creates five distinct narrative voices in *Mama Day*: George's and Cocoa's alternating first-person, past-tense narrations; Mama Day's third-person, limited-omniscient, present-tense narration; a communal (or "village voice") narrator speaking in the first-person-plural, present tense but relating events that have already occurred; and finally, a third-person, omniscient, past-tense narrator occasionally distinguishable from the other third-person narrators. George's, of course, is the voice of rationalism; one of Naylor's singular achievements in *Mama Day* is to render this masculine, rationalist voice sympathetic. Miranda speaks for non-rationalism, but from the vantage point of one fully conversant in rational thought as well. The communal narrator—the voice of the Willow Springs community—accepts the supernatural as fact but is an observer, not a practitioner, of the magic occurring in Willow Springs. Cocoa is positioned in the middle: Growing up as a Day in Willow Springs, she has witnessed Miranda's supernatural abilities firsthand and has developed a few of her own, yet she has chosen to leave Willow Springs and live in rationalist, urban Euro-American culture. While the multiple narrators fragment the novel to some extent, the polyvocality they contribute precludes a narrow absolutism, building into the text a full range of responses to the supernatural.

Amy Tan employs a different narrative strategy in her 1995 magic realist novel *The Hundred Secret Senses*. Unlike Naylor, Tan chooses the rationalist in her story as the sole narrator.[3] This strategy sounds dangerous—narrating a story about the margins entirely from the center—but Olivia, the protagonist/first-person narrator, is a Chinese American with one reluctant foot in the margin and the other positioned uncertainly in the center; she can speak for those in the margins, those in the center, and those like herself caught in between. Olivia's narration details her own strong resistance but eventual conversion to a belief in the nonrational, particularly in the ontological reality of ghosts, or "yin people," with whom her Chinese half sister Kwan constantly communicates. Like the other supernatural occurrences in the novel, the appearance of ghosts from the World of Yin is part of the realist landscape of the text, part of everyday life for Kwan—and ultimately for rationalist Olivia as well.

In her resistance to the nonrational, the narrator of *The Hundred Secret Senses* is intended to represent the position of the typical, rationalist U.S. reader responding to unsettling antinomies. Thus the destabilization of the reader, a postmodernist strategy for opening readers to alternative ontologies, is deliberately conflated with the destabilization of the narrator. The destabilizing element in all magic realist narratives is the magical, which, in Wendy B. Faris's words, "exists symbiotically in a foreign textual culture—a disturbing element, a grain of sand in the oyster of [. . .] realism"

(168). In choosing a rationalist as her narrator, Tan effectively anatomizes the reader's response to the disturbing supernatural by putting the reader's words into the narrator's mouth—literally, it seems, because the narrator speaks in the first person. Faced, like Olivia, with "seeming contraries"— mutually exclusive occurrences presented in the text as equally real, equally valid—readers are disturbed, destabilized, forced to question their bedrock cultural assumption that reality is ultimately knowable, stable, and predictable, that it operates within known (or knowable) physical laws.

Olivia's opening words announce, with amused irony, the destabilizing ontological conflict: "My sister Kwan believes she has yin eyes. She sees those who have died and now dwell in the World of Yin, ghosts who leave the mists just to visit her kitchen on Balboa Street in San Francisco" (Tan 3). Evidently, Olivia is as skeptical about Kwan's ghosts as the reader is likely to be. Tan thus establishes an immediate complicity between narrator and reader at the outset of the text. At once irritated, amused, and disturbed by Kwan's unusual supernatural abilities (which include, but are not limited to, her "yin eyes"), Olivia views her half sister as "wacky" (22), "odd" (23), and "crazy" (92), touchingly devoted as a sister but annoyingly persistent in her efforts to put Olivia in contact with ghosts and past lives. In 1992, when the present-tense narration begins, the Berkeley-educated Olivia is thirty-eight years old, a successful commercial photographer and businesswoman, a rationalist who, according to her mother, "analyzes every single detail to death" (22). She is extremely reluctant to accept the supernatural—Kwan's or anyone else's—as ontologically valid, insisting upon evidence, proof, and verification in the finest tradition of empiricism.

Particularly jarring for Olivia is the disjunction between her own rationalist and Kwan's nonrationalist ontologies, which she unconsciously perceives as a disjunction between "first-world" scientific logic and "third-world" superstition, imagination, and dreams.[4] As a person of mixed ancestry (her mother is American, her late father Chinese) born and raised in the United States, Olivia is so invested in being entirely "American," particularly as a child and teenager suffering peer pressure, that she distances herself from everything "Chinese," embodied by Kwan and her World of Yin, to the point of refusing to credit her own experiences with the supernatural. That even the rational, skeptical Olivia believes—however reluctantly—in the nonrational by the end of the novel lends credence to the existence of multiple ontologies, multiple realities beyond what one can see, hear, and touch.

Important though multiplicity may be, the defining postmodernist characteristic of *The Hundred Secret Senses* is liminality. Among U.S. magic realist narratives, probably only Perry's *Stigmata* contains as many border crossings between worlds as *The Hundred Secret Senses*. While Olivia finds flexible boundaries between worlds strange and disturbing, Kwan finds them entirely normal. Kwan's typical conversational opener is, "Libby-ah, [. . .]. Guess who I see yesterday, you guess." "And," says Olivia, "I don't have to guess that she's talking about someone dead" (3). Kwan speaks of and to the yin people she sees exactly as she speaks of and to the living. Yet Kwan does not appear to be psychotic, even when Olivia's stepfather commits the newly immigrated Kwan to a mental institution for six months to rid her of her ghosts.[5] Olivia makes a point of noting that "most of the time, Kwan is like anyone else" (21)—except when she entertains visitors from beyond the grave and remembers her past lives. From the outset, then, we understand that Kwan has, in her own mind at least, erased the boundary between the worlds of the living and the dead, and between her present life and her past lives.

Shortly after her arrival from China, eighteen-year-old Kwan first "introduces" six-year-old Olivia to the yin people who come to visit Kwan in the bedroom that the sisters share. Olivia is so frightened that she tells her mother about Kwan's ghosts, leading to electroshock treatments for Kwan in the psychiatric hospital, and Olivia's lifelong guilt over the pain she has caused Kwan. Upon Kwan's return from the hospital, Olivia, determined to say nothing to anyone about Kwan's ghosts, becomes accustomed to Kwan's "jabbering away in Chinese" (13) to her "many, many good friends" (16) from the World of Yin; Olivia even learns Chinese as a result of Kwan's conversations with and stories about yin people. Before long, Olivia is seeing yin people too—but the adult Olivia, the narrator, has a rational explanation for this border crossing: To stay out of the mental institution, Kwan must pretend that that she doesn't see ghosts, and to help Kwan maintain this pretense, Olivia in turn pretends that the ghosts *do* exist. "I tried so hard to hold these two contradictory views," Olivia explains, "that soon I started to see what I wasn't supposed to" (55). (Clearly she is speaking from a rationalist position here.) Besides, she adds, "most kids, *without* sisters like Kwan, imagine that ghosts are lurking beneath their beds" (55). Couched in these terms, Olivia's ghost sightings appear reasonable, logical—a trick of the mind, the workings of a child's imagination.

Nevertheless, despite her rationalist undercutting of the evidence of the supernatural that she herself offers, Olivia does provide eyewitness testimony to the reality of Kwan's ghosts: "I saw them," she states unequivocally

(55). The yin people she sees "looked alive. They chatted about the good old days. They worried and complained. I even saw one scratching our dog's neck, and Captain thumped his leg and wagged his tail" (56). The actuality of these liminal, boundary-crossing visitors from another world is brought home to the eight-year-old Olivia when a Chinese-speaking ghost girl appears one day, borrows Olivia's Barbie doll, removes the doll's feather boa, and then appears to take the boa with her when she leaves to return to the yin world. "I couldn't believe that a ghost could take something real and make it disappear" (57), says Olivia, voicing the reader's skepticism—but Olivia never saw the boa again, despite an immediate, meticulous search, followed by another week of equally meticulous searching. As an adult, however, she rationalizes once again, suggesting "more logical explanations" (57) for what she saw as a child but "did not want to believe" (57).

For some of Kwan's strange magical abilities—recharging dead batteries with her fingers (18), pinpointing faults in complex electrical circuits with a touch (19), diagnosing past and present ailments in strangers by shaking hands with them (19), knowing as she talks to Olivia on the phone that Olivia is balancing her checkbook (29)—Olivia can offer no rationale at all. "[Kwan] can't explain any of this," states Olivia, "and neither can I. All I can say is, I've seen her do these things" (19). Olivia is, in fact, a trustworthy eyewitness to ghosts and magic precisely because she does *not* believe, or want to believe, in the nonrational; she reports the truth about what she sees because it *is* the truth, even though she wishes it weren't. The effect of eyewitness verifications hedged by rational disclaimers is to inscribe within the text the antinomy that neither Olivia nor the reader can resolve.

The liminality in *The Hundred Secret Senses* is twofold: Not only do ghosts regularly cross over from the yin world into the world of the living, but the boundary between past and present is blurred, or in Kwan's case, almost totally erased. Kwan has perfect recall of her most recent past life as Nunumu, a one-eyed Chinese peasant girl who was killed in 1864 in the village of Changmian with her American missionary friend Miss Banner, of whom Olivia is the reincarnation. Kwan also knows that through her behavior toward Olivia in this life, she can rectify the mistakes she made as Nunumu in her past life, mistakes that led both to Miss Banner's separation from her lover and to Miss Banner's and Nunumu's deaths. From the moment Kwan arrives in America until her "death" in China thirty-two years later, she tries to jog Olivia's memory of the past by telling her sister "bedtime stories about [. . .] yin people" (31), detailed narratives of their life together as Nunumu and Miss Banner in Changmian in the 1860s. Olivia, however, steadfastly resists the liminal. Like George in *Mama Day,* she is disturbed and destabilized by the blurring of the well-defined boundaries between worlds that her enculturation as an American has taught her to assume. As her depiction of her resistance demonstrates—"I listened to [Kwan's] stories, all the while holding on to my doubts, my sanity" (258)—Olivia shares the Western cultural assumption that sanity is associated with the rational, insanity with the nonrational.

Olivia *does,* however, have vivid, unforgettable dreams of "see[ing] a thousand spears flashing like flames on the crest of a hill [. . .] touch[ing] the tiny grains of a stone wall while waiting to be killed [. . .] smell[ing] my own musky fear as the rope tightens around my neck" (31). As a child, she learned from Kwan to think of "dreams as other lives, other selves" (31). Nevertheless, Olivia refuses to see any connection between her dreams and Miss Banner's life, even though she knows that Kwan wants her to make that connection. She clings instead to her "logic and doubts" (358), wanting to believe that her dreams are nothing more than normal dreams, not a supernormal colliding of past and present lives, an irrational liminality in which she participates as actively as does Kwan.

Rationalist that she is, Olivia is finally convinced by physical evidence to accept the reality of permeable borders between worlds. In Changmian, China—where she has never been before—at the site of Miss Banner's death, Olivia recognizes the stone wall, the landscape, the tune played by Miss Banner's music box (which Kwan has retrieved from the cave where Nunumu hid it in 1864). Inside the music box are artifacts that Kwan has mentioned in her stories—a now-brittle nineteenth-century kidskin lady's glove, Miss Banner's journal, books published in 1855 and 1859. Only as Kwan recounts the events leading up to Nunumu's and Miss Banner's deaths does Olivia allow herself to recall as a memory "what I always thought was a dream: spears flashing by firelight, the grains of the stone wall [. . .] Someone is squeezing my hand—Kwan, but I am surprised to see she is younger and has a patch over one eye" (376). Still, her "logic and doubt" propel her to reason that "it's just coincidence, the story, the box, the dates on the book[s]" (358), although she finds that explanation unsatisfactory, unconvincing.

The final, undeniable confirmation of the reality of the liminal is Nunumu's jar of "thousand-year" duck eggs that Olivia unearths in Changmian two weeks after Kwan's disappearance and presumed death. Olivia

knows from Kwan's stories the approximate location of the jars of preserved duck eggs that Nunumu had buried in the northwestern corner
of the garden of the Ghost Merchant's estate where she lived. When Olivia
does at last unearth a jar of eggs in what was in 1864 the northwestern
corner of the Ghost Merchant's garden, and when the blackened eggs
crumble to dust—as only hundred-year-old eggs would do—when she
hugs them to her, she has the final proof she seeks: empirical evidence that
verifies the permeability of the borders between worlds.

Embracing the liminal, Olivia also embraces the departed Kwan, whom
Olivia now sees not as her crazy Chinese sister but as a wise woman, a
knowledge-bringer, her true mother, whose extraordinary "connected
knowing" has made Olivia whole. Valorizing the supernatural opens a new
dimension of experience to Olivia; she can see the limitations of a strictly
rationalist epistemology for the first time in her life. "I now believe,"
Olivia states at the end of the narrative, "that truth lies not in logic but in
hope[. . .]. [H]ope [. . .] can survive . . . all sorts of contradictions, and
certainly any skeptic's rationale of relying on proof through fact" (398).

When Olivia finally accepts Kwan's—and her own—ability to cross
the boundary between worlds, she recognizes that she has always viewed
Kwan from a colonialist perspective. Olivia's Orientalism, developed as a
child, was an unconscious strategy of identification with the "privileged
center" by casting her Chinese half (represented by Kwan) as separate
and "other." This recognition paves the way for Olivia to embrace the part
of her that is Chinese and to gain the self-understanding that she has
always lacked. She even takes Kwan's last name; finally, she knows who she
is—and Kwan is part of her identity. When she speaks for the ontological
validity of the supernatural at the end of the novel, she brings Kwan's
ex-centric discourse into the center and makes it her own: "believing in
ghosts—that's believing that love never dies. If people we love die [. . .] we
can find them anytime with our hundred secret senses" (399). The postmodern multiplicity in *The Hundred Secret Senses* ultimately extends beyond
the ontological to the narrator's subjectivity, which is seen as a kind of
liminal collective comprising Olivia, Miss Banner, Kwan, Nunumu, and
Olivia's baby Samantha—the past, the present, and the future.

Though *Mama Day* and *The Hundred Secret Senses* are especially instructive examples, all magic realist texts foreground the ontological, expanding the boundaries of "the real" by describing supernatural events as
empirical fact. U.S. magic realist texts also pointedly critique rationalist
ideology by dramatically illustrating the limitations of rationalist "separate

knowing," which isolates individuals, in contrast to nonrationalist "connected knowing," which creates community. Like other postmodernist modes that deliberately "wage a war on totality" (Lyotard 186), and, as Carpenter and Kolmar indicate, like other U.S. literature of the supernatural, particularly women's ghost stories and Gothic fiction of the Victorian and Edwardian periods (12), magic realism subverts the conventions of realism and challenges the hegemony of rationalism by interrogating Cartesian binaries, erasing or at least blurring the border between the natural and the supernatural, the living and the dead, the past and the present, the knowable and the unknowable. By contesting what Natoli and Hutcheon term "the comforting security—ethical, ontological, epistemological—that 'reason' offer[s]" (ix), magic realism destabilizes the reader, opening the door to realities inexpressible within the confines of rationalist discourse. U.S. magic realist writers in particular are also invested in recovering the erased histories and nonrationalist voices of the marginalized groups to which they themselves belong. In challenging and stretching the limits of the knowable in these ways, U.S. magic realism vividly demonstrates its postmodern "commitment to doubleness."

NOTES

1. I am aware that Latin American magic realist writers consider their primary marginalization to be in relation to world literature (presumably because they are not from First World countries), not as individuals or groups in relation to their own societies.

2. The deposing of her uncle, Salvatore Allende, as president of Chile may have pushed Allende and her family into the political margins, but by race and class, hers is a centrist rather than an ex-centric voice. P. Gabrielle Foreman argues in "Past-On Stories: History and the Magically Real, Morrison and Allende on Call" that "Allende's magical realism [in *The House of the Spirits*] gives way in the end to political realism [. . .]. [She] employ[s] magic realism as a bridge to a history recoverable in the political realm, a history that she will ultimately constitute in her text as distinct from the magical" (286). Allende's use of magic realism as a "bridge" is very similar to other writers' use of it as a "ruse" or "trick."

3. Although Kwan narrates in the first person stories about her past life as Nunumu, these stories are narrated to Olivia, who places them within her own first-person narration by quoting them at length in the text, just as she quotes conversations she has with Kwan or Simon or Du-Lili, the woman who helped raise Kwan. with her. Olivia is thus presented as the sole narrator in *The Hundred Secret Senses* even though Kwan/Nunumu's first-person, past-tense stories occupy one-quarter of the text.

It is interesting to note that Kwan has two distinct voices in the text: her pigeon English, which is entertainingly ungrammatical and never lets the reader forget that

Kwan is "a foreigner," and Olivia's English translations of the stories of Nunumu that Kwan tells in Chinese, which are grammatically perfect, well-polished narratives.

4. Here, too, Olivia speaks for the reader by revealing an unconscious colonialist ideology. Olivia has always wished that Kwan were "more normal" (21), speculating that "maybe in another country Kwan would be considered ordinary. Maybe in some parts of China, Hong Kong, or Taiwan she'd be revered" (21). Olivia's wistful supposition demonstrates her underlying Orientalism. She has cast Kwan, and Chinese people in general, as "other," people from the mysterious Orient with nonrationalist customs, beliefs, and superstitions. Olivia's implication is clear: In U.S. culture, Kwan is *not* normal, not ordinary, not revered.

Only when Olivia visits China does she learn, to her great surprise, that Kwan's supernatural powers are nearly as unusual in rural Changmian as they are in urban America. The residents of Changmian, and even Du-Lili, always regarded Kwan as unusual, even within their culture, which does recognize a permeable boundary between the worlds of the living and the dead. The villagers are "frightened" (231), or as Simon describes them, "freaked" (232), when Kwan suddenly begins weeping and conversing with the ghost of Big Ma, her foster mother, who had left the village—very much alive—that morning to go meet Kwan. The "news"—we note that Olivia does not call it a "rumor"—quickly spreads that Kwan has seen Big Ma's ghost; no one is surprised when Kwan's "yin eyes" are confirmed some hours later by officials who arrive to inform the family of the death of Big Ma that morning in a traffic accident.

5. The binary "sane/insane" is explored in a number of U.S. magic realist texts. In *Mama Day*, for example, George believes that Miranda is literally insane for seeking to cure Cocoa by nonrational means. In Phyllis Perry's *Stigmata*, Lizzie spends fourteen years in mental institutions after the spontaneous "stigmata" she suffers—bleeding wrists and ankles from the chains her African great-grandmother wore during the Middle Passage—are interpreted as a suicide attempt.

WORKS CITED

Carpenter, Lynette, and Wendy K. Kolmar, eds. *Haunting the House of Fiction: Feminist Perspectives on Ghost Stories by American Women*. Knoxville: University of Tennessee Press, 1991.

D'haen, Theo L. "Magic Realism and Postmodernism: Decentering Privileged Centers." In *Magical Realism: Theory, History, Community*. Edited by Wendy B. Faris and Lois Parkinson Zamora, 191–208. Durham, N.C.: Duke University Press, 1995.

Faris, Wendy B. "Scheherazade's Children: Magical Realism and Postmodern Fiction." In *Magical Realism: Theory, History, Community*. Edited by Wendy B. Faris and Lois Parkinson Zamora, 163–90. Durham, N.C.: Duke University Press, 1995.

Foreman, P. Gabrielle. "Past-On Stories: History and the Magically Real, Morrison and Allende on Call." In *Magical Realism: Theory, History, Community*. Edited by Wendy B. Faris and Lois Parkinson Zamora, 285–303. Durham, N.C.: Duke University Press, 1995.

García Márquez, Gabriel. Interview with Plíno Apuleyo Mendoza. Quoted in "Sources of Magic Realism/Supplements to Realism in Contemporary Latin American Literature," by Scott Simpkins. In *Magical Realism: Theory, History, Community*. Edited by Wendy B. Faris and Lois Parkinson Zamora, 145–59. Durham, N.C.: Duke University Press, 1995.

Hutcheon, Linda. "Beginning to Theorize Postmodernism." In *A Postmodern Reader*. Edited by Joseph Natoli and Linda Hutcheon, 243–72. Albany: State University of New York Press, 1993. Kerr, Howard, John W. Crowley, and Charles L. Crow, eds. *The Haunted Dusk: American Supernatural Fiction, 1820–1920*. Athens: University of Georgia Press, 1983.

Lyotord, Jean François. Excerpts from *The Postmodern Condition: A Report on Knowledge*. In *A Postmodern Reader*. Edited by Joseph Natoli and Linda Hutcheon, 71–90. Albany: State University of New York Press, 1993.

McHale, Brian. *Postmodern Fiction*. New York: Methuen, 1987.

Natoli, Joseph, and Linda Hutcheon, eds. "Introduction." In *A Postmodern Reader*. Albany: State University of New York Press, 1993.

Naylor, Gloria. *Mama Day*. New York: Vintage, 1989.

Perry, Phyllis Alesia. *Stigmata*. New York: Random, 1998.

Ringe, Donald A. *American Gothic: Imagination and Reason in Nineteenth-Century Fiction*. Lexington: University Press of Kentucky, 1982.

Slemon, Stephen. "Magic Realism as Postcolonial Discourse." In *Magical Realism: Theory, History, Community*. Edited by Wendy B. Faris and Lois Parkinson Zamora, 407–26. Durham, N.C.: Duke University Press, 1995.

Tan, Amy. *The Hundred Secret Senses*. New York: Ballantine, 1995.

Weinstock, Jeffrey A.. Introduction to *Spectral America: Phantoms and the National Imagination*. Madison: University of Wisconsin Press, 2004.

Wilson, August. *The Piano Lesson*. New York: New American Library, 1991.

Zamora, Lois Parkinson. "Magical Romance/Magical Realism: Ghosts in U.S. and Latin American Fiction." In *Magical Realism: Theory, History, Community*. Edited by Wendy B. Faris and Lois Parkinson Zamora, 497–550. Durham, N.C.: Duke University Press, 1995.

Zamora, Lois Parkinson, and Wendy B. Faris. "Introduction: Daiquiri Birds and Flaubertian Parrot(ie)s." *Magical Realism: Theory, History, Community*. Edited by Wendy B. Faris and Lois Parkinson Zamora. Durham, N.C.: Duke University Press, 1995.

Melodramatic Specters

Cinema and
The Sixth Sense

KATHERINE A. FOWKES

I. INTRODUCTION

Say the word "ghost" and most people think of Halloween and horror
stories. But recent Hollywood ghost films are much more likely to feature kindly, romantic, or comedic ghosts than scary ones. This essay will
consider such films, ultimately focusing on *The Sixth Sense* (2000) as a
vehicle for more fully illustrating the conventions common to Hollywood
ghost movies. For despite its horror-genre overlay, *The Sixth Sense* belongs
to a tradition of ghost movies that has become common in the past twenty
years, departing from Gothic and horror ghost traditions and instead
employing ghosts as full-fledged characters in melodramatic, romantic,
and/or comedic narratives. In fact, following a larger trend, many recent
ghost films tend to blur or combine otherwise well-delineated genres. The
1990 box-office phenomenon *Ghost* is perhaps the best-known example,
typifying the trend through its whodunit/suspense plot combined with
both melodramatic and comedic elements. And as most people now realize, *The Sixth Sense* is not quite what it seems. This applies both to its
plot and to its apparent genre since its initial "horror" premise is ultimately defused in favor of melodrama. Melodramatic and/or romantic
treatments of the occult are equally evident in movies released directly
prior to *The Sixth Sense*, such as *City of Angels* (1998), *What Dreams May
Come* (1998), and *Meet Joe Black* (1998). And a comedic sensibility is combined with otherwise romantic/melodramatic plots in *The Preacher's Wife*
(1996) and *Michael* (1996). Throughout the 1980s and 1990s, Hollywood
released a score of such films, revisiting its own ghostly themes from the

1930s and 1940s when supernatural comedies and melodramas enjoyed popularity (*Topper* (1937), *The Ghost and Mrs. Muir* (1847), etc.).

While anomalous in its "trick" construction, *The Sixth Sense* nevertheless belongs to this company of ghost films whose purpose is other than merely scaring the bejeebers out of the audience. Furthermore, the gimmick of *The Sixth Sense* depends on the viewer's being familiar with both general cinematic conventions and traditional ghost-story conventions. It therefore provides a handy case study for discussing some of the intersections between ghost stories and the cinematic medium. As this volume on ghosts illustrates, fictional ghosts belong to well-established oral, literary, and dramatic traditions (campfire stories, *Hamlet*'s ghost, etc.), so there is nothing about film that makes it the *necessary* "medium" for a successful ghost story. However, the visual and aural properties of the cinema and the conventions of Hollywood narrative are uniquely suited to certain aspects of ghost stories. For example, the emphasis on ghosts as visual apparitions intersects nicely with the cinema's photographic base. And cinema's ability readily to disconnect and recombine audio and video mimics the ability of ghosts who may sometimes be seen and not heard, or vice versa. Furthermore, since a question often posed by traditional ghost stories concerns whether or not ghosts are real, cinema's manipulation of fictional story worlds through aural and visual techniques has the potential to be quite compelling in dramatizing this conundrum for the viewer. *The Sixth Sense* is an interesting film to examine precisely because it relies on the viewer's familiarity with other ghost stories and with Hollywood cinema to create and then thwart the viewer's expectations.

II. Themes and Conventions in Recent Ghost Films

While there is considerable variety among recent supernaturally themed movies, some important commonalities emerge. Instead of using the supernatural to shock and scare the audience, many recent films employ ghosts and angels almost exclusively as vehicles for romance. These stories are less about fearing death than they are about appreciating life, and this appreciation is inextricably linked to true love and an emphasis on the heart rather than the mind. Perhaps more importantly, these romances are constructed explicitly upon the concept of second chances. While an untimely death may cut short the promise of love, a second chance will be provided

either through the return of the loved one as a ghost, through the minis-
trations of an angelic spirit, or through a journey to the beyond. Furthermore, while there are variations in the roles that ghosts or angels may play
within each narrative, it is common for angels to serve as magical facilita-
tors to the main character's romance and/or for ghosts to be the manifestation of a living character's lost love. In many cases, the ghost is a man
who returns to earth for a second chance to express his true love for a girlfriend or wife. Although the characters' goals will ultimately be fulfilled,
the male ghost often finds himself compromised and emasculated due
to his ghostly state. In my recent book, *Giving Up the Ghost: Spirits, Ghosts
and Angels in Mainstream Comedy Films,* I examine these trends in depth,
beginning chronologically with *Heaven Can Wait* (1978) and including
twenty or so other ghost and angel films throughout the 1980s and early
1990s.[1] Since I have covered those earlier films in that volume, I will reca-
pitulate some of those trends here in the context of more recent mainstream movies. These films reiterate and provide variations to the original
pattern described there, and serve as a backdrop to a closer analysis of *The
Sixth Sense.*

Meet Joe Black (a remake of *Death Takes a Holiday* [1934]) is an example
of a film that offers a supernatural love story, but provides a twist to many
earlier films by casting the "dark spirit" as Death himself. This supernatural love story employs the "second-chance" trope by establishing a glimpse
of true love for a young woman, Susan, when she encounters a charming
young man in a coffee shop. It seems clear that he could be the love of her
life, but the romance is dashed when he is killed by a car. When Death,
in the form of Joe Black, occupies the body of the young man (Brad Pitt
plays both characters), he not only falls in love with Susan, he also eventually gives a second chance to the original romance when the young man
is magically restored to his own body at the end of the film. The viewer,
who risks being deprived of a satisfying conclusion to the intense relationship between Joe and Susan, thereby also gets a second chance. By having
Brad Pitt play both Joe *and* the young man, the identity of Joe Black and
her (original) true love are magically merged for both the character and for
the audience.

An important hallmark of recent ghost films is their tendency to establish a narrative goal at the beginning of the film that is *other* than the
culminating romance, thereby temporarily obscuring or complicating the
thematic focus of the film. Thus, in *Meet Joe Black*, the title character's

original reason for inhabiting another's body is merely to experience the world of the living.[2] But while the initial pleasures of the flesh begin with simple bodily sensations such as tasting and savoring peanut butter (a minor running gag), the ultimate benefit of Joe's bodily incarnation will be found not in the physical pleasure of the five senses, but in the romantic fulfillment that it facilitates.

Both *City of Angels* and *Michael* provide variations on the idea that heavenly spirits crave earthly sensations. Whether it be the taste of peanut butter in *Meet Joe Black*, sugar and pie in *Michael*, or a juicy pear in *City of Angels*, the physical sensations of the mortal plane are emphasized at the beginning of each story, only to be eclipsed in importance by the more ethereal joy of romance.[3] For while the angel Seth craves the unknown taste of food and the touch of a woman in *City of Angels*, he is only willing to "take the fall" and become mortal because he has "fallen" in love with a mortal woman. Although the film does give Maggie and Seth a second chance when he becomes mortal, this is one of the few films that seem to end unhappily through the death of Maggie. However, as with other ghost films, once the existence of an afterlife has been established, the romance can still be fulfilled (at least hypothetically) upon Seth's eventual death.

In *Michael*, the angel does not himself fall in love, but—as is often the case with angel characters—instead facilitates romance between two other characters. At the opening of the movie, a cynical tabloid reporter named Frank remarks that he possesses brains but no heart. He suggests to his colleague, Huey, that with *his* (Huey's) heart, they might together make up a complete man. Since the initial narrative goal is to find out if the rumors about the existence of an angel are true, this "throwaway line" doesn't become truly relevant until later in the film when the angel, Michael, succeeds in helping Frank "get back his heart." The object of Frank's affections will turn out to be his new colleague, Dorothy, who is posing as an angel expert. In facilitating the romance between Frank and Dorothy, Michael also mends Dorothy's heart, broken three times from unhappy marriages and bitter divorces. By the end of the film, the angel disintegrates before their eyes, thus preventing Frank and Huey from achieving their original goal of delivering him to the newspaper. But as Michael begins to fade, it looks as if he, too, has failed in his mission. His attempts to bring Dorothy and Frank together are ruined when Frank learns that Dorothy has lied to them and will, in fact, become Frank's replacement at the newspaper. This revelation and Michael's disappearance sets the characters back to square one, and Frank and Dorothy go their separate ways. As the characters question their experience and the reality of angels, Frank's old cynicism returns and he denies that Michael ever existed. But the movie is not over yet! Michael—being an angel—is not really dead! He makes a sudden and mysterious reappearance, leading Frank down an alleyway where he bumps into Dorothy. This second sighting of Michael and the coincidence of running into Dorothy now make a believer out of Frank. He regains his heart and is thus free to believe in both love and angels. Frank's inability to remain cynical in the face of a true angel is thus linked to his capacity to love.[4] Frank promptly proposes marriage, Dorothy accepts, and the film ends happily. The (supposed) original goal of the film—to deliver Michael to Chicago for a media spectacle—is thus eclipsed in importance by the romantic story line fulfilled at the film's conclusion.

Another commonality of these films is the tendency to put the male protagonist in a passive role—an uncharacteristic position for Hollywood male leads. Specifically, if the male protagonist of the film dies and returns as a ghost, his role as active, narrative agent is severely compromised. Male characters who return from the dead may still be actively goal-oriented, but their ghostly status tends to emasculate them for the majority of the film, rendering their actions futile until the film's conclusion. In other cases, the male character may not be a ghost, but may be visited by an angel with magical powers to which he must submit.[5] *The Preacher's Wife* is a recent film that illustrates this point while also dramatizing the theme of a second chance. In this film (a remake of *The Bishop's Wife* [1947]), a couple's floundering marriage is given a second chance through the help of an angel.[6] As with the original film, the story at first appears to be about a minister's struggle to raise money for his church, and the angel originally "appears" to be the catalyst for the resolution of this problem. As the narrative evolves, however, a strange love story emerges as the focus, and the angel's more important mission is thus revealed—to revive Frank and Dorothy's dying romance. Before this is achieved, however, the husband is repeatedly undercut by the angel's savvy ways, as the angel surpasses him in both business meetings and in marital duties. As in *City of Angels* and *Meet Joe Black*, a forbidden romance between a mortal and an angel is ultimately used to emphasize the value of true love here on earth. But as in stories in which the husband dies and returns as an ineffectual ghost, here the husband earns his second chance only after an emasculating interlude, orchestrated by the angel who threatens to take his place.

The second-chance love story and passive positioning of the male protagonist dovetail with a final, curious trend in many of these films. Specifically, many of the stories emphasize difficulties in relationships between
men and women, and the problem of distant husbands or fathers. In *Ghost*
and other films such as *Always* (1989); *Truly, Madly, Deeply* (1991); and even
Ghost Dad (1990), a man and woman have difficulty communicating with
one another. To be more specific, a male ghost character has difficulty expressing himself to a (living) female companion and/or his family. Of
course the problem of communicating is any ghost's central dilemma as
it attempts to haunt the living. Nevertheless, it is fascinating that ghostly
haunting has been transformed by Hollywood into a dilemma of poor gender relations, often blamed upon distant or absent husbands and fathers.[7]

What Dreams May Come is a good example of a second-chance-for-love
story combined with the guilty father/distant husband theme. As in earlier films such as *Made in Heaven* (1987) and *Defending Your Life* (1991),
much of the story takes place in the afterlife rather than on earth. The
setup features Annie and Chris as a romantic couple ("soul mates") whose
children are killed in a car crash. Not long after, Chris is also killed in a
crash. The film follows Chris into the afterlife where he eventually learns
that his wife has committed suicide out of grief. Instead of a tearful
reunion in heaven, Chris learns that his wife's suicide has caused her to go
to hell and that he will never be able to see her. But Chris vows to rescue
her, ignoring the pessimistic advice of several helping "angels" who later
turn out to be his own dead children. It is only through reevaluating his
failure as a father that Chris comes to recognizes the true identity of these
spirits, thereby simultaneously redeeming his relationship with them. Chris
comes to understand that not only was he a flawed father, but he was a
flawed husband as well. Because he had been unable to support Annie and
join fully in her grief over their lost children, he is implicated in her loneliness and subsequent suicide. In the course of his journey, Chris repeatedly talks about "not giving up" in his quest to rescue his wife from hell.
While rescuing a female is a classic Hollywood activity for a male character, this film nevertheless adheres to the formula of other ghost movies by
providing a different spin on what is meant by "not giving up." Not coin-
cidentally, the title of my book *Giving Up the Ghost* refers, in part, to the way
in which the male ghost character relinquishes his control either to another
character or to his destiny.[8] And indeed in this film it turns out that "not
giving up" actually comes to mean the opposite. Instead of fighting to

extricate Annie from hell, Chris gives up and decides to stay with her. When he says to another spirit (significantly, a former father figure from earth), "I'm giving up, just not the way you think," he is referring to the fact that he will finally give himself up completely to Annie and join her in all her emotions, including her grief. This gesture of self-relinquishment succeeds where no active measure could. Instead of dooming them both to a hellish existence, they are miraculously transported to a heavenly world. Now safely together, Annie tells Chris that nothing worked "until you tried joining me."[9] The supernatural and emasculating interlude provides the vehicle to redeem the distant father/husband while simultaneously providing the requisite second chance for true love.

There is one final similarity in the films discussed here, and one that will be particularly relevant to an analysis of *The Sixth Sense*. Unlike traditional horror/ghost stories, most of the movies mentioned here do *not* revolve around the question of whether a supernatural phenomenon is real. In most cases, the narrative and cinematic techniques are used to establish the reality of the ghost for the audience, and instead employ the incredulity of the (other) characters for comedic or dramatic purposes. For example, *Ghost* and *Ghost Dad* both exploit invisibility as a device to create comic situations. The comedy depends upon the audience's accepting the reality of the ghost while enjoying the amazement of characters who can find no plausible explanation for strange phenomena. In *The Preacher's Wife*, a number of comic scenes involve the angel's attempts to convince the preacher that he is, in fact, a real angel. *City of Angels* and *Meet Joe Black* establish the reality of the angelic spirits but create dramatic situations for the female characters who must come to grips with the true identity of their lovers. And *Michael* provides a comedic twist by introducing an angel who is so unlike the usual stereotypes (he drinks, smokes, etc.) that some viewers may temporarily share in the characters' skepticism. But as in most of the other films, this doubt is necessarily erased early in the film.

This last trend in ghost films is particularly relevant to *The Sixth Sense*, a film that employs familiar cinematic techniques to lull the audience into complacency regarding the reality of the ghosts, only to switch gears at the last minute. And as the film adheres nicely to the thematic trends discussed above, the following discussion should serve to elucidate further the conventions and common themes of recent "comedy/romance" ghost films.

III. CASE STUDY: *The Sixth Sense*

By now, the basic plot and the surprise twist to *The Sixth Sense* should
be no secret to the readers of this essay. But a quick summary of the plot
may be helpful to establish the context for a discussion of the details. The
story begins with a private evening of celebration enjoyed by a slightly
tipsy couple. The husband, Dr. Malcolm Crowe (Bruce Willis), has been
honored by the city for his work as a child psychologist. An undercurrent
of tension is introduced, however, when his wife Anna (Olivia Williams)
mentions that his obsession with work may have caused him to neglect
her. But this is a brief lull in the celebratory mood and they soon maneu-
ver themselves into the bedroom for a roll in the hay. Unfortunately, they
are immediately interrupted by an intruder who reveals that he is a former
patient of Malcolm's. The teenager, Vincent (Donny Wahlberg), is distraught and accuses Malcolm of failing to help him. He claims that he
is "still afraid." Whatever psychological demons may have "haunted" the
teenager, the doctor was apparently unable to drive them away. He then
shoots Malcolm in the stomach before killing himself.

The film then cuts to a later date (the next fall, as indicated by a sub-
title) and we observe that Malcolm has survived the shooting but not the
psychological fallout from the event. He believes that the shooting and the
young man's suicide are his own personal failures. He is now shown trying to make contact with a new patient who reminds him of the shooter
when he was a boy. We soon come to understand that Malcolm sincerely
wishes to help the new boy but, at the same time, also hopes for a kind of
redemption for himself if he succeeds. Unfortunately, his obsessive desire
to make good further exacerbates the trend in his relationship with Anna.
The two become increasingly distant, almost like "strangers," as Malcolm
describes it.

During the first half of the movie, we learn that the boy, Cole Sear
(Haley Joel Osment), bears many similarities to the shooter.[10] He is the
troubled child of divorce. He lives alone with his mother and suffers from
a variety of disturbing symptoms. He has no real friends and draws violent
pictures at school. Like Vincent, he is often afraid and describes himself
as a freak. What Malcolm doesn't know right away is that Cole is plagued
by paranormal disturbances. As the movie progresses, it is revealed that
the boy sees ghosts, or dead people (as he puts it). He doesn't see just any
old dead people, of course; he sees scary dead people, the ghosts of those
who appear to have suffered from a violent or unjust death. Malcolm

desperately wants to help Cole, but he is understandably skeptical when Cole reveals that ghosts are the true cause of his troubles. As a psychologist, Malcolm's initial interpretation is that Cole must be hallucinating and that the boy's psychological damage has gone far beyond what one would expect from the trauma of a divorce. As far as the audience is concerned, however, Malcolm's diagnosis will not be complete until he comes to understand that the ghosts are real and not just figments of Cole's imagination. The clincher of course is that, by the end of the film, the audience learns that the doctor himself is a ghost. For Malcolm, believing in ghosts becomes the prerequisite for realizing that he himself is one. But for the audience, believing in Cole's ghosts is a kind of a red herring because it causes us to focus only on the story elements that will lead Malcolm to believe Cole. The story is thus constructed as a mystery surrounding the little boy and the protagonist/physician's quest to solve it, rather than as a story about a doctor who discovers that he is a ghost—the "real" revelation of the film.[11]

As is common to mystery narratives, the protagonist's goal here is to find clues and then properly interpret them. It's not too different from the way in which some television detective shows operate (*Columbo*, some episodes of *Monk*, etc.). In each episode, the viewer first learns the "truth" (the identity of the murderer), and then watches to see how the detective will put the pieces of the puzzle together. Similarly, in *The Sixth Sense*, we learn the truth about Cole before Malcolm does and watch Malcolm struggle to make sense of the facts. And as in standard mystery formulas, we eventually learn the "motive" behind the hauntings via Malcolm's investigation, namely that the ghosts wish to communicate something to Cole about their untimely death. Once again, the audience is probably familiar with this story element, since many film ghosts haunt in order to reveal (or avenge) their unjust demise.[12] And as in other recent films the audience understands that the ghosts are "real" but watches as other characters come to grips with their existence. Many recent ghost films follow this formula, and *The Sixth Sense* is no exception—at least not initially. Typically, a ghost character is given the task of communicating effectively to the living. This goal is then combined with the need for the subject of the haunting to accept the reality of the ghost (which Cole already does) and properly receive its message (which Cole will eventually do). But although *The Sixth Sense* presents this dual process and goal as its central focus, this convention—which is so familiar from other ghost movies— also serves as a clever tactic to distract the viewer from the true nature of our hero's dilemma. Not only is our hero *himself* a ghost, but his problems with his wife stem *not* from his work obsession, but from his unrealized ghost status.

This last revelation returns us to the theme of faulty relationships between men and women and the difficulty of communication. Just as in *Ghost* (which bears an "uncanny" similarity to *The Sixth Sense* both in its "sleeper" status and in its portrayal of gender roles),[13] the audience is cued to accept the reality of the ghosts, and both feature a man and woman with a communication flaw in their relationship. In *Ghost*, Sam cannot tell his wife that he loves her.[14] His difficulty in expressing his emotions becomes exacerbated as a ghost, as he desperately tries to communicate with her. As noted, this theme is repeated in scores of other ghost films that draw on and work through difficulties in gender and stereotypical relationships between men and women.[15] The films repeatedly portray men as obsessed or distracted by work, distant from their wives and children and unable to express their emotions. In *The Sixth Sense*, Malcolm has failed to keep up his end of the marriage, putting Anna "second," as she reminds him in the film's opening exchange. Furthermore, both Vincent's and Cole's problems are ostensibly the result of divorces that have deprived them of their fathers. Since these scenarios are likely to resonate with viewers, the audience is unlikely to attribute Malcolm's poor marital skills to anything but the usual gender stereotypes. Once Malcolm is revealed as a ghost, however, it becomes clear that the formula for recent ghost films is once again fulfilled: Miscommunications between men and women and relationship problems are repeatedly combined and conflated with male ghosts. And, as in *Ghost*, it is precisely this thematic that will eventually eclipse the initial focus of the film. For while *Ghost* first appears to be a suspenseful whodunit, it is just as much a story about Sam's being allowed to tell Molly that he really loves her. Here, Sam's ghostly status can be seen as a kind of exaggerated dramatization of his ineptitude in the relationship. In *The Sixth Sense*, Malcolm's ghostly status becomes the explanation and justification for his neglect. His ghostly state is not just symbolic of his poor relationship skills, but, by the end of the film, also serves as an alibi for his poor behavior. Significantly, in both films (as well as others, such as *Always* and *Ghost Dad*), the conclusion of the film features a male ghost finally succeeding in articulating his love for his wife, girlfriend, and/or family.

As we have seen, the narrative questions initially posed by *The Sixth Sense* concern Malcolm's ability to diagnose Cole's problem properly, thereby helping Cole while simultaneously redeeming the former's own past failure. But Malcolm's correct diagnosis of Cole hinges on resolving a dilemma that is intrinsic to ghost stories, namely—are the ghosts real? As Tzvetan Todorov describes it, this uncertainty is the hallmark of the fantastic genre. In order for a ghost story to be wholly fantastic, the reader/viewer must remain uncertain as to the reality of the ghost (or other supernatural phenomenon). Often, but not always, this uncertainty is shared by one or more of the characters. *The Sixth Sense* trades on this hesitation in several ways. To begin with, the story is framed by the notion that there may be a psychological explanation for the ghosts since our protagonist's main goal is to wield his psychological acumen to help his patient. The purely psychological explanation (that the boy is merely disturbed) is countered, however, by the film's visually illustrating and thereby "proving" the nature of Cole's problem.

As Todorov describes it, the fantastic asks whether or not a phenomenon is an illusion and therefore *outside* oneself, or instead a problem of imagination and therefore *inside* oneself (36). While a hallmark of the fantastic genre, this dichotomy also lends itself perfectly to a story about a psychologist. The possibility of a psychological explanation for mysterious phenomena provides an excellent motivation for the protagonist to investigate the reality of ghosts. However, it also serves as a foil to the viewer, distracting the audience from the possibility that Malcolm is himself a ghost. Furthermore, the psychology motif extends far beyond merely providing a motive for Malcolm's interest in Cole and his ghosts. It helps to mend a rift in the dichotomy created by Todorov's dichotomy of "inside-versus-outside" or "subjective-versus-objective" explanations for supernatural phenomenon.

Consider for example the nature of the ghosts that haunt Cole. Their mangled and bloody bodies make them terrifying to Cole and perhaps to the audience as well. If horror films tend to concern themselves with fear of disease, death, or the unknown, then these ghosts seem to indicate initially that this is, indeed, a horror film (Kaminsky 122). Certainly the vomiting ghost girl seems like a character right out of a horror film (and she's suspiciously reminiscent of Linda Blair's infamous character in *The Exorcist* [1973]).[16] But by the end of the film it becomes clear that the vomiting ghoul is far from a minion of the devil. In fact, she seems sad and frighten*ed*, not frighten*ing*. Her behavior and appearance derive not from an inherent malevolence but are instead the symptoms of a terrible trauma. In other words, what the ghosts in this film need is not an exorcism but a good therapist. And, in fact, this is more or less exactly what they get when Cole finally *listens* to the ghosts' problems. Although he is able to help the poisoned girl in a very material way by showing her father proof of her murder on videotape, it is unlikely that there will be simple solutions to appease the other murdered ghosts. It is implied that Cole will placate them merely by listening to their stories, a kind of talking cure of the crypt rather than of the couch.

Interestingly enough, it is precisely the popularity of psychology and psychoanalysis that prompts Todorov to claim that the fantastic genre will eventually disappear or become unnecessary. Because supernatural tales are often said to provide a handy way of exploring taboo subjects such as sexual desire, Todorov contends that "psychoanalysis has replaced (and thereby has made useless) the literature of the fantastic" (160).[17] Whereas people may have once believed that spirits and devils were entities external to themselves, psychoanalysis provides a plausible, internally based psychological explanation for apparitions and hallucinations. But *The Sixth Sense* provides a bridge to Todorov's inside/outside dichotomy. While the story features a psychologist, it refuses to replace the supernatural explanation with a psychological one. Instead, the movie actually uses the psychological motif to *support* the supernatural explanation. Cole *is* troubled, but he is troubled because he is haunted. The haunters are compelled to haunt because they *themselves* are troubled. Luckily, it turns out that therapy can be applied to the troubled in both the living and the occult realm.

The concept of psychological healing also extends to the film's key reversal. Throughout the film, Malcolm has been trying to help his patient, Cole. But Cole soon proves to be quite mature and well adjusted for a kid who is constantly subjected to scary ghosts. By the end of the film, it is understood that it is not Cole but Malcolm who is the real patient. In fact, Malcolm suffers from the same problem as the other ghost-patients in the film: denial. He doesn't know that he is dead because he only sees what he wants to see. Since the term denial is often used to refer to one's inability to accept another person's death, it is an ironic twist that it is here applied to the dead themselves. Furthermore, denial of death is one of the most common reasons given to explain the supposed appeal of ghost films. We don't want to admit that loved ones might die, so we create stories in which the dead people can still be with us.[18] According to this view then, fictional ghosts are usually the denial, wish-fulfillment product of the living. In this film, however, denial is the wish-fulfillment product of ghosts!

The phrase "they only see what they want to see" is an important clue that Cole reveals about Malcolm, but the seeing metaphor is also important for its function as a pun. As Cole departs from his very first encounter with Malcolm in the church, he says to the doctor: "I'm going to see you again, right?" Here the word "see" is understood in the sense that one "sees a psychiatrist" for treatment. Later, however, the viewer comes to understand the double meaning in Cole's statement since Cole "sees" ghosts. This doubleness runs throughout the whole film, providing two possible readings to every scene and underscoring the generic doubleness of all ghost films that seem to be about one thing (murder, death, ghosts) but end up instead (or also) being about something else (love, communication, gender). The doubleness also extends equally to the fact that ghost films often seem to be about one character, while actually being about another.[19] Thus, while *Ghost* may at first seem to be about Molly's grief and denial at Sam's death, the movie actually focuses on Sam. *The Sixth Sense*, of course, follows the pattern perfectly, and as the viewer eventually learns, this other focus (Malcolm, not Cole) underlies the gimmick that is the hallmark of the film.

While *The Sixth Sense* delivers a pun about sight and seeing as a clue to its conflation of psychiatry and the occult, seeing is important on a meta-textual level as well. One of the strengths of the cinema in telling a story of the fantastic is that the photographic image carries immense power. Despite the ability to create illusions and special effects, the indexical quality of film provides a profound reality effect. Because film serves as an "index" that there was really something there to be photographed, the viewer is encouraged to take for granted what she sees on the screen, provided that the story world is internally consistent.[20] Even though the audience understands that this is a fictional story, the story world is constructed as fact, and various techniques are used to encourage the acceptance of certain events, no matter how bizarre. And despite recent innovations in cleverly altering and therefore "faking" photographic images, the photographic image still suggests to most people that "seeing is believing." This quality of the cinema (combined with careful story and production elements) allows the film to introduce the hesitation of belief that is central to the fantastic genre, only to direct that hesitation away from the viewer's response and confine it instead to Malcolm.

Consider the following scene that occurs early in the film: Cole's mother leaves the kitchen for a few seconds only to find, upon her return, that every single drawer and cupboard has been opened. It is one of the eerie moments in the film in which the camera work combines with the visuals to lead the viewer to the ever more certain hypothesis that the supernatural phenomenon exists. The camera follows her into the laundry room and back to the kitchen where Cole remains seated at the breakfast table. Clearly, there could not have been enough time for Cole to execute this prank, and yet the evidence that it happened is right before our eyes. The camera's continuous pan (as opposed to an edit point) makes this effect even more believable. This is coupled with other visible evidence, such as strange scratches on Cole's arm, that provide further proof of the external reality of the phenomenon. And there is additional photographic proof of Cole's "gift" as we are shown a strange light surrounding Cole in family snapshots. The photographs serve to double the reality effect since the audience not only sees the phenomenon photographed on the big screen but also understands that within the film, photographs provide external, "objective," and documentary evidence. *The Blair Witch Project* (1999) (a low-budget horror film released before *The Sixth Sense*) also relies on this phenomenon, using video cameras within the film to suggest the "documentary" nature of the story.[21] The sound track supplies additional, almost subliminal, confirmation when ghosts are present, providing an aural counterpart to the visuals, as the eerie orchestration occurs at each ghostly visitation.

Once the audience has been encouraged to believe that Cole is not hallucinating, the first step in the hoax has been completed. By hoax I mean the fact that (if the film succeeds) we never suspect that Malcolm is a ghost, and we are just as surprised as he is to learn the truth. Consider yet another series of scenes that are cleverly constructed to be interpreted one way, while supporting an alternate or double reading by the end of the film. Several times throughout the film, Malcolm attempts to enter the cellar. Each time, he is surprised to find that the door has been locked. Each time, the camera cuts away before he is able to find the key and open the door. Since the camera later shows him in the cellar, the audience *infers* that each time he eventually finds his key. This type of inferred cause-and-effect sequence is a mainstay of Hollywood's so-called invisible or continuity editing that can easily collapse time/and or space in order to delete nonessential events. For example, in a sequence in which a person rides an elevator to the top of a skyscraper, a typical shot might begin at the entrance to the elevator and then cut to the character's exit at the top floor. Since the seconds it would actually take to make the journey are probably irrelevant to the story, there is no reason to include them in the film. This type of elliptical editing is so common to viewers that the audience is not likely to question Malcolm's entry into the cellar. It only stands to reason that if he's in the cellar, he must have found the key.

Only later in the movie do we understand that the locked door was actually a clue to Malcolm's ghostly state. The clue works in two ways. First, the audience may wonder why the door is always locked and why we are repeatedly shown his attempts to enter. Since the beginning of the film reveals only wine in the cellar but later features Malcolm's office desk and supplies, a plausible hypothesis is that his strained relationship with his wife has caused him (or her) to move his office to the basement. Exasperated by his repeated neglect and late evenings, perhaps Anna locks the door in his absence before going to bed alone. Upon learning that Malcolm is a ghost, the sequence of scenes yields a totally different meaning. His office has been moved to the basement, not because Anna is angry, but because Malcolm is dead and Anna has stored his unused belongings there. Furthermore, the supposition that Malcolm has obtained the key each time is now proven wrong. He doesn't need a key because ghosts don't need keys. As everyone familiar with ghost stories knows, ghosts go through walls! This long-established tradition in ghost stories dovetails nicely with Hollywood cinema's emphasis on doors as entry points for story action or reversals, and once again shows how the film cleverly conflates conventions from both ghost stories and cinematic traditions.[22]

Editing and camera work also continue to support the tendency of the audience to believe that the story is really only about watching Malcolm uncover the "truth" about Cole's ghosts. For example, when Cole sees people hanging from the gallows in his school corridor, the camera first shows us what Cole sees in order to establish their presence. It then cuts to Malcolm and then away, this time showing an empty stairwell. This sequence follows a standard editing technique that establishes the temporary point of view of a character. The audience understands from this sequence that Malcolm is unable to see the ghosts. We also see a shot of the stairwell from behind the ghosts, and see an "objective" view of Malcolm and Cole looking at the empty hallway. This has the effect of linking Malcolm's perception to "objective reality" rather than to his purely subjective point of view.[23] Indeed, most films use camera work to establish an objective viewpoint for the audience, creating the effect that the audience is eavesdropping on the scene.[24] Although a film may temporarily cut to a subjective perspective, it is understood that that the objective view is the default to which we will always return. The viewer's unquestioning familiarity with this process is essential to the "trick" element of *The Sixth Sense*. And, indeed, it is a trick that has an excellent chance of succeeding precisely because the same editing technique is used by almost every movie the viewer has ever seen.[25]

Because the occurrence of the supernatural is ratified by the camera's objective presence and the internal coherence of the cause-and effect, linear story world, it is not necessary to believe in ghosts in the real world to believe that ghosts are real in a fictional story. In fact, most recent ghost films would be classified by Todorov as "marvelous" (or fantastic/marvelous) for this very reason—the films establish the credibility of the occult world for the viewer and the story proceeds from there. As we have seen, recent movies (including *The Preacher's Wife*, *What Dreams May Come*, *City of Angels*, and *Meet Joe Black*) spend very little time asking the audience to question the plausibility of the supernatural premise, but a lot of time exploring the characters' reaction to it.

The manipulation of subjective and objective reality is also crucial to one of the most important scenes in *The Sixth Sense*. When Malcolm arrives at the restaurant where his wife is celebrating their anniversary alone, the viewer is supposed to understand that Malcolm has once again let his obsession with work interfere with his marriage. His wife is understandably cold and aloof when he finally arrives and apologizes with a stupid joke, "I thought you meant the other Italian restaurant where I asked you to marry me." After this lame attempt at communication and a monologue about his progress with Cole, the waiter brings the bill and Malcolm reaches for it. Anna snatches it up and turns away, muttering sarcastically, "Happy Anniversary." In hindsight, we realize that her aloofness is the result of the fact that she is unaware of his presence. She is celebrating their anniversary alone not because her husband is an insensitive cad, but because her husband is dead. The scene is shot from behind her so that for the better part of the scene we are not shown her face. We aren't given the chance to notice that she is looking past him (or through him) or that she probably looks sad rather than mad. Furthermore, this angle mimics a standard "over-the-shoulder" shot that in Hollywood films is usually taken to be the point of view of the character whose back is to the camera. This standard camera technique once again causes the viewer to infer that Anna can see him and is looking right at him. Of course, if it really were her point of view, then Bruce Willis would not be in the scene at all and, like Malcolm's "reaction shot" of Cole's gallows-ghosts, we would see only an empty space.

The depiction of time is another important element in the film, and its clever manipulation again plays on the viewer's familiarity with cinematic convention. The elliptical editing mentioned earlier explains why audiences probably made inferences regarding the cause and effect relationship between scenes. But this standard editing technique that helps to propel movie narratives along in an efficient cause-and-effect manner, in this film also conceals what would otherwise be a logical flaw in the plot. That is, why doesn't Malcolm notice that no one but Cole interacts with him? Where does he spend his time when he's not with Cole? These are some of the questions that caused some skeptical viewers to find it implausible that Malcolm wouldn't realize that he was ghost. As one viewer put it, all he had to do was try to order food at a McDonalds and he would have been tipped off. However, the movie *does* address this by having Cole explain that ghosts: "live in their own world . . . they don't see each other . . . they only see what they want to see." Malcolm's existence as a ghost is not a linear one but is instead perceptually linked only to those events that are relevant to his particular spiritual dilemma. When Malcolm attempts to explain to Anna why he is obsessed with Cole, he says: "I feel like I'm being given a second chance." Although Malcolm is referring to his ability to help Cole, the scenes with Anna are all crucial for allowing Malcolm to resolve his "real" problem, namely getting a second chance with Anna. By showing scenes with only Cole and selected scenes with Anna, the movie is not, therefore, cheating (as some have suggested). The audience merely experiences the same interludes as Malcolm does. (As Malcolm explains to Anna when he is late for dinner, he has trouble "keeping track of time.") While the intermittent depiction of time is motivated by Malcolm's ghostly state, it also handily mimics the type of selective editing that all films use when they show us only relevant scenes in the life of a character. For this reason, the audience is unlikely to question the selection or omission of scenes outside the main story line. Like Malcolm, viewers end up only seeing what they want to see (or what the movie wants them to see), mainly that Bruce Willis is our screen hero who must rescue the little boy. It probably doesn't occur to most viewers that our hero could be the one in trouble. As with other recent ghost movies featuring a male ghost, there is dramatic value in casting a macho action star in the role of an ineffectual ghost. In other films, such casting provides a handy alibi for audiences to root for an otherwise weak, male protagonist. Here, the familiar technique also serves to distract the audience from the possibility that our rescuer himself needs rescuing.

There are numerous clues that reveal the truth about Malcolm through-out the movie, of course, and once the viewer realizes that Malcolm is dead, they are all too obvious. But there are two bits of anecdotal evidence that also serve as allegorical or metaphorical clues to the nature of the movie. The first is the bedtime story that Malcolm attempts to tell Cole. The story is about a prince who goes on a long drive. He is "driving, driving, driving a lot. . . . They drove so much that he fell asleep. Then he woke up and he realized that they were still driving." Despite the sup-posed ineptitude of the narrative, the story actually reveals Malcolm's lack of progress in his *own* narrative. Like the prince, he is unclear of his final destination and finds himself in a prolonged, repetitive state. He thinks he is awake and is surprised to find that he is still . . . driving. But this scenario would come as no surprise to other film ghosts who suffer long periods of repetitive and ineffectual action before the resolution of their respective narrative goals. Of course, the film takes Cole's advice about storytelling and provides a twist to the story (although not soon enough, according to some viewers).[26]

The "magic trick" that Malcolm shows Cole marks another telling moment in the film. The trick with the penny is a joke that refers to the conventional magician's technique of visually distracting the audience so that they won't know the true whereabouts of the penny. The audience of *The Sixth Sense* is likewise distracted by the visuals and other story ele-ments in this film and therefore doesn't realize the truth. Just as the penny never left Malcolm's hand, neither did the primary event of the movie change (the catalyst for all subsequent action), namely that Malcolm was shot and killed in the first few minutes of the film. The truth has been under our noses the whole time, if only we had been paying attention. Upon a second viewing, the audience realizes what Cole has known all along—that both the penny trick and the film's narrative are, in essence, a joke. The punch line is similar in both cases—we have been driving, driving, driving . . . only to learn that we have, in fact, been taken for the proverbial ride. At the end of the film, the audience finally joins Cole in his precocious perception and gets the joke. In fact, the audience has shared in Cole's extrasensory perception all along without knowing it. For, like Cole, WE see ghosts! We see ghosts because the movie allows us to—otherwise how could we see a movie about a ghost character who is invis-ible to everyone in the movie but Cole?

The cinema is, in this "sense," the true sixth sense. In the real world, people use their five senses to provide them with a sense of day-to-day reality, but this is a world that rarely features ghosts and spirits. Yet we are able to suspend our disbelief and accept the reality of ghosts when watching a movie. The cinema becomes like an extra sense, allowing us to experience and accept the most improbable jumps of space, time, and perspective and to participate in fantastic scenarios. The spectral properties of the cinema are uncanny in their ability to endow the viewer with Cole-like powers of perception. The images flit across the screen like phantoms, their presence evidence of an absence—for like ghosts, the actors are no longer with us. We see, therefore we believe. We don't need to believe in ghosts to believe in the power of movies.

IV. Conclusion

It is true that *The Sixth Sense* derives its fame more from its tricky construction than its love story. However, I hope I have shown that the gimmick owes its success to established conventions that the film exploits and then thwarts to create a powerful effect. To the extent that recent ghost movies require an acceptance of the supernatural, they do so for the same reasons dramatized in the stories they convey. This has less to do with authenticating the world of the occult, and everything to do with engaging a cynical audience in a version of romance that sometimes seems impossible (or at least improbable) in the modern era. Just as the characters must shed cynicism and find their "heart," these films use ghosts and angels as vehicles for engaging the audience in believing in and accepting the possibility of true love. And if, in accepting the most improbable cinematic happenings that cinema allows, the audience simultaneously accepts the romantic message of the movie, then Hollywood combines two of its greatest strengths. Ghost stories and love stories were popular long before the advent of cinema, but both require a willing suspension of disbelief—a goal at the "heart" of Hollywood cinema.

NOTES

1. Although the book focuses on recent films, I also discuss several older films from the thirties and forties such as *The Ghost and Mrs. Muir, Topper, The Bishop's Wife, A Guy Named Joe* (1943), and *The Canterville Ghost* (1944).

2. The plot is further complicated because Joe has made a deal with William Parish, Susan's father. He agrees to keep Parish alive in exchange for being his earthly guide. The extension of life also effectively gives Parish a second chance to express his love for his daughter, thus correcting the guilty-and-distant-father syndrome described below.

3. Through their emphasis on "spirit," most comedy ghost films tend to down-play physical pleasures or horrors. These later films thus represent an interesting new variation. The "food" examples given here all seem to be prerequisites for the pleasures of sex. Both *City of Angels* and *Meet Joe Black* have prolonged sex scenes, and *Michael* features a running gag surrounding his sex appeal. Although we never see him have sex, it is implied that he did on at least two occasions, once with a judge and once with a waitress.

4. The emphasis on "heart" as a metaphor for love and emotional openness is made explicit both in the titles and content of earlier ghost movies such as *Heart Condition* (1990) and *Hearts and Souls* (1993). The metaphorical reference is combined with actual hearts in *Meet Joe Black* in which Death saves William Parish from death by heart attack, in *City of Angels* in which Maggie massages a man's heart during surgery while another patient (a former angel) is being treated for a heart attack, and again in *Heart Condition* in which a heart transplant recipient is haunted by the dead man whose heart he has received.

5. I elaborate on this theme throughout my book *Giving Up the Ghost*. There I use the term "masochistic" to describe this tendency of the male ghost character. I am avoiding that term here since it has complicated psychoanalytic connotations that are not relevant to this discussion.

6. Many recent ghost films are remakes of older films, providing a kind of "second chance" for old Hollywood films.

7. As such, the films appear to be expressing current anxiety about changing gender roles, particularly among men. This thematic aspect also relates directly to the specifically melodramatic emphasis found in many other ghost films, since traditional melodrama concerns not just love and loss, but missed opportunities for communication, often the expression or revelation of love (Doane 91). In addition to the films mentioned here, also see, for example: *Kiss Me Goodbye* (1982), *Heart Condition*, *Made In Heaven* (1987), and *Hearts and Souls*.

8. Furthermore, the title phrase "giving up the ghost" also refers to the way in which the film viewer relinquishes control of the story and willingly suffers with the characters with the understanding that their "destiny" (the film's ending) will be happy.

9. Along with receiving a second chance in heaven, the characters are given the chance to be reborn and fall in love again on earth. Second chances through birth, re-birth, and reincarnation are common motifs in ghost movies. See, for example, *Made in Heaven; Truly, Madly, Deeply; Defending Your Life; Switch* (1991); and *Dead Again* (1991).

10. The boy's name appears to be a thinly disguised reference to Cole's aspect as a "seer" (Sear) and the coldness (Cole) associated with the ghosts. Coldness is associated with ghosts in other films too. See for example, *Truly, Madly, Deeply; Heart Condition;* and *The Haunting* (1963).

11. Malcolm's last name (Crowe) might also be seen as a reference to his position at the end of the film in the sense that one who finds that he is badly mistaken is said to "eat crow." Thanks also to Jeffrey Weinstock for pointing out the possible references to the occultist Malcolm Crowley as well as to the movie *The Crow* (1994).

12. Many recent film ghosts also want to fulfill a goal that their untimely death has

prevented them from achieving. Their efforts to communicate with the living are often appeals for help in resolving their personal narrative goals. As described above, this goal is often either explicitly linked to a second chance at romance or else will be surpassed in importance by a romance.

13. The terms "sleeper" or "surprise hit" were commonly employed in the popular press to characterize the film's unexpected success. (See for example, Davis and Chang and "Sense-ation.")

14. When Molly tells Sam that she loves him, he is unable to reciprocate and is only able to say the word "ditto." This is a point of contention between them before his death.

15. This tendency applies even to films that don't feature actual ghosts but do concern angels and/or the afterlife. See for example *The Preacher's Wife* and even *Switch* (which puts a slightly different spin on the problem but nevertheless features a male character who must atone for his crass behavior toward women). Difficulties in gender go beyond stereotypical gender differences and miscommunications between men and women. In *Giving Up the Ghost*, I employ a psychoanalytic perspective to discuss the inherent instability of gendered identities. Male film ghosts seem to dramatize this instability and highlight a desire to erase gendered differences.

16. Some promotional material even described the film as *Ordinary People* (1980) meets *The Exorcist*.

17. This is a highly debatable prediction (witness the sexually charged vampire stories of Anne Rice).

18. See, for example, Howe and Valenti.

19. This is what Carol Clover calls "dual-focus narratives" a term she applies to occult films that seem to be about a possessed woman, but prove to be more about a male crisis (Clover 70).

20. Internal consistency is crucial to Hollywood films, and audiences will accept quite unbelievable scenarios provided this condition is met.

21. In addition, when ghosts approach Cole, the thermostat provides an objective validation of Cole's shivering response. The use of mechanical instruments is a mainstay of the science-fiction genre, in which computers and electronic gizmos lend scientific credibility to otherwise improbable scenarios. For an excellent analysis of the science fiction genre see Vivian Sobchack's book, *Screening Space*.

22. This is what the film critic Andre Bazin once called "door-knob cinema." Film ghosts routinely call attention to this convention each time they breach it. For an in-depth discussion of this and other Hollywood conventions see: Bordwell, Staiger, and Thompson's *The Classical Hollywood Cinema*.

23. Lynette Carpenter has remarked that this scene recalls a moment in Eisenstein's film *Potemkin* (1925) in which a sailor doomed to die at the gallows sees ghostly figures hanging from the yardarm. It is the only scene in the film that provides the subjective viewpoint of a character by making the hanged figure "invisible" to the viewer. This is an interesting piece of intertextuality, especially considering the fact that Eisenstein is known (along with Vertov, Kuleshov, and others) for his influential and pioneering work in the manipulation of reality through editing techniques.

24. Films routinely use what is called an "establishing shot," a wide shot of the set that orients the viewer's sense of space and the characters and objects within it. All of

the other shots in the scene (close-ups, reverse angles, etc.) are understood merely to provide different views of this same shot.

25. As David Bordwell writes, very few Hollywood films deviate from this convention: "Whereas art-cinema narration can blur the lines separating objective diegetic reality, characters' mental states, and inserted commentary, the classical film asks us to assume clear distinctions among these states. When the classical film restricts knowledge to a character, as in most of *The Big Sleep* (1946) and *Murder My Sweet* (1944), there is nonetheless a firm borderline between subjective and objective depiction" (162).

26. See, for example, McCarthy, and also "Screen."

WORKS CITED

Bordwell, David. *Narration in the Fiction Film.* Madison: University of Wisconsin Press, 1985.

Bordwell, David, Janet Staiger, and Kristin Thompson, eds. *The Classical Hollywood Cinema.* New York: Columbia University Press, 1985.

Clover, Carol. *Men, Women, and Chain Saws: Gender in the Modern Horror Film.* Princeton: Princeton University Press, 1992.

Davis, Alisha, and Yahlin Chang. "Spicy Literature, From 'Sixth Sense' to Sixth Grade." *Newsweek* 134, issue 11 (Sept. 13, 1999): 71.

Doane, Mary Ann. *The Desire to Desire: The Woman's Film of the 1940s.* Bloomington: Indiana University Press, 1987.

Fowkes, Katherine A. *Giving Up the Ghost: Spirits, Ghosts and Angels in Mainstream Comedy Films.* Detroit: Wayne State University Press, 1998.

Howe, Desson. "Death Takes a Holiday: Why Are We Just Dying to See Movies about the Afterlife?" *Washington Post,* August 1990, C3.

Jackson, Rosemary. *Fantasy: The Literature of Subversion.* New York: Methuen, 1981.

Kaminsky, Stuart M. *American Film Genres.* Chicago: Nelson-Hall, 1985.

McCarthy, "The Sixth Sense," *Variety* 375, no. 11. (Aug. 2, 1999): 33.

"Screen." *People Weekly* 52, no. 61. (Aug. 6, 1999): 33.

"Sense-ation: Haley Joel Osment Makes a Large Impact as the Small Medium in the Sixth Sense." *People Weekly* 52, no. 8. (Aug. 30, 1999): 143.

Sobchack, Vivian. *Screening Space: The American Science Fiction Film.* New York: Ungar, 1987.

Todorov, Tzvetan. *The Fantastic: A Structural Approach to a Literary Genre.* Translated Richard Howard. Cleveland: The Press of Case Western Reserve University, 1973.

Valenti, Peter. "The 'Film Blanc': Suggestions for a Variety of Fantasy, 1940–1950," *Journal of Popular Film* 6, no. 4. (Winter 1978): 295.

Stephen King's
Vintage Ghost-Cars

A Modern-Day Haunting

MARY FINDLEY

He could hear the car's engine, suddenly revving up. That horrible, unearthly shrieking of the undercarriage on the cement again. Moochie turned around, panting harshly. Christine was reversing back up the gutter, and as it passed him, he saw. He saw. There was no one behind the wheel.

—*Christine*, 239

They are not made of flesh and bone. They are made of steel, iron, and chrome. They have headlights for eyes, snarling grilles for mouths, and wheels for legs. They are both of this world and detached from it. They represent the past, expose the fears of the present, and proclaim doom for the future. They are not typical of the ghosts that haunt modern-day fiction, television, or film, but they are, indeed, ghosts. Stephen King's vintage ghost-cars, the 1958 Plymouth Fury in *Christine* (1983), and the 1954 Buick Roadmaster in *From a Buick 8* (2002), explore a peculiarly modern kind of haunting: one that examines American individual and collective identity in terms of relationships with cars, and one that examines an alternate history of the automobile—a tarnished one that reveals the destructive power of these mechanized beasts. King's ghost-cars raise frightening questions: Who's driving whom? Are we in control of technology or is technology in control of us? Ultimately, King's spectral automobiles figure the contemporary American fear of spiritual loss in the face of technological advancement.

Make no mistake about it—cars have power. Their power, however, is not measured by horsepower alone but also by the images they project in American culture. Bursting onto the scene in the first decade of the twentieth century, at roughly the same time that the motion picture was invented, cars have left an indelible mark in film, photographs, and advertisements, and on the American psyche. Few things, in fact, are able to conjure up an image of the "American spirit" (both literally and figuratively) as quickly and succinctly as an image of the vintage American automobile. The Ford Model T, the Studebaker President Roadster, the '55 Ford Thunderbird—they represent decades of glamour, decadence, innocence, and raw power. The American love affair with cars speaks to a nation of mobile people. "The heretic who dares to doubt the splendor of these automobiles doubts America itself," says Harvard professor Jonathan Veitch. "And it follows," he continues "in the iron-clad logic with which this country was founded—that if America is called into question, then God's very plans for the world are in jeopardy" (650). Whether spoken ironically or not, Veitch's comment speaks directly to the undeniable love affair and the intimate link between America and its automobiles.

Stephen King may not be privy to God's plans for the world, but he qualifies as a heretic on the basis of Veitch's definition. Perhaps more than any contemporary author, King questions the splendor of America's automobiles and explores their influence on our individual and collective consciousness through novels like *Christine* and *From a Buick 8* and short stories such as "Trucks" (which inspired the cinematic flop *Maximum Overdrive* [1986]) and "Uncle Otto's Truck." The automobile, King suggests, has forged an undeniable link in the chain of our identity, our history, and our future. Like it or not, our cars have become a part of who we are. And King, through his ghostly vintage cars, reminds us that, although the advance of technology holds great promise, it holds great peril as well.

Literary discourse concerning societal fears of technological advancement, which is essentially what King's car stories represent, is not new (see Mary Shelley's *Frankenstein,* for one), but the utilization of the car as the main locus of terror is a recent development. Although fleshy apparitions and supernatural phenomena accompany these stories, the cars themselves perform the physical act of "haunting." In these stories, the cars themselves are the ghosts from the past that reach into and disrupt the present.

I. *Christine*: THE INTERCONNECTEDNESS OF CAR AND IDENTITY

The car suddenly spat an almost feline burst of static.
"Don't worry," Arnie whispered. He ran his hand slowly over the
dashboard, loving the feel of it. Yes, the car frightened him sometimes.
And he supposed his father was right; it had changed his life to some degree.
But he could no more junk it than he could commit suicide.

—*Christine*, 253

In contemporary America, we are what we drive. One's choice of a car speaks volumes about his or her financial and social status, as well as personality. But, as King uncovers in *Christine*, the automobile's influence on our identity has the potential to be immensely destructive.

King's decision to put Arnie Cunningham, a geeky, awkward, high school senior in the driver's seat of a vintage '58 Plymouth Fury—a car whose name alone suggests violence and mayhem—is a suggestive move in itself. What better way to demonstrate the car's power over identity than to turn a stereotypical loser into the popular guy at school? Arnie's relationship with Christine begins as any red-blooded teenager's fascination with newfound freedom and power behind the wheel of a first automobile, but it quickly becomes a frightening, self-sacrificing obsession as the vintage Plymouth he buys from an evil old man named Roland LeBay begins to exhibit abnormal powers. From the moment Arnie sees Christine, beaten and battered in LeBay's yard, his mind is under her control. "I saw that car—and I felt such an attraction to it[. . .]. I can't explain it very well even to myself," he says (29).

In the beginning, Christine acts as a catalyst that transforms Arnie from a stereotypical high school nerd into one of the most popular guys at school. With the strength and freedom he equates with not only having his own car but having Christine in particular, he gains confidence, and stands on his own against his overbearing parents and a handful of dime-a-dozen school bullies. He even lands the hot new girl in school, Leigh Cabot, a feat attributed to Arnie's new image—an image brought about mainly by Christine.

Christine not only represents independence and freedom for Arnie, she offers strength, status, power, and control. She is an outward symbol of what Arnie wants—acceptance and a respected position in the hierarchy of secondary education. For the first time, Arnie believes he is in control of his life and life is finally going his way—but this merely shadows the truth. On the inside, an emotional and psychological storm is brewing. Arnie's soul is being taken over by Christine. While behind the wheel, he views life through her "eyes" that distort reality and take Arnie back to the pristine world of 1950s America. His view of the world, and his place in it, are obscured. She acts as a selfish lover, slowly draining his psychological, emotional, and financial bank accounts by placing demands on his time and energy. His life revolves around her as he spends countless hours in Will Darnell's garage puttering her into perfection.

It soon becomes overtly apparent that Christine is not just a car—she is an "other." She hovers in the vampirical realm of the undead. Her mechanical rendering and lack of a physical body and/or soul categorize her as the dead, the inanimate, but she is clearly alive, possessed with powers beyond the realm of human understanding. She is, in fact, a ghost—an entity from the past, the 1950s, that has come to haunt Arnie's world of the present—the 1970s. Like all ghosts, she escapes the passage of time. Her odometer runs backward and she regenerates, much like the infamous, indestructible Freddy Kruger of the *Nightmare on Elm Street* movies. Christine doesn't die.

To the naked eye, Christine is nothing but a vintage car, but she has the ability to think, monopolize, destroy, kill, and possess. She is the ultimate killing machine and Arnie is her pawn. Though he physically drives Christine, her psychological hold over him clearly puts her in the "driver's seat." She dictates how Arnie will spend his time, who he will date, and, most importantly, who will pay for wrongs done to the both of them. Her hold over his identity is unparalleled. While leading him to believe that she has acted as a positive influence in his life by elevating his social status and giving him a sense of self-confidence, the reader comes to understand that she has really done nothing of the sort. She has instead made Arnie a slave to her will. She ruthlessly murders the bullies that defile them both, and, in a fit of jealous rage, attempts to murder his girlfriend Leigh, breaking the lover's triangle. Once away from Arnie, Leigh voices her suspicions about Christine—suspicions the reader knows are correct: "I think that somehow that car is alive," she says. "More alive every day. I think it's some kind of horrible vampire, only it's taking Arnie's mind to feed itself. His mind and his spirit" (278).

As Arnie's obsession with Christine grows, his relationships with his parents and his only friend, Dennis, deteriorate. Everything that once held meaning for him is replaced by Christine. She becomes his focus, and her power over him becomes absolute. She not only drains his energy, she transforms him into her first owner, and/or lover, Roland LeBay, in an effort to recapture that once-perfect first love. The loss of identity suffered by Arnie should presumably be something of which he is acutely aware, but, as Dennis states, he is oblivious to his transformation. Dennis recollects, "The car, the car, the car, that's all he could talk about. He was starting to sound like a broken record. And, worse, it was always her, her, her. He was bright enough to see his growing obsession with her—it, damn it, it—but he wasn't picking it up. He wasn't picking it up at all" (80).

If contemporary American culture is viewed through the lens of King's car-owner relationship as illustrated in *Christine,* it is possible to see the detrimental relationships that Americans have with their automobiles. Often unable to pay in full for these mechanized modes of transportation, Americans become slaves to monthly car payments, not to mention the plethora of expenses that go along with car ownership—insurance, maintenance expenses, gasoline, and all too often, with accidents, the expense of hospital bills, as well as physical, emotional, and psychological pain. Car owners are tied to their vehicles by unseen financial chains, but contemporary American existence obscures these disadvantages, and what was once a luxury item has become a necessity as more and more people find the hassle and lack of public transportation prohibitive.

The hold that vehicles have over contemporary Americans is not as threatening as Christine's hold over Arnie, but cars can be viewed as providing a false sense of security, power, and freedom on both individual and collective levels. As King points out, the individual freedom, power, and dependence we believe cars offer is nothing more than a smoke screen—a well-marketed image that has been ingrained in the collective American psyche. What we believe cars represent, according to King, is not the whole picture, and his vintage ghost-cars come back to speak the truth we're unwilling to accept. Comparable to the ghost of Hamlet's father, who represents the voice of truth in a world of deceit, King's mechanized ghosts force us to step beyond the illusion we've created and recognize that technology breathes a life of its own—a life that is powerful and potentially fatal.

II. Behind the Mirror: History Reinvented

We went back in time, I have said, but did we? The present-day streets of
Libertyville were like a thin overlay of film—it was as if the Libertyville of the
late 1970s had been drawn on Saran Wrap and laid over a time that was
somehow more real, and I could feel that time reaching its dead hands out
towards us, trying to catch us and draw us in forever.

—*Christine,* 416–17

If one lesson is to be learned from Christine's ghostly rage it is this: There
is an alternate history at work here. There is a darker image to what the
car represents—one that overshadows the car as power, status, and the all-
things-desirable image embedded in our collective psyche. Using the vintage car as, literally, his vehicle, King points a finger at the past and drags
it into the future, blurring the distinction between the two. Vintage cars,
and the glamorous image that they project of the decades that they represent, are shown to have a dark side, one that represents death, destruction,
and chaos.

King, it seems, is mindful of the fact that the image-driven society in
which we live paints a one-dimensional picture of what the vintage car
represents. Our nation's historical landscape is teeming with cars that
symbolize the decadence of the past. As mentioned earlier, the automobile
and the motion picture industry both celebrated their births during the
early part of the twentieth century and have been inseparable from the
start. Since its beginning, we have been fooled into believing that the car
represents all that is good in the world. "Along with the female face, the
cigarette and the gun, the car became one of the great, glamorous things
that somehow works as an object of fantasy and desire on the big screen
in the dark" (French xxiv).

The car's glamorous image may have begun on the silver screen but it
was certainly not confined to the darkness of the movie theater. It soon
became obvious that as moviegoers walked out of the theaters and into the
streets, this image of car-as-glamour went with them. The image of James
Dean, for example, personified the idea of youth struggling to be heard,
of young people longing to find a place in the world. But the minute he
purchased a 1955 silver Porsche Spyder—a racing car he nicknamed "The
Little Bastard"—the power and masculinity of Dean's image was magni-
fied. His decision to team up with the 1955 silver Porsche Spyder showed
the world that it truly was possible to have it all—youth, fame, power, and

speed. From our contemporary perspective, it's as if the photograph of Dean standing beside his Porsche naturally represents an era of innocence and good—and the fact that Dean was killed while embracing the power of that car hardly tarnishes the symbolic meaning that the conjoined image of the two have come to represent. The outward projection of power, perfection, and greatness, in other words, supercedes the truth behind the story—that both Dean and his Porsche ended up a mangled, twisted mess along a hot, dusty road in California. Veitch emphasizes the spiritual fulfillment that automobiles seem to afford when he claims that "the automobiles of the 1950s have been regarded with a reverence that represents a pagan adulation of machinery, with actor James Dean [. . .] fulfilling the role of martyr" (650). And it is just this sort of nostalgic reverence surrounding automobiles that King's intentional use of vintage cars as ghosts of the past interrogates. Through King's ghostly cars, he examines the scratches and dents beneath the familiar historical representation of the "good ol' days."

Christine may be a vintage car in mint condition but she is also a violent, destructive killing machine. The deaths she deals out are not quick and easy, but brutal, painful, prolonged, and often messy, as she pins people in her headlights, smashes into them full force, runs them over, or forces them (through her supernatural powers) into a prolonged death by choking. Among her victims are a small girl, a troop of school bullies, a police detective, a garage owner, Arnie's parents, and, ultimately, Arnie himself. Not only does she kill but she also claims her victims, sentencing them to an eternal death ride trapped in her cab. Her victims become the unwilling passengers and coconspirators in future killings—and their rotting corpses more than offset her outward image of vintage perfection. Though she is able to regenerate, popping out dents, fixing cracked windshields, erasing scratches, inflating tires, and regrowing antennas, her glamorous image is defiled by the deaths she perpetrates and by the presence of her victims in the cab. She feeds off them like a vampire feeding off its victims. King connects something here that automotive marketers have known, and capitalized on, for years—that cars and violence go hand in hand:

[T]he very names Detroit managers gave to their cars reveal quite plainly the industry's appeal to motives of violence and aggression. Consider the Oldsmobile Cutlass, the Buick Le Sabre, the Plymouth Fury, the Plymouth Barracuda, the Chevrolet Corvette Stingray, the Ford Mustang Cobra, the

American Motors Matador, the Mercury Lynx, the Mercury Bobcat, and Mercury Cougar—killers all[. . .]. The theme of violence in these names has a cunning economic logic behind it. As we now know, Detroit management's guiding theology during the postwar era was: big car, big profit, small car, small profit. And what better way to sell big, powerful cars than to link them in the public's mind with the libidinal release of destructive impulses. (Blumberg 12)

As consumers, we are so inundated by the image of the automobile symbolizing glamour, status, and power that we are rendered impervious to the truth beneath that power, even when it is made painfully obvious. Cars are deadly. King's haunted cars issue a wake-up call to the car-buying public, revealing the dark, ugly side to technological progress. The destructive, unconscionable behavior of Christine reminds us that automobiles— and, by extension, the 1950s—also represent violence, death, and destruction. King reminds the reader that the decade that gave America poodle skirts, Elvis, and "Mr. Sandman" also brought the Korean War, McCarthy's Communist witch-hunt, the construction of the hydrogen bomb, and the launching of the first nuclear submarine.

III. *From a Buick 8*: A TECHNOLOGICAL COEXISTENCE

The imitation lives we see on TV and in the movies whisper the idea that human existence consists of revelations and abrupt changes of heart; by the time we've reached full adulthood, I think, this is an idea we have on some level come to accept. Such things may happen from time to time, but I think that for the most part it's a lie. Life's changes come slowly.

—*From a Buick 8*, 307

If *Christine* explores the interconnectedness of cars and identity and offers an alternate interpretation of the car-as-glamour facade permeating our modern media, then King's *From a Buick 8* drives home the final point, at our apex of fear—that technology is careening out of control. There is no escaping the fact that technological advancement has brought with it all manner of disadvantages. Cars, computers, cell phones, and other technological gadgets we once believed would make our lives less complicated have burrowed into the fabric of our lives. Humankind, King seems to say, no longer holds dominion over machine, but is forced into coexistence with it at best, or subordination to it at worst. King adapts the traditional ghost story to reflect the changing world around us and the pervasive sense of technology out of control. His ghosts, in fact, become technological constructs with apocalyptic overtones.

An obvious difference between *Christine,* published in the twentieth century, and *From a Buick 8,* published in the twenty-first century, is King's treatment of control over technology. In *From a Buick 8,* members of the state police in Pennsylvania's Troop D come into possession of an abandoned vintage '54 Buick Roadmaster that soon proves to have other-worldly powers. Troop D, however, is largely spared from the gruesome, violent deaths inherent in *Christine* because, unlike Arnie, these twenty-first-century warriors connect the dots and respect the Roadmaster's obvious power—a connection Arnie is never able to make, and one that King's audience may not have been willing to accept in 1983, but is perhaps more willing to accept in 2003. King's new ghost-car in *From a Buick 8* is a powerful force that must be respected and revered, not harnessed, controlled, and destroyed, like Christine. The locus of control clearly lies with the Buick and, at best, coexistence is the only option for King's police force.

While Christine represents a dangerous poltergeist in the throes of raw and destructive adolescent power, King's Buick Roadmaster presents the flip side of a technological ghost twenty years in the making—one that has matured and come into its own power in the modern world of technological acceptance. The ghostly Buick Roadmaster exudes a calm reserve—an understanding that its power comes not from what it does, but from what it represents, a conduit into another world, a dimension of raw power with the potential for the destruction of humanity. The spectral Buick in *From a Buick 8* is so powerful that exorcism is not even an option for the humans within its haunted realm. They cannot escape the power of this ghost. The best course of action they can pursue is not to disturb it and, if they do, to tread lightly in its path. This ghost is too real and speaks a truth too powerful to ignore—technology cannot be avoided and must be respected, but it is dangerously close to careening out of our immediate control.

From a Buick 8 represents not only King's coming-of-age story for his vintage ghost-cars but also can be considered a more general commentary on modern technology. Unlike *Christine,* which joins a teenage loser in a one-sided relationship with a ghost-car, King purposely pits his ghostly Buick Roadmaster against a group of characters that epitomizes the apex of authority and control—state troopers. A far cry from the powerless, teenage Arnie in *Christine,* these characters have little to gain from owning a vintage Buick. They already have status, authority, power, and control. Instead of proclaiming one side stronger than the other, King's twenty-first-century novel puts his human characters on an even playing field with his spectral technological construct.

Responding to a routine call, Pennsylvania State Troopers Curtis Wilcox and Ennis Rafferty arrive to find what they believe is a mint-condition '54 Buick Roadmaster abandoned at a local gas station. What they discover begins for them, and the rest of the troopers of Troop D, a prolonged co-existence with a piece of high-performance, otherworldly machinery whose power they cannot harness and do not understand. The workings of the car, which was driven into the station and abandoned by a mysterious (possibly not-of-this-world) man, defy logical explanation. It has an engine but "it's all wrong. There are eight plugs, four on each side and that's right—eight cylinders, eight sparkplugs—but there's no distributor cap and no distributor [. . . ,] no alternator either" (39). The car also contains a battery with no cables, an empty radiator, an ignition key that is nothing more than a long piece of metal, dashboard controls that are fake, an exhaust system made of glass, and no glove compartment (39–41). King's vintage Buick, we soon learn, not only has a mind of its own, like Christine, but a *life* of its own that eludes human understanding. Like Victor Frankenstein's patched-together monster, the Buick that should not be able to run exhibits unmistakable signs of life when the troopers secretly house it indefinitely in Shed B behind the barracks. "From where we sat on the smokers' bench," explains Sandy Dearborn, one of King's many trooper-narrators, "We could see bright, soundless explosions of light going off inside [the shed]. The row of windows in the roll-up door would be as black as pitch, and then they'd turn blue-white. And with each flash, I know the radio in dispatch would give out another bray of static" (73). These lightshows not only symbolize the Buick's unharnessed power but portend a power beyond humankind's control. Once again, the image of the vintage car serves as nothing more than a smoke screen for something else. In this case, it represents a technological ghost from the past that has emerged into the present to issue a warning to society's protectors—a warning that a dangerous storm is coming if technological advancement is not kept under control.

As with Arnie (minus the love angle), Wilcox soon becomes obsessed with the Buick and quickly claims guardianship over it. It is important to note, however, that Wilcox is aware of his obsession, which limits the control it might otherwise have over him. It is equally important to point out that Wilcox's guardianship over the Buick is a more mature guardianship than Arnie's ownership of Christine. Unlike Arnie, Wilcox understands and respects the car's power, hence, he is safe from the kind of blinding psychological spell that claims Arnie's body and soul. Although he and other members of Troop D fall under a temporary spell when in direct contact with the Buick, it is never long-lasting and they are always aware of its power. "In the twenty-odd years that followed that day, he would go inside Shed B dozens of times," Dearborn explains, "[b]ut never without the rise of that dark mental wave, never without the intuition of almost-glimpsed horrors, of abominations in the corner of the eye" (65). It's as if King is giving his characters credit for understanding and acknowledging the psychological hold technology has over them. Once that hold is understood, its power dissipates to a certain extent. He is, however, also clear in his assertion that the Buick symbolizes a questionable future as it offers "almost-glimpsed horrors of abominations in the corner of the eye."

That the Buick stands on its own as a ghost is also not at question here. Unlike *Christine*, in which King never really acknowledges Christine's evil beginnings but leaves it up to the reader to ascertain the cause of the car's haunting presence, he lays the cards on the table with the Buick. It is definitely a "shadowy third" from another dimension, one that is neither of this world nor detached from it. "If your Dad believed anything," a trooper tells Curt Wilcox's son Ned, "It was that yonder machine came from some other dimension" (149). With that said, the question remains: What message does this ghost bring? Even though Wilcox dies as a result of his protection of the Buick, he assumed his role willingly with the hope of unraveling the car's mystery and understanding its power. Without this understanding, he knows that the Buick can destroy not only Troop D but possibly the world as well. Unfortunately, after years of safeguarding the Buick, Wilcox is killed while stopping a truck in the line of duty (a death that is quite brutal but not necessarily linked to the Buick), and he never solves the mystery of the Buick's power. However, his teenage son, Ned, soon shows up at Troop D to volunteer and, more importantly, to learn about his father. As he is told the story of the Buick, it becomes clear that Wilcox, and the rest of Troop D, have kept the Buick's existence a secret. They have chosen to watch it, guard it, and coexist with it in order better to grasp its destructive ability. The Buick's representation as an otherworldly visitor is clear, and King's decision to keep his characters safe from lasting psychological harm offers hope in the face of our collective fear of technology gone crazy.

Offsetting this hopefulness, however, is the unsettling progeny of the Buick. King's vintage vehicle spews forth vile creatures and strange items from its trunk in a birth-like compulsion that portends the future mutation of humanity in a world dominated by technology—a world so distant from fulfilling spirituality that it is projected as robotic, foreign, and cold. A dead bat-like creature whose "face seemed to peel back, revealing a dead and glassy eye that looked as big as a factory ball bearing" (112), strange leaflike items that are "smooth and soft, but in a bad way" (153), flowers as "pallid as the palms of a corpse" (221), and a "thin and wrinkled yellow nightmare with a head that wasn't really a head at all but a loose tangle of pink cords" (261) find their way into the shed.

However, unwilling to kill the messenger and unable to destroy its power, the troopers engage in an uneasy coexistence with the Buick and attempt to understand the extent of its power and define the degree of human power, if any, that they have over it. Wilcox carefully dissects the bat-like creature, only to be faced with its rapid decomposition. Before the creature fully decomposes, however, he is given a glimpse of a number of "rough black pellets [. . .] wrapped in a swaddle of gray membrane" (169). Each pellet has a blankly staring eye and resembles the future of a mutated generation of creatures.

With his haunted Buick, which is similar to Christine in the fact that it is a car-ghost with powers beyond explanation, King takes a more rational, more mature look at our interaction with technological inventions. There is no snarling grille or instances of death in which humans are overtly pulverized in jealous fits of rage. It's as if King is saying that we've made an uneasy peace with the fact that cars, and technology more generally, are here to stay. The 1980s technological explosion of computers and endless computerized gadgetry (especially pertaining to cars) has defined our way of life, and we have adjusted. We are more rational and less reactive to this age of technology that is undeniably here to stay, but now what? Our decision to live with it does not dismiss the mounting anxiety and fear interwoven with this forced and unnatural state of coexistence. The looming question posited in the beginning of this essay still remains in *From a Buick 8*: Who's driving whom? King's entire point in the text seems to be to grapple with this question. Yes, King seems to say, Americans are no longer exhibiting the raw, reactive fear of two decades ago—as shown by the respect the law enforcement officers of Troop D give the Buick—but the fear is still there, enmeshed within the American psyche.

More than anything, King's haunted Buick—which is referred to throughout the story as a possible conduit into another world—represents the dangerous precipice of contemporary technology. We are aware of its position and importance in our world, our dependence on it for our existence, and our powerlessness to stop it. Dearborn, King's predominant narrative voice in *From a Buick 8,* puts it perfectly: "The Buick wasn't about what you knew, but what you didn't" (94). King reminds us that we don't know the full power of the technological beasts we have created—we can only hope they don't claim our humanity.

IV. The End of the Road

There are moments in life that don't matter and moments that do and some—maybe a dozen—when everything is on a hinge.

—*From a Buick 8,* 208

King's ghost-cars speak volumes about contemporary American society. Our world is, indeed, "on a hinge"—the hinge of a technological takeover that supersedes the importance of human touch, understanding, and spirituality. The fact that King's ghost-cars are technological constructs underlies the undeniable presence of technology in our physical world and our collective psyche. The birth of the automobile literally changed the American landscape, covering the green grass with the black tar of technology; and our reliance on our vehicles, and technology in general, has spawned a society at once technologically advanced and individually independent while collectively dependent on oil-producing countries. King explores this complex connection between vehicle, owner, and identity by showing how the lines between them blur. The Arnie Cunningham who was at peace and able to live with others in the world elevates his status and is more socially acceptable on an outward level behind the wheel of Christine—but he self-destructs. What lies behind the car's image of freedom, power, and control is revealed by King to be a harried tale of dependence and false identity.

King's ghost-cars capture the essence of our changing relationship with technology, from the hormonal excitement of journeying into new dimensions, to a cautious reserve highlighting the deliberate coexistence that we embrace with it as we stand on the brink of an uncertain future. His vintage-ghost-car novels, it seems, are as yet unfinished. This series should be a trilogy: We know what happened at the beginning, we know where we are now, but where will we end up? King himself seems unsure of the final destination. "I think the fireworks are over," Ned Wilcox tells Sandy Dearborn about the Buick's power at the end of *From a Buick 8*. "I think we're going to hear one last big steel clank and then you can take the pieces to the crusher." "Are you sure?" Dearborn asks. "Nah," he said, and smiled. "You *can't* be sure" (351). Perhaps the good news is that we are now able to recognize the unbridled power of technology and recognize our responsibility to harness that power before it careens out of control, but the question remains: Will we? "I turned back to my own window, cupping my hands to the sides of my face to cut the glare," Dearborn says. "I peered in at the thing that looked like a Buick Roadmaster 8. The kid was absolutely right. Sooner or later . . ." (351).

WORKS CITED

Blumberg, Paul. "Snarling Cars: How an Industry Undid Itself." *The New Republic* 188 (1983): 12.
Edmundson, Mark. *Nightmare on Main Street: Angels, Sadomasochism, and the Culture of the Gothic.* Cambridge: Harvard University Press, 1997.
French, Sean. "An Open Road and a Silver Screen." *New Statesman* 127 (1998): xxiv.
King, Stephen. *Christine.* New York: Signet, 1983.
———. *From a Buick 8.* New York: Scribner, 2002.
Naisbitt, John. *Megatrends 2000.* New York: William Morrow, 1990.
Veitch, Jonathan. "Angels of the Assembly Line: The Dream Machines of the Fifties." *Southwest Review* 79 (1994): 650–51.

Ghosting HIV/AIDS

Haunting Words and Apparitional Bodies in Michelle Cliff's "Bodies of Water"

DIANA M. DAVIDSON

Organized political responses to the American HIV/AIDS phenomenon, and literary representations of the epidemic demand that we examine cultural constructions of gendered and sexualized bodies. In the more than twenty years since HIV/AIDS was first written about in the June 6, 1981, edition of the *San Francisco Chronicle* as "a pneumonia that strikes gay males," AIDS, and later HIV, materialized in American culture in specific bodies (Associated Press 4). In 1981 the Atlanta Centers for Disease Control (CDC) divided AIDS/ARC (AIDS Related Complex) patients into the "Four H's": homosexual men, heroin users, hemophiliacs, and Haitians (see Shilts 197). While this early categorization was quickly abandoned in favor of HIV risk-assessment models that focus on one's behavior as opposed to identity, AIDS has nevertheless materialized in Western culture within specific bodies viewed as "other." HIV/AIDS has been seen as a disease of a gay male body, a disease of an intravenous drug-using body, a disease originating in a black Caribbean and/or African body, and as a disease of a prostituted or promiscuous body. HIV/AIDS has also been constructed as a plague threatening the conservative body politic, a sickness threatening the body of the family, and an illness decimating the body of urban youth. Both individual cultural critics, like those quoted in this essay, and communities, like the founders and contributors to the AIDS Quilt NAMES Project, testify and try to alert their readers and viewers to the ways in which HIV/AIDS is also a disease of abject, absent, silenced, and forgotten bodies. The language used in popular American culture to talk about HIV/AIDS can "ghost" people living with the syndrome. "Ghosting" makes bodies and words absent but also ensures them a haunting presence. This short essay investigates the trope of "ghosting" or apparitionality in Michelle Cliff's 1990 short story "Bodies of Water." Cliff's narrative exposes how the body of a person living with AIDS can be culturally "ghosted," or made to disappear. "Bodies of Water" also uses the figure of the ghost as a catalyst; apparitional presences become sites through which the story's characters relate to the world around them and to one another. Cliff's trope of "ghosting" in her AIDS narrative demonstrates how the use of language can have significant political and personal repercussions for people's material and spiritual existences.

While the idea of a ghost may seem familiar and obvious to most readers, it is worth noting that the definition of a ghost is multiple and fluid. Ghosts disappear and appear in many forms. The *New Oxford Dictionary of English* defines a "ghost" as:

> 1. An apparition of a dead person which is believed to appear or become manifest to the living, typically as a nebulous image. 2. Appearing or manifesting but not actually existing. 3. A faint trace of something. 4. A spirit or soul. (771)

"Ghostly" is further defined as: "pertaining to the spirit or soul; spiritual. Opposite to *bodily* or *fleshly*; occas. to *natural*" (771). In "Bodies of Water," Cliff uses the trope of apparitionality as a rhetorical device with which to write about ghosts and AIDS and a constellation of issues surrounding both.[1] Cliff's story features both literal and symbolic phantoms. Memories haunt characters, characters see ghosts, certain words are absent, unwritten words hover over written words like specters, and characters describe their own experiences and existences through the trope of apparitionality. Cliff's narrative constructs the character Bill as someone to be remembered and his sister Jess as someone to do the remembering. Jess narrates her recollections of Bill's youth, and, in particular, his struggle within their family to control readings of his homosexual identity. Through Jess and Bill's exchange of letters, we learn that Bill is suffering from unnamed illnesses that we can decode to be late-stage AIDS. The construction of Bill as a memory, the fact that we learn about him through Jess, and the absence of his body in the narrative lead us to read him as ghostlike. This essay asks why HIV/AIDS is defined in Cliff's story by absence and makes connections between the physical absence of gay bodies and bodies-affected-by-AIDS and the story's gesture that these "queer" aspects—homosexuality and AIDS—are unnameable secrets that are spoken and written about in codes and coverings.[2] The trope of apparitionality raises a constellation of linguistic and social issues: how the ghosting of bodies in language reflects and/or contributes to the ghosting of material bodies within a culture, how the story uses and questions a cultural understanding of homosexuality as illness, how the refusal to name and specify either AIDS or homosexuality can be read as both reactionary and revisionary, how the female body is ghosted in the Western AIDS phenomenon, and how writing about AIDS positions itself as activist.[3] Ghosts, both literal and symbolic, become a way for the characters and narrative in "Bodies of Water" to discuss sexuality, cultural oppression, death, dying, and AIDS.

Until the development of protease-inhibitor drug therapies in 1996, AIDS-related illnesses had a high fatality rate. The person and body with AIDS were viewed as occupying a space between life and death; in other words, a person with AIDS was viewed as a living ghost. Partly because of its associations with death, HIV/AIDS itself is often constructed in popular discourse as "haunting" and "ghostly." In an April 18, 1983, "AIDS Epidemic" report in *Newsweek*, Vincent Coppola wrote that "ironically, the freedom, the promiscuity, the hyper masculinity that many gays declared an integral part of their culture have come to *haunt* them" (80, italics mine). Even in the optimistic piece "When Plagues End," which appeared in the November 18, 1996, edition of *New York Times Magazine*, Andrew Sullivan described his HIV diagnosis as an "experience [that] can never be erased. Blurred, perhaps, and distanced, but never gone for good" (62). Rhetoric of ghosts and haunting creates a mournful and frightening tone in AIDS discourse. Words like "haunt" and phrases like "never be erased" gesture toward a reading of HIV/AIDS as both macabre and ever-present in recent American consciousness.

However, the representation of HIV/AIDS and the HIV/AIDS-affected body as a ghost and/or as a ghostlike memory in journalism and literature must be read as more than a linguistic reflection of death or haunting. Spectral representations of HIV/AIDS in writing signal that there is no linguistic space wherein the material, living HIV+ body can fit into the "symbolic hegemony," to use Judith Butler's phrase, of American culture (16). The exclusion of the HIV+ body from this "symbolic hegemony" can be attributed to the fact that the HIV+/AIDS-affected body is not only diseased, but it is "other." We can read an HIV+/AIDS affected body as "other" in multiple ways. The cultural memory and perception of HIV/AIDS as a "gay disease" is still apparent in many of the ways in which HIV/AIDS is figured in popular culture, scientific study, activism, and art. Homosexuality is still viewed as "other" in many public discourses. Furthermore, any body that is HIV+ is ascribed a new and potentially threatening sexuality because it is viewed as polluted and contagious. The HIV+ body is seen as "other" in the sense that it is seen as outside the "norm." The HIV+ body and/or AIDS-affected body is "other" when it is viewed as a "living ghost," or a body so near to death that it is distinguished from the normal realm of the living. All of these readings of the HIV+ body and AIDS-affected body as "other" are present in "Bodies of Water." The character Bill, who is a gay man with HIV/AIDS, is written about as if he is a phantom, he is remembered by his sister Jess as if he is a ghost, and he even positions himself (in his letters) as apparitional. The narrative never specifies if Bill is living or dead at the time of the story, and we can read his temporal limbo between the present and the afterlife as nothing if not ghostlike. While Bill's apparitional status could be read as a linear narrative event— Bill is gay, Bill has AIDS, Bill dies, and Bill becomes a ghost because he dies a tragic death—Cliff's use of apparitionality is more complicated, and more political, than it may initially appear.

Cliff introduces ghosts and the trope of ghosting before she introduces us to Bill or opens up possible readings of AIDS. "Bodies of Water" is a story that begins and concludes around ghosts. The narrative first connects ghosts to readings of female and, specifically, lesbian identity. The first paragraph describes a mystical and apparitional old woman sitting in the center of a lake, "singing to bring in the fish" (Section I, 121). As the older woman sings, "mist escapes her mouth" and her voice can be "caught in the winter light" (I, 121). A younger woman watches the older woman on the lake and "the younger woman fancies a shape, not able to make it out, the wind swirls it so" (I, 126). The ethereal opening description of the older woman is soon connected with her "queerness." The older woman recalls how her niece "had erupted most recently when another old woman died, and her aunt was named—for all the world to read—in the weeklies and dailies of the valley as the 'sole survivor'" (I, 124), to which the niece's husband assured her "any reasonable person will see for what it is[. . .]. Two old maids. That's all" (124). Cliff's opening immediately establishes the older woman's lesbian relationship and identity as unseeable, as "any reasonable person will see [. . .] it" for precisely what it is not. If one refuses to see something, one essentially "ghosts" it, as one makes it "an unsubstantial image; hence, a slight trace or vestige" (*Oxford English*

Dictionary 791). Not only does the narrative ghost the older woman's lesbian relationship but also, by representing the older woman's relationship with "it," the story establishes homosexuality as unnameable.

Cliff's opening description of the ghostlike older woman on the lake establishes gay identity as spectral, and this association becomes crucial to readings of HIV/AIDS in the story. However, the idea that a lesbian identity is spectral is not unique to Cliff's story; Terry Castle argues it is well established in Western and specifically American literature and culture. In the introduction to *The Apparitional Lesbian*, Castle writes:

> When it comes to lesbians—or so I argue in the following chapters—many people have trouble seeing what's in front of them. The lesbian remains a kind of "ghost effect" in the cinema world of modern life: elusive, vaporous, difficult to spot—even when she is there, in plain view, mortal and magnificent, at the center of the screen. Some may deny she exists at all[. . .]. The lesbian is never with us, it seems, but always somewhere else: in the shadows, in the margins, hidden from history, out of sight, out of mind, a wanderer in the dusk, a lost soul, a tragic mistake, a pale denizen of the night. She is far away and she is dire. (2)

It is possible to see how "queer" bodies could be represented as ghosts in a culture in which the white male heterosexual body has been made the "norm." If "queer" bodies are made absent and apparitional, then they do not have to be acknowledged, respected, or given a place within a "symbolic" or practiced hegemony. The representation of the older woman as ghostlike forces us to ask why there is not more cultural space for "queer" bodies and to wonder why certain bodies are seen and others are only glimpsed within the space of a "symbolic hegemony."

While "Bodies of Water" gestures us toward a Castle-like reading of an apparitional lesbian in the first section of the story, the narrative also introduces the ambiguity of an apparition's absence-but-presence. The narrative assures us that this older woman, who we can read as an apparitional lesbian, is also corporeal. She drinks "whiskey-laced tea" that she pours on the ice for the ghosts in the lake and "she is fighting sleep" (I, 126). Apparitions do not drink tea and they do not need sleep, so the woman's hunger and fatigue establish her as embodied. Just as the older woman's drinking and sleeping establish her as embodied, so, too, does her fear of being institutionalized. The older woman describes a retirement home her niece wants to send her to as "a room (shared with a stranger,

strangers) where she would be spoon-fed—everything mashed beyond
texture or recognition. Probably tied to her bed by night, her chair by day.
Where the stench of urine would be as unrelenting as a bank of lilac in
bloom" (124). Specifically, the older woman knows that if she is institutionalized, she will lose control over the place of her body: She will be
"tied to her bed by night, her chair by day." She also fears losing control
of her bodily boundaries: She fears what will enter her body (unrecogniz-
able food) and what will exit and surround her body (the stench of urine).
There are connections between the older woman's observation of life in
an institution as a loss of bodily control and the loss of bodily control associated with HIV/AIDS. Boundaries, and particularly, the fear about crossing boundaries, are useful when thinking about what HIV/AIDS means
to both individual and collective bodies.

If, as Butler outlines in her preface to *Bodies That Matter* "not only [do]
bodies tend to indicate a world beyond themselves, but this movement
beyond their own boundaries, a movement of boundary itself, appears to
be quite central to what bodies 'are'" (ix), then we may interrogate how
these boundaries are defined when applied to bodies affected by HIV/
AIDS. In American culture, HIV/AIDS is constructed in terms of boundaries: We distinguish between which bodies are and are not at risk for HIV
infection, we are obsessed with how to create barriers between infected
and noninfected bodies to prevent transmission and control contagion,
we limit sexual activities and assess them as "safe" and "unsafe," and we
draw boundaries to distinguish different levels of HIV/AIDS infection
(window period, HIV+ status, asymptomatic and symptomatic HIV, full-
blown AIDS, post-protease AIDS, and end-stage AIDS). Boundaries are
often determined and crossed by fluids and, hence, HIV/AIDS is talked
about in terms of fluidity. HIV transmission and prevention are talked
about in terms of bodily fluids, HIV infection is determined by the presence of antibodies in a sample of blood, and the health of HIV+ people is
often determined by the presence of T cells in the blood. Keeping in mind
the complex relationship HIV/AIDS has with boundaries and fluidity, it
is crucial to explore how the lake and sexuality are connected in "Bodies
of Water."

The title and opening section of Cliff's story use fluidity as a metaphor
for human sexuality. The story establishes sexuality as natural, secretive,
and ever changing or mutable. We are told that Jess is "drawn to lakes, yet
afraid of water" as she remembers how at "twelve, or thirteen" the water
"lap[ed] at her and the black snakes of a mountain lake whisper[ed] past

her[. . .]. Hard black waterbugs play[ed] around her legs. That is the picture in her mind" (I, 122). The description of her "rising womanly from the waters" (I, 122) invests the lake with magical, transformative powers, and it appears that the water has the ability to transform a girl into a woman, to change some sort of bodily boundary. Jess also remembers how her mother yelled, "Mind! Snakes!" and so she "ran out of the water, convinced a snake had wrapped around her legs; a water bug made its way into the tangle of her sweet new hair—of which her parents were ignorant—and in that instant, giving way to her mother's warning, the delicacy of her relationship with snakes, bugs, water, weeds, had been violated, changed. That simple" (I, 122–23). However, the meanings of this comparison between water and an emerging sexuality are anything but "simple." Jess recognizes that her mother's verbal warning changes a natural, almost mystical experience into something to be "minded" and feared.

The same passage in "Bodies of Water" that connects sexuality to the mystical and fearful qualities of water also introduces the gay male body as absent. As a young girl, Jess realizes that her attraction to water and her changing body cannot be discovered by her parents, for then she too might be sent away to "a tough place" (I, 121) and made absent as her brother is made absent. Jess remembers how her brother "reads too much" and how that "summer at the mountain lake he had not been with them. Sent to some tough place, while she had her parents to herself" (I, 122). Jess's brother is introduced by memory, and, specifically, by Jess's memory of his absence. It is much later in the story, in the fifth section, that the narrator explains why her brother, named Bill, is sent away to a "tough place" where "they taught [him] carpentry" (123): He is sent away because he is gay. Jess remembers that her parents discovered fourteen-year-old Bill's journal where in "the blank space for *subject* [was] written DIARY— PRIVATE PROPERTY," and they ha[d] highlighted the phrase "I think I am" (V, 140). The narrative explains, "Bill had not even spoken to the other boy about it, just noted in the diary, *I think I may be. I think I am.* Following those speculations with the only word he had ever heard to describe it" (V, 143–44). By reading Bill's private writings, his parents deduce that he is attracted to other men and immediately panic about what to do with their son and his "unacceptable" sexuality.

Bill's discovery of his sexuality, through writing, holds two things in common with Jess's complex awareness of her sexuality in the lake: Transformation and secrecy mark both. However, Bill's discovery of sexuality has devastatingly different consequences within their family. Bill is not submerged in the fluidity and natural bodily transformation of the lake as Jess is and, in fact, soon after his sexuality is discovered, Bill becomes dehydrated and loses control of his body. The discovery of Bill's sexuality, signaled by the presence and absence of the words "I think I am" in his diary, leads his parents to enclose him. He is locked in a glass porch in which

> The sun is magnified in the glass and seems to pinpoint the child on the closed-in porch, his skin reddening. There is no shade[. . .]. Sweat gathers at his temples. On his top lip. He drips. The sweat curls his dark-brown hair. There is no relief in this heat, light. He draws a breath and feels his throat closing. He gags in the heat and the light. Vomiting orange juice and milk and shredded wheat onto the floor of the porch. (V, 140)

For both Jess and Bill, water and fluidity are conflated with the danger of discovering sexuality: It hides Jess's secret transformation from a child into a woman from her parents, and its absence makes Bill's enclosure on the porch viscerally painful and humiliating. Water, in the form of fog, also "embraces" Bill when he is forced to endure electroshock "treatments" for his sexual "sickness" (V, 144).

Bill's parents treat his unnameable homosexuality as a disease. The narrative tells us: "The father silenced the son. [. . .] Jess heard the noises of tears, whispers. A sudden shout from their mother: 'Goddamit! Stop it! 'Goddamit! Stop it! Don't you know it's a sickness?'" (VI, 141). Indeed, Bill's parents not only view his homosexuality as a disease, which they assume by reading the words "I think I am" written in his diary, but they attempt to "cure" his "illness" through electroshock therapy. Jess remembers how "Bill took his treatment one afternoon a week" (V, 143). Jess also remembers how the treatments "failed," as they led to more questions than answers to the problem of "I think I am"; Bill's body reflects this realization when the treatments "curved his spine into a question mark" (V, 144).

Male homosexuality has long been associated with illness, and, by extension, death, in North American culture. Lee Edelman points out in his chapter "Equations, Identities, and 'AIDS': The Plague of Discourse" from *Homographesis: Essays in Gay Literary and Cultural Theory* that "the culturally specific and phobically inflected identifications of homosexuality with illness and contagion" are "implicated in ideological operations"

(80) and claims that "long *before* the phenomenon of 'AIDS,'" there existed a "historic equation of homosexuality with the unnatural, the irrational, and the diseased" (86). The construction of homosexuality as an illness not only gives homophobic culture ammunition with which to delegitimize gay rights but it also enables the dominant culture to try to "cure" and "treat" homosexuality, in other words, to medicalize and police homosexuality. We can see how the discovery of Bill's adolescent epiphany, "I think I am," leads to his parents' treatment of him as ill and diseased, and consequently to their attempts to contain him on the porch, send him to a place to make him "tough" (and thereby, it is implied, masculine), and "heal" him with electroshock therapy. Through the construction of his sexuality as a disease, Bill's later physiological illness, which as readers we assume to be HIV/AIDS, becomes an extension of this equation that homosexuality equals illness.

In the introduction to *Death, Desire, and Loss in Western Culture*, Jonathan Dollimore explains how the connections between homosexuality, illness, and death manifest as and in cultural history. He writes:

> Male homosexual desire has been regarded in diverse ways by gay people themselves—as death-driven, as revolutionary, as benign, as redemptive, as self-shattering, as impossible of fulfilment, to name but some. Several of these ways of thinking about it clearly disturb those striving to establish an affirmative gay identity politics. And not surprisingly: on the one hand, this connection of homosexual desire and death has been made by those who want homosexuals literally to die; on the other, it is also part of homosexual history, as it is part of a more general cultural history. (xi–xii)

Dollimore also explains how these associations between male homosexuality, illness, and death have taken on particular political currencies since the appearance of HIV/AIDS in the early 1980s. He writes, "[I]n certain hostile representations of AIDS, homosexuality and death have been made to imply each other: homosexuality is seen as death-driven, death-desiring, and thereby death-dealing" (ix). We can see how a reading of homosexuality as death-desiring and death-driven can become part of the equation that AIDS is simply an extension of the "illness" of homosexuality. Since, until very recently, AIDS was viewed as invariably and unfailingly fatal, the equation became homosexuality=illness=AIDS=death.

It is easy to see how—keeping in mind the association of AIDS with a gay male identity, and the cultural conceptions of homosexuality as an illness—"AIDS" has come to be seen in American culture as a death sentence. The difficulty of treating AIDS-related illnesses and the devastating ability HIV has to weaken a body's immune system make AIDS an often-fatal syndrome. The equation that AIDS=Death, has been crucial in the cultural conceptions of HIV/AIDS: Bumper stickers and T-shirt slogans proclaim everything from scare-tactic educational messages like "100% Fatal & 100% Preventable" to hateful homophobia like "AIDS kills fags dead."[4] In *AIDS and Its Metaphors*, Susan Sontag explains how this equation has been created by AIDS "experts." She writes:

> Estimates of the percentage expected to show symptoms classifying them [patients with HIV] as having AIDS within five years, which may be too low—at the time of this writing, the figure is 30 to 35 percent—are invariably followed by the assertion that "most," after which comes "probably all," those infected will eventually become ill. [. . .] This figure, which will presumably continue to be revised upward, does much to maintain the definition of AIDS as an inexorable, invariably fatal disease. The obvious consequence of believing that all those who "harbour" the virus will eventually come down with the illness is that those who test positive for it are regarded as people-with-AIDS who just don't have it . . . yet. It is only a matter of time, like any death sentence. (117–18)

It is important to acknowledge that the equation between AIDS and death, whether we read it as consequential or constructed, has political effects on popular consciousness. This "narrative of irreversible decline," to use Steven Kruger's phrase, creates a sense of urgency and immediacy to take action on "AIDS" (see Kruger 73). The seeming certainty of death scares people into either becoming educated or remaining ignorant (sometimes both). But it also entrenches people living with HIV/AIDS as being "lost to the battle" or else as being brave martyrs facing the "inevitable." Becoming a living ghost, or a dead ghost for that matter, is on the same continuum as this "narrative of irreversible decline."

Bill constructs himself as ghostlike and connects this both to his "leaving" and to the naming of the ghostlike older woman Jess sees at the beginning of the story (whom Bill identifies as Miss Dillon). Bill asks Jess to stay in his house while he is gone, and he never tells her (or us) where he is going. He writes to her, in a letter dated "January something, the year of the piano," that "It's been too long not seeing each other, but you'll glimpse me here. More than glimpse" (III, 130) and advises her, jokingly, on places in the city where she can channel spirits (III, 131). Bill constructs himself as an apparitional presence to be glimpsed and felt in the house he once inhabited. His reluctance to date his letter and to specify the length of "not seeing each other" may be attempts to outdo time, to stop the "irreversible decline" of "this"—meaning AIDS or death, and perhaps both. This letter in which Bill ghosts himself also includes codes and silences in which we can infer the presence of AIDS. In reference to smoking, Bill writes, "[O]ne good thing about this, I won't have to quit after all. I can turn my fingers burnt sienna if I please" indicating that whatever "this" is, it will affect his life more significantly than would any disease associated with smoking (heart disease, emphysema, lung cancer just to name a few). He asks Jess to "pray that this thing doesn't get me in the head" (III, 131), which could be his articulating a fear of AIDS-related dementia. In a strange passage following the diversion about channeling spirits, Bill writes, "I should be burned at the stake, like Joan of ARC" (III, 131). This seemingly flippant reference to a Western cultural icon who lived in fifteenth-century France holds complicated readings if we acknowledge that Joan was executed officially for heresy and partly for gender transgression (two "sins" often conflated with homosexuality). Saint Joan's martyrdom may signal the view that the gay, male body was "sacrificed" by the dominant culture's lack of action to solve the AIDS crisis, and the capitalization of ARC may be a pun on the term "AIDS Related Complex" a term used until the late eighties to describe a stage between initial HIV infection and an AIDS diagnosis.[5] This coded reading is supported by the fact that Bill never names AIDS or homosexuality in his letters to Jess.

Bill expresses his frustration at not being able to bring himself to name AIDS or homosexuality when he writes to Jess about Miss Dillon, the older woman Jess watches in the story's opening sections, who I have argued can be read as an "apparitional lesbian." Bill describes Miss Dillon's paintings as ghostlike, ethereal, with their "skeletal trees," and "surreal" scenes of the lake. In the letter, Bill tells Jess:

> You will no doubt see Miss Dillon fishing on the lake. As I write this I can see her[. . .]. I know her by sight and from things overheard at the PO [post office]. [. . .] I gather her life-long friend passed on (Jesus! Why can't I just say died?) a while ago. The friend (and why, for God's sake, can't I say lover?—the old girl *was* listed in the obits as "sole survivor") was a school-teacher, Miss Straniere. (III, 132)

In his letter, Bill acknowledges his inability to speak about homosexuality and death. The closest he comes to discussing his illness, and its gravity, is when he tells Jess, "You know and I know why I can't say 'died.' So much easier to thinking of passing, floating, dancing on a fucking moonbeam. It's like waiting for a fucking car to crash" (132). Bill's self-ghosting may be feeding into the narrative of "irreversible decline." It is also a way of acknowledging the possibility of AIDS-related death without dealing with the corporeal messiness of death. Bill restricts his discussion of AIDS illness strictly to dementia, which affects the space of the mind and personality.

Bill's self-ghosting may not only be an acknowledgment of the "narrative of irreversible decline" but may also be a way of controlling the perceived contagion of his body. As Steven Kruger points out in *AIDS Narratives: Gender and Sexuality, Fiction and Science*, the narrative of "uncontrollable spread" often accompanies a narrative of "irreversible decline." He explains:

> The "worst-case scenario" (which is generally the one presented) shows an apocalyptic spread of disease depicted as especially disturbing in its abandonment of particular "risk groups" (gay men, intravenous drug users, haemophiliacs, blood transfusion recipients, "minority" communities, sex workers) for the "general population," with the assumption being, of course, that gay men, drug users, African Americans, Caribbeans, and Latina/os, and poor men and women do not belong to that "general population." (76)

Images of contagion and confinement of the "queer" body are present throughout "Bodies of Water." Miss Dillon fears being institutionalized by her homophobic "unimaginative," "suspicious," "dangerous" niece (I, 123) and she "retreats in winter to one room at the back of the eight-chambered house" (I, 126). Bill is contained in the glass porch of his parents' house after his "queerness" is discovered via his diary (V, 140), and he separates himself by making himself absent from Jess and his family. By virtue of their "queerness," Miss Dillon and Bill's families want to contain them because their sexualities are seen as threatening the body of the heterosexual nuclear family. This idea of contagion is especially present in the pages describing Bill's enclosure on the porch while his parents enclose Jess in their car and drive toward "the Medical Arts building, brick with Tudor detail" (V, 140). The porch is glass, so Bill can be seen; but the "panes are painted shut," so Bill becomes entrapped (V, 139). The porch is on the outside of the house, and if we read the house as a metonym for the family structure, we can read Bill, because of his secret sexuality, as outside of that family structure. The narrator describes Jess's memory: "The whole scene could be a postcard, [an] advertisement for a heartbreaking state of well-being—but for one thing. The father presses the gas pedal and the car moves forward—carefully. Away from the house. Away from her brother" (V, 140). In their leaving their home to find a "cure" for their son's "illness," Jess remembers how her parents wore "their best clothes, the ones they had worn to the great-grandmother's funeral the year before" (V, 142). The parents' mourning clothes suggest that they have lost something; more to the point, the funeral clothes suggest that Bill, because of his sexuality, can no longer be their son. The parents are simultaneously grieving his lost status as their son and trying to cure or save him from his "illness."

Bill's self-ghosting in his letter to Jess may be an acknowledgment of the narrative of "irreversible decline," it may be an attempt to control contagion, and it may be read as an attempt at revising the meanings of "homosexuality" and "AIDS." Jess is not only the very person Bill fears contaminating but she will also be the one left behind to remember him and provide testimony to his experience. We may ask what Cliff's story is telling us about the role of "the family" in the AIDS crisis, and more specifically, the role of women in "the family" in the AIDS crisis. Jess's mother tries to intervene in the father's interrogation of Bill when his diary is found, but her intervention potentially does more harm than good. After all, Bill's mother's insistence that homosexuality is an "illness" that "he can't help" leads to Bill's weekly "treatments" with electroshock therapy. Jess faces a similarly gendered and complicated role in dealing with Bill's perceived and actual illnesses—his homosexuality and his HIV+ status—because the story positions her as the caretaker of Bill's house, and as the collector of memories of Bill. Neither of these jobs is easy. The best she can do is "try to raise his scent" from the letter because even in trying to contact Bill in writing, she has no forwarding address, that is, Bill is either dead and in an unaddressable place or she does not know where he is, and "for the moment she allows this to stop her" from making contact with him (IV, 138). Jess is positioned from the very start of the story as an outsider looking in (as we learn she is the younger woman who watches Miss Dillon on the lake), and we may ask if her position can be tied to a larger reading of women's positions in the American AIDS phenomenon.

The reluctance to acknowledge women's potential to become HIV+, it can be argued, has led to women's becoming one of the highest "risk

groups" for new HIV infections in the twenty-first century. As editors
Andrea Rudd and Darien Taylor write in the introduction to *Positive
Women: Voices of Women Living with AIDS*:

> Today [1992] women have more information at their disposal, particularly
> in North America and some European countries[. . .]. But we [HIV+
> women] have had to struggle for all of this information. In many instances,
> we have had to create it ourselves because we live in a society that is in denial
> about the links between women and AIDS. Women with HIV and AIDS
> threaten society's ideas about sexuality, particularly the sanctity of hetero-
> sexuality with its close ties to reproduction. We raise age-old fears about
> illness and death. (14–15)

Jess's gender, in the crisis of a gendered and sexualized disease, may render
her a ghost in the fight against HIV/AIDS. Cliff's constructions of Jess
and Miss Dillon point out that "woman," as both affected and infected by
HIV/AIDS, is ghosted throughout the whole phenomenon in American
culture.

Women have not only been "ghosted" and ignored as patients and persons at risk for HIV but women have also often been relegated to the
feminine role of caretaker in the short history of the epidemic. This pervasive notion of woman-as-caretaker has led to a lack of specificity and
diversity in AIDS services for women in the West. Women can be viewed
as secondarily or indirectly affected by the disease, in a way that men are
not. Robin Gorna argues that women's HIV/AIDS experiences and needs
"get squashed into statements like, 'We are all living with AIDS.' This
is not true[. . .]. How can a mother recall burying her son to a woman
who has just got over PCP [Pneumocystis carinii pneumonia]? Or a sister
grieve and rage that she will lose her beautiful brother, with a woman
who is thinking positive and praying that her unborn child will not be
infected?" (156).[6] Despite the serious negative and reductive associations
of women and caretaking in the AIDS epidemic, links between femininity
and caretaking have also manifested in positive and activist ways. American AIDS-care associations, such as *Project Open Hand* in the San Francisco Bay area, and *With God's Love We Deliver* and *Mothers' Voices* based
in New York City, associate the traditionally feminized activities of cooking and cleaning with a nurturing and healing potential. The NAMES
Project AIDS Memorial Quilt associates the "plague" of AIDS with the
comfort and warmth of maternal domesticity, reaffirming and disturbing

what we read when we see a quilt. The quilt, created in San Francisco in 1987, remains the largest and most public monument to and for those affected by HIV/AIDS around the globe (see Ruskin's book *The Quilt: Stories from the NAMES Project*). The NAMES Project becomes a complex narrative that pieces together problems of feminizing and effeminizing storytelling, of creating communal and cultural memory, of revising ideas of monument, of naming the anonymous, and of giving voices to the silenced dead. It is one of the most powerful images and statements to emerge from the AIDS activist movement.

Cliff codes a reference to the AIDS quilt in the second fragment of her story. Miss Dillon "covers herself with a quilt pieced by another woman, for which she herself cut the template" (II, 128). We assume that the woman who pieced together the quilt is Miss Dillon's dead lover, so immediately the quilt is associated with death, femininity, and "queerness." Incidentally, Miss Dillon's covering of herself with the quilt is the first time her lover Bessie is *named* in the story, which, in a narrative coded in references to HIV/AIDS, could easily be interpreted as a reference to the NAMES Project. It is also when we learn Miss Dillon's first name, Anne, as we are told how "on this cold night the snow flies around a mailbox at the side of the road. ANNE DILLON. ISABELLA STRANIERE. She has not had the heart to remove the other name" (II, 129). The erasure of Bessie's name would signal a finality Anne is not willing to face. Similar to the way we might see the meanings of the quilted names in the NAMES Project, Anne sees Bessie's name on the mailbox as a memorial and testimony to their relationship. Bessie becomes another one of the "queer" ghosts of "Bodies of Water." Furthermore, the narrative's coded reference to the AIDS quilt brings the NAMES Project's dual purposes as a memorial and as a tool of activism into "Bodies of Water." Miss Dillon's memory of her lover Bessie is the first instance in "Bodies of Water" in which the narrative mentions activism.

The AIDS quilt makes death, of both the forgotten and abject bodies and of the loved and remembered, present to encourage its viewers to mourn and to take action. In "Bodies of Water," the ghostly presences of Bessie and Bill become sites at which the people who loved them, Anne and Jess, can remember them. In remembering their loved ones, and in sensing their presence after death, Anne and Jess also acknowledge the pain and ostracism that their loved ones faced while living in a homophobic and AIDS-phobic culture. Hence, Bessie's and Bill's ghosts also communicate a need for change and a need for action. Anne remembers:

Bessie taught her about quilts. They spoke of cartography, biography, history, resistance. Drunkard's path. Road to California. Underground Railroad. Mohawk trail. Bessie taught her about patterns, taught her how to cut, let her watch as she threaded the needle, leading steel ad thread through cloth, stopping to consider direction, contrast, harmony, shade, colour. (II, 128)

Cultural references to American activist movements are also present in a passage in which Jess is remembering Bill, specifically when she remembers that their great-grandmother believed in ghosts (VIII, 146). The story tells us that Jess "tacks postcards to the white wall above the desk: Billie Holiday; Chief's robe from the third phase; The Second Bible Quilt of Harriet Powers; ANC women. See, Bill—also the resisters—and the artists. People like you. How long it has taken for her to say that" (VIII, 146). Jess's postcards position her as a one-time political activist, and thereby a person with a one-time investment in the process of resistance and its potential for change.

The postcards that Jess tacks to the "white wall" document specific histories of African American activism in the United States. Billie Holiday was an African American musician, Harriet Powers was an emancipated slave who created quilts, and ANC is the acronym used by the African National Congress. Some readers may see the postcards as gesturing toward a racial identity for Jess and Bill; however, these postcards cannot "prove" identity and, rather, their detail draws attention to the fact that Bill and Jess's race is another ambiguous presence in the story. Because of the complicated visibility of gay white men as people with AIDS in the 1980s and early 1990s, many readers might assume Bill is white. Because in regard to her postcards of prominent African American artists and organizations, Jess says, "See Bill—also the resisters—and the artists. People like you," some readers might read Bill as black (VIII, 146). Some might see the postcards as forming a colorful quilt against a "white" wall—signifying the difficult ideological status of the United States as a melting pot. Many readers will see that Cliff forces us to question and deliberate the racial identities of Bill and Jess, and, in doing so, leads us to question how and why race matters. In leaving the race of her characters unnamed, along with their sexualities and the presence of AIDS, Cliff again uses narrative to challenge how identities operate, are silenced, and are apparitional in the dynamics of HIV/AIDS.

Change, for the characters in "Bodies of Water," is not easy to enact. Despite the reading of Bill's and Bessie's ghosts in the story as messengers of proactive change for those who are left behind in the world of the living, there is another competing ghosting in the story that implies that change of any kind is going to be difficult. Despite their cultural connections, AIDS and homosexuality are never explicitly named in Cliff's story. The words "AIDS" and "gay" are haunting presences in the narrative that does not utter them. So not only is the "queer" body absent through the ghosting of Miss Dillon, Bessie, and Bill, but so too is the public assertion or the naming of "gay" and of "AIDS." Because the word "AIDS" is never mentioned, unlike "Cancer" (III, 135), Cliff's narrative forces us to associate disease with homosexuality in particular ways: We realize our own assumptions when we can link Bill's unnamed sexuality with his unnamed illness as AIDS. Our ability to assume that Bill's "illnesses" are homosexuality and HIV/AIDS may be problematic to some readers, but this ability and the association of these three signifiers—disease, homosexuality, and AIDS—lead one to conclude that the words "homosexuality" and "AIDS" are strategically ghosted in Cliff's narrative. The unnameability of "homosexuality" and "AIDS" in Cliff's story may signal the political, social, and personal meanings and consequences that these words carry in North America. There is a very real possibility in many American communities of violence, loss of employment, and abandonment by family and friends when one "comes out" as gay, lesbian, bisexual, or transgender, or as affected by HIV/AIDS. The highly publicized torture and homicide of Wyoming university student Matthew Shepard in the late 1990s signals just how murderously material homophobia can become.[7] Because of the material threats homophobia poses to our bodies, and, as Eve Kosofsky Sedgwick points out, because "the fact that silence is rendered as pointed and performed as speech, in relations around the closet, depends on and highlights more broadly the fact that ignorance is as potent and multiple a thing as there is knowledge" (4), Cliff's choice to silence the word "AIDS" cannot be read superficially. We can read Cliff as communicating the effects of homophobia by choosing to "ghost" the words "homosexual" and "AIDS," and this can lead to a rather unhopeful reading of "Bodies of Water."

In a more proactive reading, the ghosting of "homosexuality" and "AIDS" can be viewed as an attempt to revise their meanings, and, at the least, as a tactic that forces readers to realize what our cultural constructions of these words entail. Cliff's choice to leave "homosexuality" and "AIDS" unnamed forces her readers to realize that our language and culture construct "homosexuality" and "AIDS" in ways that are detrimental to those affected by the disease and living with the disease. In *The History of Sexuality Volume One,* Michel Foucault writes that "silence itself—the thing one declines to say, or is forbidden to name, the discretion that is required between different speakers—is less the absolute limit of discourse, the other side from which it is separated by a strict boundary, than an element that functions alongside the things said, with them and in relation to them within over-all strategies" (27). This reading of silence as functioning within discourse, rather than opposing it, further allows us to read "homosexuality" and "AIDS" as hovering and haunting the spaces in Cliff's story. Bill's reluctance to name "AIDS" can be read as a revisionary tactic both within and outside the story to disassociate "AIDS" and "homosexuality": If "it" is never named, then "it" can never be defined. After all, Bill's adolescent writing in his diary, "I think I am" (V, 141), "following those speculations with the only word he had ever heard to describe it" (V, 144), leads to electroshock therapy "treatments," containment, and ostracism. It also signals that one forfeits privacy—as his diary is marked PRIVATE PROPERTY—when one discloses one's sexuality (whether it is named or implied). Accompanying this forfeiture of privacy when disclosing or defining sexuality is a forfeiture of rights: as Bill mutters into his breakfast, "And don't I have any rights?" (V, 141). There may be a linguistic space in which Bill, by not naming his "illnesses," may be able to redefine the meanings of these words and thereby prevent his being defined by other people's readings of them.

To write a story that can be read as an AIDS narrative is in itself an activist move. The people and communities who initiate awareness and expose ideological inaction on AIDS issues are often those who do it out of political and medical necessity; activism is generated when the bodies in the community, and sometimes the body of the community, are (sometimes quite literally) fighting to survive. Besides answering the activist call to "ACT-UP" and recognize the possibility that "SILENCE=DEATH," speaking out about the ignorance surrounding homosexuality and HIV/AIDS in North American culture is brave. It is easier to be silent, and ignorant, until absolute necessary, and, more specifically, until one identifies as a "them" rather than as an "us." The developments in "Bodies of Water" demonstrate just how complicated it is to name "homosexuality" and "AIDS" in American culture, let alone take an activist (whether reactive, proactive, or both) stance on either or both of the subjects. Jess expresses this difficulty in a letter to Bill when she writes, "'I am in the world to change the world,' the grown-up version of that little girl told you once,

and you called the words (and me too?) 'impossibly dangerous.' Why didn't
I that morning do something? If I could fight for a stranger why couldn't
I fight for you?" (148). Cliff's Jess expresses something many people
affected by HIV/AIDS ask themselves and struggle to answer.

Cliff best represents the difficulty of writing about "AIDS" and its surrounding issues in the last section of her story. Sedgwick writes in *Axiom*
7 in the introduction to *Epistemology of the Closet* that in questions about
"someone's strong group-identification across politically charged boundaries, whether of gender, of class, of race, of sexuality, of nation [. . .] what
these implicit questions really ask for is narrative, and of a directly personal sort" (60). Cliff provides us with this narrative of a "directly personal
sort" by constructing her story around the exchange of letters between
Jess and Bill. Both Bill and Jess self-censor their writings; Bill apologizes
for allowing even the ghost of "AIDS" to hover in the ellipses as he writes:
"no . . . God . . . I didn't mean to lay that out here" (III, 131) and assures
Jess that "this is the fifth draft of this letter. I am trying not to be morbid.
Bear with me" (III, 132). Just as Jess witnesses Miss Dillon on the lake, we
witness Jess struggling to compose a letter to Bill. She starts by apologiz-
ing for beginning her letter with the mention of Memorial Day: "nothing
like beginning a letter with a *memento mori*—sorry" (IX, 147). Cliff's story
ends with Jess's ripping up the letter she has composed to Bill and remark-
ing, "I thought for a moment I saw your ghosts" (IX, 149). This is crucial
to reading the story, as writing as an innermost privacy and sanctuary is
challenged in "Bodies of Water" when the discovery of Bill's private diary
"outs" him as "queer." The utterance of "queer" words, such as "homosexuality" and "AIDS," opens these words up for multiple readings and
multiple political implications. Jess admits that she is "not ready to compose an answer" (145) to the unspoken questions implicit in her and her
brother's exchange of letters and memories. Jess may not be willing to
write exactly how she will keep Bill's house and manage in his community. She cannot explain how she will fulfill, resist, or change her role as a
woman within the crisis of a gendered and sexualized disease. Ultimately,
Jess resists writing down how she will deal with Bill's absence and his
ghosts because writing would be an acknowledgment of her loss. By putting these answers in writing, she somehow finalizes them or inadvertently
opens them up for multiple (and possibly detrimental readings by others).
Jess's self-censoring suggests that there may not be a language accessible
to her, or to Cliff for that matter, to talk about the "queerness" of AIDS
and to memorialize those lost to "AIDS," without reproducing the very

discourses that lead to threats of containment, ineffective "treatments," and ignorance.

In the decade since the publication of "Bodies of Water," much has changed in HIV/AIDS activist rhetoric and political movements. Many activists, readers, and members of American culture would like to think that we have "come a long way" in the fight against AIDS. We have, but there is still a long way to go before HIV/AIDS is no longer an epidemic of disastrous proportions. The use of protease-inhibitor treatments since 1996 has helped many people in the West who were bedridden by AIDS-related illnesses to resume normal lives. News report titles about the epidemic in the United States have changed from "The Change in Gay Life-Style: As Nightmare Rumors Become Fact, Fear of Contagion Prompts A Slowing Down of Life in the Fast Lane" (*Newsweek*, April 18, 1983) to "When Plagues End" (*New York Times Magazine*, November 18, 1996) to "The Four Letter Word We All Forgot About" (*Esquire*, March 1999). Throughout its American history, AIDS has been written about as a ghost, but this metaphor or trope has changed dramatically in recent years. Sullivan's description of his HIV diagnosis as a ghost, in the previously quoted 1996 essay "When Plagues End," exemplifies an alarming trend in recent American consciousness. Partly due to the improvement in treatment options and falling mortality rates, AIDS discourse since 1996 often makes HIV/AIDS into a ghost of the past. While Sullivan's piece reflects a much-needed political movement to emphasize living with HIV rather than dying of AIDS, his piece and others like it may come at the expense of erasing and ghosting the past and thereby ensuring a similar future. To ghost AIDS as a disease that affected mostly white, gay men in the 1980s further silences the multiple and diverse identities of those struggling with the disease today. Furthermore, to write that "AIDS" is ending seems irresponsible, considering that worldwide HIV infection rates in all "risk" groups are rising each year worldwide and current treatments are being questioned as long-term options. The recent view of HIV/AIDS as a manageable disease, in the United States and in the West in general, is ghosting the whole epidemic and the people it continues to affect.

HIV/AIDS is a phenomenon entangled in silences, early and tragic death, loss and mourning, and the hope for a different future. It seems logical that we would want to talk about it in terms of ghosts and specters. Cliff's use of ghosts and apparitions to talk about sexuality and AIDS in "Bodies of Water" raises many questions, not the least of which is how to navigate beyond the devastations of AIDS in America. It is within their negotiations between speaking out, in writing, and remaining silent, in writing, that the fictional Jess and her creator Cliff are the most activist and radical: Both women are suggesting that the activisms, memorials, constructions, and languages that we use at present to talk and write about the "queerness" of "AIDS" are not enough. Cliff's "Bodies of Water" first forces readers to consider how "HIV/AIDS" and "homosexuality" are constructed in American culture, and then asks us to examine how we, as readers living in Western culture, have become implicated in these constructions. Cliff uses the figure of the ghost and the trope of apparitionality to encourage us to think about how certain bodies are written and viewed in the HIV/AIDS epidemic. Through a personal narrative, in a literary text, we readers become part of a community in which we struggle along with Jess, Anne, and Bill. We all search to find the words to convey the loss and courage implicit in identifying with "queerness" and in living with, dying with, and surviving HIV/AIDS.

NOTES

1. "Trope," as defined by Harry Shaw in *Dictionary of Literary Terms* as "any literary or rhetorical device (such as metaphor, metonymy, simile, etc.) which consists of the use of words in other than their literal sense," may seem to be a benign, encompassing, and fluid definition. However, other literary terms do not adequately describe what Cliff is doing. The use of ghosts to talk about AIDS in "Bodies of Water" is a rhetorical move that is more than metaphorical, as the narrative does not treat ghosts and AIDS as two unlike things that are identical, and it is a comparison that is more than symbolic, as the narrative's use of ghosts is more than representative. Nor is Cliff's use of ghosts a conceit, as the story's complicated shifts in temporality and the ever-evolving characterizations make it clear that while the trope may be elaborate, it is not "far-fetched" (Baldick 230). "Tropes," according to the *Oxford Dictionary of Literary Terms*, "change the meanings of words by a 'turn' of sense," and this is how I read Cliff's story working on a rhetorical level: The use of ghosts to talk about AIDS turns readers' perceptions and readings of the disease and experience of AIDS. Like a ghost, the term "trope" is open to multiple readings.

2. I am using the term "AIDS-affected" to include people living with HIV/AIDS in multiple ways: people infected with HIV, people suffering from AIDS-related illnesses, people who have lost friends or families to AIDS-related illnesses, people involved in AIDS activism (in any of its forms), people whose communities are affected by AIDS, and people who make life choices based on the reality and risk of HIV infection. In recent years, many theorists and activists have debated the usefulness of terms such as "queer," "gay," and "lesbian," pointing out that these terms have diverging multiple meanings and, hence, cannot be read to mean a singular thing. I am using the term "queer" with quotation marks to signify its multiple meanings. Specifically, I want to call readers' attention to the term's history of being both a pejorative

label and a recovered signifier of identity in a gay rights movement and in AIDS activism.

3. Many thanks to Steven Kruger, who helped shape this essay's direction in its earliest stages and who introduced me to "Bodies of water" as an AIDS narrative.

4. John Gordon and Clarence Crossman discuss the activist reaction to an "AIDS kills fags dead" T-shirt in their essay "'aids . . . kills fags dead': Cultural Activism in Grand Bend" in *Fluid Exchanges: Artists and Critics in the AIDS Crisis* (1992), edited by James Miller.

5. In *AIDS and Its Metaphors* (1989) Susan Sontag uses the term ARC as the second of three stages of AIDS (HIV infection, ARC, AIDS) and also discusses the potential phase out of the term. In a footnote she explains: "The 1988 [American] Presidential Commission on the epidemic recommended 'de-emphasizing' the use of the term ARC because it 'tends to obscure the life-threatening aspects of this stage of illness.' There is some pressure to drop the term AIDS, too. The report by the Presidential Commission pointedly used the acronym HIV for the epidemic itself, as part of a recommended shift from 'monitoring disease' to 'monitoring infection'" (116).

6. PCP stands for Pneumocystis carinii pneumonia and is one of the first AIDS-defining illnesses to be identified and included by the Atlanta Centers for Disease Control and, consequently, the World Health Organization. Although PCP can be prevented with antibiotics, it is also a potentially fatal condition for those with full-blown AIDS.

7. Matthew Shepard was a University of Wyoming student who was abducted, beaten, and tortured by two student-aged men who suspected he was gay. These men tied Matthew to a fence and left him to freeze and die on the side of the road. This incident occurred in late 1998 and received international media attention.

WORKS CITED

Associated Press at the *San Francisco Chronicle*. "A Pneumonia That Strikes Gay Males," *San Francisco Chronicle*, June 6, 1981, 4.

Baldick, Chris, ed. *The Concise Oxford Dictionary of Literary Terms and Literary Theory*. Oxford: Oxford University Press, 1990.

Butler, Judith. *Bodies That Matter*. New York: Routledge, 1993.

Castle, Terry. *The Apparitional Lesbian*. New York: Columbia University Press, 1993.

Cliff, Michelle. "Bodies of Water." In *Bodies of Water*. New York: Dutton, 1990. 121–49.

Coppola, Vincent, and Richard West. "The Change in Gay Lifestyle," *Newsweek*, April 18, 1983, 80.

Dollimore, Jonathan. *Death, Desire, and Loss in Western Culture*. New York: Routledge, 1998.

Edelman, Lee. *Homographesis: Essays in Gay Literary and Cultural Theory*. New York: Routledge, 1994.

Foucault, Michel. *The History of Sexuality: Volume One: An Introduction*. Translated by Robert Hurley. New York: Vintage Books, 1978.

Garrett, Laurie, and Wilkinson, Alec. "The First Crisis of the Twenty-First Century." *Esquire Magazine* 13, no. 3 (March 1999): 102-10.

Gordon, John, and Clarence Crossman. "'aids kills fags dead . . .': Cultural Activism in Grand Bend." *Fluid Exchanges: Artists and Critics in the AIDS Crisis.* Edited by James Miller, 241–54. Toronto: University of Toronto Press, 1992.

Gorna, Robin. *Vamps, Virgins and Victims: How Can Women Fight AIDS?* London: Cassell, 1996.

Kruger, Steven F. *AIDS Narratives: Gender and Sexuality, Fiction and Science.* New York: Garland, 1996.

Pearsall, Judy, ed. *The New Oxford Dictionary of English.* Oxford: Clarendon, 1998.

Rudd, Andrea, and Darien Taylor. "Introduction." In *Positive Women: Voices of Women Living with AIDS.* Edited by Andrea Rudd and Darien Taylor. Toronto: Second Story, 1992.

Ruskin, Cindy. *The Quilt: Stories from the NAMES Project.* New York: Pocket Books, 1988.

Sedgwick, Eve Kosofsky. *Epistemology of the Closet.* Berkeley: University of California Press, 1990.

Shaw, Harry. *Dictionary of Literary Terms.* New York: McGraw-Hill, 1972.

Shilts, Randy. *And the Band Played On.* New York: Penguin Books, 1987.

Sontag, Susan. *AIDS and Its Metaphors.* London: Penguin Books, 1989.

Sullivan, Andrew. "When Plagues End," *New York Times Magazine,* November 16, 1996, 58–84.

Salem's Ghosts and the Cultural Capital of Witches

BRIDGET M. MARSHALL

Every day is Halloween in Salem, Massachusetts. On an average day in Salem, costumed vampires, werewolves, and witches roam the streets, recordings of ghoulish sounds emanate from outdoor speakers, and drawings of witches on broomsticks adorn nearly every street sign and storefront. Before the strange events of the year 1692, the town of Salem was probably much like any other Puritan town of its day. But following the events of the now well-known witch trials, Salem became a town haunted, if not by the ghosts of the unjustly executed "witches," then by the guilt and regret of the accusers and judges. Three hundred years later, the story of Salem still haunts America's national imagination as a foundational trauma and a fascinating story. Today, Salem's tourist industry caters to the public's curiosity about this story, attracting more than a million visitors each year (Fox 3). The focus of this tourism is not Salem as it exists today, but Salem as a haunted site, a place where a particularly horrible event in American history is publicly remembered and displayed. Ultimately, Salem's hyperactive marketing of itself as "Witch City" capitalizes on its haunted history at the same time that it distorts and evades that history. Salem markets its trauma without actually confronting and dealing with that trauma.

Modern Salem is more than just a historic site; it is a profit center. According to the local press, "Witches have been good business in Salem" ("Witches Good"). This success has led to even more investment in the tourist-industry machine. As Joan Formally, director of the Salem Chamber of Commerce, explains, "For the number of people who come to Salem there could be twice as many who would come if they knew more. *What*

Salem desperately needs is packaging" (quoted in "Witches Good," my emphasis). Salem has worked for some time on its "packaging." Despite its being the location of the events of a rather dark chapter of American history, modern-day Salem has found a way to capitalize on what might otherwise be considered a public-relations nightmare. Instead of hiding its past connections with witchcraft, the town has created a thriving heritage-tourism destination. Teeming with witch-themed products and attractions, Salem disguises the real horror of the past with sites and performances that offer the visitor a manufactured horror that only scares for entertainment and fails to convey a real sense of the town's tragic history. Salem's entertaining sites are a collective strategy of evasion, a misremembering of the past that denies the horrors that happened here.

As described in Barbara Kirshenblatt-Gimblett's study, *Destination Culture: Tourism, Museums, and Heritage*, "Heritage is a mode of cultural production in the present that has recourse to the past. Heritage thus defined depends on display to give dying economies and dead sites a second life as exhibitions of themselves. A place such as Salem, Massachusetts, may be even more profitable as an *exhibition of* a mercantile center than it was *as* a mercantile center" (7). At present, Salem's mercantile center is its witch tourism, a $30 million industry in 2001 (Haskell). In enacting such an exhibition, Salem pretends to offer the visitor access to the past. But by commemorating the events of three hundred years ago, it also denies that anything has happened since that time and ignores the process of its own creation. Moreover, Salem's heritage production actually conceals the horror of the real historical events by creating a carnivalesque, Halloween-themed entertainment park on the site of twenty murders and hundreds of injustices committed by the Salemites of the seventeenth century.

Salem's past is not actually something Salemites (or tourists) will experience in the city's heritage productions. As Kirshenblatt-Gimblett explains, "Both heritage and tourism deal in the intangible, absent, inaccessible, fragmentary, and dislocated" (167). These general qualities of heritage tourism are particularly applicable to Salem's tourism sites, as the story of the Salem witch hysteria is widely known, yet the details of the dramatic events are ultimately "intangible, absent, inaccessible, fragmentary, and dislocated." While much of Salem's industry is dead, its heritage tourism thrives and continues to grow as more and more exhibits are created to tell the story of Salem and attract the money of Salem tourists.[1] Performances of witch trials, displays of witchcraft documents, and haunted houses create narratives about history that can be sold to the tourist. Salem foregrounds its witch heritage on everything from streets (Witch Hill Street) to businesses evoking the witch theme (Witch City Auto) to the town newspaper and nearly every sign in "Witch City," which feature the logo of a witch flying on a broomstick. But such names and images refer to Halloween-style, broomstick-riding figures, not actual murdered people hanging from trees. Salem's images and evocations of the "witch" trade on the entertainment value of mythical witches while ignoring and even denying the true horror of the historical figures.

I made my first visit to Salem in August 1999, when I visited the Witch History Museum and the New England Pirate Museum and explored the Halloween costume party that is the downtown open-air mall area. The streets of Salem are filled with stores selling books on witchcraft, souvenirs featuring witches and black cats, and men and women walking around in seventeenth-century costumes and encouraging crowds to come to the (live reenactment of a) witch trial to be held later in the day. Brochures, museums, and plaques inform the visitor about the many "historical" and "educational" sites of interest. But ultimately, in this incredibly commodified version of history, I felt very little of the true horror of Salem's past. I returned in July 2000 for a few days of further investigation, during which time I toured most of the museums and sites, and made a visit to the neighboring town of Danvers. This visit only increased my feelings of uneasiness with Salem's packaged heritage as I learned that Salem's thriving heritage-tourism sites have contributed to the loss of many of the actual historical sites in the town. While these heritage creations claim to offer visitors the chance to go back in time and witness history, the sites actually prevent any true confrontation with the horrors of the past; instead of a documentary, we get a horror movie (and a B horror movie, in most cases). While such fun and camp may have its place, we must question why Salem would choose this manner of commemoration and consider what it tells us about our relationship with the past.

My first visit to Salem as an average heritage tourist began with a walk on "Heritage Trail," a 1.7-mile long route through the city, marked on the sidewalk with a red line. One of the first sites of interest on the Heritage Trail is the Witch House on Essex Street. According to a Heritage Trail guidebook, "The Witch House is the only home still standing in Salem with direct ties to the Witch Trials" (Francoeur, Fox, and McAllister 23). While the house is indeed a real artifact from the period, its name is something completely fabricated by the community long after that period. As a guidebook from 1902 explains, "[T]he only pretext for calling this the

'Witch House' is a tradition that some of the preliminary examinations for commitment took place therein" (Hunt 6). When I arrived for a tour, the guide (in period costume) immediately informed me that the presentation was "not about witchcraft," but rather provided information about the rooms and furnishings of the house and details about how the Corwin family lived. Another tour, called "The Real Witch Trials," offered through the Peabody Essex Museum uses a similar marketing technique in its brochure, *Peabody Essex Museum: New England's Roots Start Here*, which explains, "The 1684 John Ward House, once situated next to the Salem jail, was witness to the life-and-death struggle that gripped Salem during the witchcraft accusations in 1692" (5). A tour guide explained that the house was not actually associated with the witch trials; rather, it is a house set up to illustrate what life was like in the seventeenth century. The tour centered on presenting artifacts of the past—beds, dishes, cookware, furniture—and no mention was made of the witch trials until I asked about the connection.

Although the Corwin ("Witch") House and the John Ward House sites are "authentic" in that they show some actual artifacts from the period, their ties to the witch hysteria are constructions of the marketers of witch-hysteria tourism in Salem. In the past, these particular buildings were just two private residences among many other buildings. Now they stand with far greater importance to represent "the real thing" from the past, and they purport to provide the experience of time travel back to that period. These sites only use witch history as a marketing ploy; they discuss the history and lifestyle of the period while completely ignoring the witch hysteria. This separation of daily life from information about witchcraft trials supports the idea that the hysteria was an inexplicable anomaly in Salem's history instead of considering how the experiences and daily lives of the early Salemites contributed to and erupted in the trials and executions. As John Putnam Demos explains in *Entertaining Satan: Witchcraft and the Culture of Early New England*, witchcraft "belonged to the regular business of life" during these times (vii). The lifestyle tours could provide context for explaining the witch hysteria, but instead they completely separate the "normal" lives of the colonists from the witch trials. Our understanding of both their daily lives and the trials is diminished by this decontextualization.

I. Creating New Sites: Salem's Museums

Museums in Salem are nothing new; indeed, Salem's Peabody Essex Museum is "the oldest continually operating museum in the country"

(Francoeur, Fox, and McAllister 21). Today, the Peabody Essex Museum features a one-room exhibit called "The Real Witchcraft Papers." Glass cases display a selection of the original warrants and trial depositions, as well as four items that once belonged to condemned witches: two canes, a chair, and a sundial. But aside from these few papers and objects, there is little evidence of the 1690s. The many preserved documents do not do enough to reflect the "heritage" or provide a clear picture of what life was like during Puritan times. For this, Salem tourists and heritage-seekers must turn to a wide variety of other museums, many of which have been established in the last thirty years.

The Salem Witch Museum, in operation since 1972, is one of the town's most established attractions of this type. Little has changed in its presentation since that time: For a six-dollar admission fee, visitors are offered a twenty-five-minute long presentation on the history of the witch hysteria. The audience, seated in the middle of an auditorium, is surrounded by stage sets populated by mannequins representing the inhabitants of Salem in the 1690s. As the lights illuminate various sections, a prerecorded narration explains the significance of each scene. A recent brochure for the Witch Museum claims that it is "Salem's most visited museum" and tells the reader: "You are there. Witness the testimony of the hysterical girls, the suffering of the blameless victims, and the decisions of the fanatical judges who sent innocent people to their deaths" (*Salem Witch*). What the tourist actually witnesses is a diorama with a sound track. The "experience" of the Salem Witch Museum is based on the transcripts of trial documents, but clearly there is much more to the story than these records provide.[2] This interpretation is no more "real" than the wooden (and increasingly worn-out) mannequins on the stage. The apparatus of the presentation— the canned sound effects; the recorded voice-over; and the mannequins' mechanical, repetitive movements (in those cases in which there is movement)—call attention to the exhibit's production, not to the real people who were involved in the real events of the past.

There is no single story that gives the true history of Salem; a variety of narratives serve to explain different aspects of the events. A survey of just a few titles of some seminal texts on the topic, from Paul Boyer and Stephen Nissenbaum's *Salem Possessed: The Social Origins of Witchcraft* (1974) to John Putnam Demos's *Entertaining Satan: Witchcraft and the Culture of Early New England* (1982) to Carol F. Karlsen's *The Devil in the Shape of a Woman: Witchcraft in Colonial New England* (1987), indicates the variety of approaches used in the study of Salem. Whether these studies (and many, many more) are concerned with class struggles, cultural and religious shifts, or gender politics, they ultimately show that there is no single version of what happened. However, one must remember that visitors to any individual site in Salem will see only one simplified and limited version of what happened and will not be told that numerous historical lenses can be used to understand the events.

The most recent addition to the Salem museum scene, the Witch History Museum, opened in July 1999. According to its brochure, it offers "'[t]he untold stories,' told through a live presentation and tour (Including Modern Animated Techniques)" (*Witch History*). The museum's pamphlet invites the visitor to "[c]ome and experience life in the wilderness of 1692 . . . where wolves, Indians and wild witches roamed the nearby woods" (*Witch History*). In creating this experience, the museum produces a narrow, highly specific, and perfectly self-contained narrative. While the Witch History Museum stresses the connection with Indian massacres and the proximity of Native Americans, other exhibits omit such references entirely. Notably, one of the most recent additions to the scholarly study of Salem focuses on this Native American connection. Mary Beth Norton's 2002 book, *In the Devil's Snare: The Salem Witchcraft Crisis of 1692*, considers the role of the colonists' ongoing battles with the Native populations in King Philip's (1675–76) and King William's (1688–99) Wars and their influence on the witchcraft accusations. Whereas scholarly sources are generally grounded in a history of the previous research on the subject, connecting new theories with older ones, the tourist sites do not include such a grounding in the multiplicity of stories and interpretations. Each museum produces a narrative that it claims is the master narrative in the single, unified, and packaged heritage it creates for the visitor. But at the next stop, that heritage is often rearranged by the presentation and displays of yet another competing narrative. Since each individually owned and operated tourist production is interested in gaining the most money from tourists, all of them vie for attention, often by trying to be more outrageous, more creepy, and more entertaining than the other productions. Each one makes claims for the superiority of its own narrative, not because its narrative is more worthwhile but because it wants to be a successful business.

While some brochures for museums and tours tout their "educational value," those describing others are clearly selling the sites as entertainment packages. According to brochures for the Salem Wax Museum of Witches and Seafarers, "300 years of sense-tingling history awaits you!" (*Salem*

Wax). Apparently, this presentation will allow us to "Feel the terror of the Salem Witch Trials of 1692" (*Salem Wax*). How exactly is this feat accomplished? The brochure explains: "You'll touch history as never before in our Gravestone Rubbing Station, dungeon, Trial Scene and much more!" (*Salem Wax*). How precisely doing a gravestone rubbing (on a fake gravestone, at that!) will cause one to feel terror is unclear. I personally felt no such terror on my visit, nor did the other visitors around me, many of whom were laughing. The Salem Wax Museum is partnered with the Salem Witch Village; you can purchase the "Salem Hysteria Pass" and visit both exhibitions for one price. The Witch Village brochure explains: "You will be confronted with the grim realities of medieval hysteria, superstition, and torture" (*Salem Wax*). Perhaps it would be more accurate to say that "you will be confronted with a grim re-creation of what was once a reality for Salem residents." The two sites also pair up to create the "Haunted Neighborhood": "During October both sites transform into the area's largest haunted attractions" (*Salem Wax*). Two hundred thousand tourists visit Salem in the month of October for its "Haunted Happenings" (Haskell), indicating just how effective Salem's spooky marketing has become.

Throughout the campy, haunted-house atmosphere of Salem, images of witches—those black-clad, pointy-hatted, broomstick-riding, green-faced, wart-nosed hags from fairy tales—are the most prevalent symbol. With so many reminders of this version of witch history, it is easy to forget that the "witches" of Salem were not running around in black pointy hats. They were not witches, but innocent citizens vilified for a variety of reasons. Yet Salem's markers for its historic district, the signs for the witch museums, and the paraphernalia sold in museum gift shops all feature the Halloween-style witch figure. Thus, these exhibits seem to imply that there actually were witches (of the sort those of us in the twentieth century would recognize) who incurred the wrath of their Puritan society. This production of "Scary Salem," does not help us understand the events and people of 1692; rather, it is a narrative of history as something to be enjoyed and consumed, a story and a site to entertain us. Walking through the darkened hallways of the exhibits, we are not frightened by the notion that witch-hunts and executions took place, but by the costumed actors who cackle behind masks and jump out to scare us.

Each new museum or tour in Salem seems less and less connected with the history of Salem and more focused on Halloween thrills. For instance, tourists can purchase "Salem's Fright Pass," a combination package of three museums: Boris Karloff's Witch Mansion, Terror on the Wharf, and Dracula's Castle. These haunted houses, reminiscent of those found in amusement parks, display props from horror movies and play scary music. The costumes of the workers are not re-creations of colonial garb, but the capes, wands, masks, and fangs of witches, vampires, werewolves, and the like. The Haunted Footsteps Ghost Tour provides a "nightly lanternlit stroll" with "costumed guides" who "resurrect Salem's bewitching history" (*Haunted*), and Mass Hysteria Haunted Hearse Tours offers "the most comprehensive occult-themed tour in all New England" in its hearse equipped to seat ten guests (*Mass Hysteria*). Such haunted houses and tours seek to capitalize on the tourist's notion that "something bad happened here"; but that event is commodified into something that can provide entertainment to visitors and profit to presenters. While these sites and tours celebrate Salem's "witch history," they utterly fail to evoke or explore any real history; indeed they bury the facts of the real events and replace them with an easy-to-enjoy thrill that requires no thinking or contemplation. Salem's amusement-park-style heritage attractions shield the visitor (and resident) from experiencing any real horror.

II. HISTORIC SITES AND HERITAGE SITES: SALEM'S MARKERS AND ABSENT CENTERS

Further complicating Salem's refusal to come to terms with the true horror of its haunted history is the loss of many real sites related to the historical events of the witch hysteria. Perhaps the single most important failure of the majority of the horror-themed attractions is that they ignore the fact that Danvers, not Salem, is the original site of the alleged witchcraft. Additionally, many sites—from Gallows Hill, to the graves of the accused, to the witch dungeons—have been lost or destroyed with little or no acknowledgment by the town's heritage productions. These sites are ignored or glossed over by Salem's exhibit- and consumption-driven heritage producers, and the average visitor gets misinformation or no information at all about them.

The Question of Which City

The events of the witchcraft hysteria did not actually occur in Salem Town proper, but in Salem Village, which has been known as the town of Danvers since 1752 (LeBeau). This will come as a surprise to the many visitors to modern-day Salem who believe that they have seen the town where the witch hysteria happened. Such a geographical error is fairly important, as several interpretations of the witch trials (including, most notably, Boyer and Nissenbaum's *Salem Possessed*) use the geography of the area and the location of the various participants as important factors in uncovering what happened in 1692. The fact that Danvers is the site where the purported "bewitchings," the first accusations, and the initial investigations occurred is easily overlooked. Danvers itself has few indicators of its ignoble past, although it does have a memorial "in memory of all those who died during the 'Salem Witchcraft Hysteria.'" I made the short drive to Danvers after a morning of touring Salem. The difference between the two towns was apparent immediately, perhaps most significantly in the fact that, on a beautiful Saturday afternoon in July, I did not encounter even one other tourist.

Danvers does little to publicize itself as an important site of interest to witch-hysteria seekers. There are no signs directing the driver to site parking, nor any visitor's center providing brochures in multiple languages. And yet the town could do this, and perhaps even do it more efficiently than Salem itself. Many of the original buildings from the period are still intact (most of them are still private residences) and are located in a circle of less than two miles in radius, making Danvers a prime candidate for a "Heritage Trail" of its own. There are certainly enough "sites" for the heritage-seeker to visit, including the Rebecca Nurse Homestead (Nurse was hanged as a witch), where visitors can tour her house and visit the graveyard in which George Jacobs, another accused witch, is buried.[3] But the Nurse Homestead is an exception in this town that otherwise seems to do nothing to enhance or exhibit its heritage. As I walked down Centre Street, I nearly missed the small sign indicating the "Samuel Parris Archaeological Site." Walking down a dirt path virtually into the backyards of residents, I came upon the foundations that were once the home of Reverend Samuel Parris, whose daughters were the first to throw fits and cry witch. Two simple signs, erected in 1974 when the archaeological dig was completed, give a brief history of the site, but it seems that few visitors will make the trip to see a few stones in a square hole in the ground. I saw no other tourists here either.

Gallows Hill: Losing Sites

The site of the Parris foundation marks the geographical starting point of the Salem witch hysteria; the site of its ultimate conclusion—Gallows Hill, where the witches were executed—is unknown to this day. A 1902 guidebook informed visitors that the hill where the witches were executed "remains in the same condition" as it was at the time of the hangings (Hunt 32–33). Charles Upham, one of the noted chroniclers of the witch hysteria, also claimed to know in 1867 the exact location of the hill. He saw the site as particularly appropriate for a visitor's notice:

> When, in some coming day, a sense of justice, appreciation of moral firmness, sympathy for suffering innocence, the diffusion of refined sensibility, a discriminating discernment of what is really worthy of commemoration among men, a rectified taste, a generous public spirit, and gratitude for the light that surrounds us and protects us against error, folly, and fanaticism, shall demand the rearing of a suitable monument to the memory of those who in 1692 preferred death to a falsehood, the pedestal for the lofty column will be found ready, reared by the Creator on a foundation that can never be shaken while the globe endures, or worn away by the elements, man, or time—the brow of Witch Hill! On no other spot could such a tribute be more worthily bestowed, or more conspicuously displayed. (379–80)

No monument was created in Upham's time, and since then the site of the hill has been worn away by the elements and passage of time, and in the memory of Salem's residents and historians.

Several studies have concluded that there is no way to determine the exact location of the sites of either execution or burial of the convicted witches (Roach 4). The loss of these sites can be attributed to numerous factors. First, there is the vagueness of the original "clues," which indicate with certainty only that the hangings were done in a public place, away from the town proper, and at such a height that they could be seen from the town. Various oral traditions have been passed down, but these too are inconsistent. Moreover, the geography itself has changed a great deal, with the filling in of salt marshes, the changing banks of the river, and the blasting of the land for railroad expansion (14). Local historian Marilynne Roach's investigation on the subject concludes that "locating the exact places of the deaths and burial would not merely satisfy curiosity. It would help to reconstruct, and so to understand, past events. But beyond that, the site contains graves and deserves the respect due any burying ground. The dead, after all, were real people—not symbols, not stereotypes, and not tourist attractions" (19). Roach's sentiments perhaps allude to another reason why no further attempts have been made to find these authentic sites: Even if they were discovered, they would not be tourist attractions.

The lure of a few gravestones could hardly compete with the entertainment of all of Salem's symbols, stereotypes, and manufactured sites.

Graves and Markers: Missing Sites

There are several places in both Salem and Danvers where we are reminded that those who died in 1692 were not symbols, but real people. Both towns have erected large memorials to the condemned witches as a group, and there are several monuments to individual victims. But despite the visibility of these markers, there are no graves; the exact site of burial of all but one of the bodies remains unknown. Most of the victims were thrown into a pit near the site of the hangings, though some bodies were recovered by family members and reburied. But even the graves of these recovered bodies were unmarked, and memory of their location has been lost over generations. The remains of only one witch (George Jacobs) have been found and identified (Hill 174). The absent center of these markers is remarkable. Presumably, a gravestone indicates the location of a body beneath it, but this is not the case for the witch memorials. On the Nurse Homestead in Danvers, I visited the monument erected in Rebecca Nurse's honor in 1885; however, her body is not located there.[4] The marker is located in a graveyard in which other markers do point to graves, including that of George Jacobs. But the Nurse monument, and others like it, is made to indicate the very absence of that grave, pointing to an absence as well as to another (unknown, unknowable) location.

Meanwhile, a key stop on Salem's Heritage Trail is the Burying Point, the oldest burial ground in the city. A sign on the fence informs visitors that "[t]he Burying Point contains the graves of Governor Bradstreet, Chief Justice Lynde, and others whose virtues, honors, courage, and sagacity have nobly illustrated the history of Salem." But the Burying Point also contains the grave of Justice John Hathorne, who presided over the witch-trial court. A few yards away from Justice Hathorne's gravestone and grave stands the tercentenary memorial to the witches, erected in 1992. The proximity of memorials for both the accusers and accused perhaps indicates that after all this time, these events must be forgiven, that in death, both must exist side by side. Generations later, however, the descendants of the witches are still trying to gain proper memorials for each of the condemned and, in some cases, to have their innocence officially acknowledged by the courts.

The monuments to the Salem witches are ultimately sites marking absences. They do not mark bodies, nor do they mark sites of action. They are located in or near graveyards, where other bodies are buried and where other markers are placed, perhaps even casting doubts on the accuracy of these other markers. These monuments, while they cannot change history, serve to mark it. Taking up a physical space, they represent a temporal place, recalling a specific and solemn moment in the past. While visiting these monuments certainly seems to be a more serious and thoughtful activity than visiting Salem's museums, a similar heritage process is at work. Like the other forms of heritage display in Salem, these monuments are intended to recall for the visitor a time in the past, but, in doing so, their own history is obscured. These created sites can be powerful scenes for the modern visitor; however, they do not actually transport us to that past being honored. Instead, they continue to remind us of the inaccessibility of that past. Peaceful contemplation of the graves at the Old Burying Ground and the Tercentenary Memorial is nearly impossible due to the Salem Wax Museum of Witches and Seafarers, which plays scary haunted-house sounds—clanking chains, ghoulish moans, and howling wolves—on outdoor speakers. Thus, while perusing the gravesites commemorating the dead, the tourist is reminded not of real ghosts or real horror, but of manufactured sideshow horror.

The Witch Dungeons: Destroying Sites

In 1957, during the construction of a New England Telephone building, the actual dungeon in which the accused witches were held was discovered and promptly razed; a large office building now stands at the site at 4 Federal Street. The remains of the dungeon might have been restored as a historic location, offering proof of the horrendous conditions in which the "witches" lived, in some cases for a whole year. One would think that this would be the site of archaeological work, of historical research—hallowed ground of sorts for those who are interested in the history of the area. Instead, only a few pieces of debris were salvaged, including a beam from the original structure that is now on display at the Witch Dungeon Museum, located a few blocks from the original site. During my tour of the museum, the guide presented the beam with much reverence and told the tour group: "Touch it if you dare!" Exactly what would be so daring about touching it was not explained. Perhaps we were to expect that it held magical power or that it was cursed by the "witches" who were once imprisoned beneath it. Even this one authentic artifact was thus used in the service of the cheap haunted-house version of Salem.

At the Witch Dungeon Museum, for a five-dollar adult admission, the contemporary visitor to Salem can see a reenactment of a portion of the trial of Elizabeth Proctor followed by a tour of the basement that is made up to look like the dungeon in which she and the other convicted witches were contained. On the front of the building (of twentieth-century construction) is a large metal plaque that reads: "Here stood the Salem Gaol Built in 1684, used until 1813, razed in 1957. During the witchcraft persecution of 1692, many of the accused were imprisoned here. One of them, the Aged Giles Cory (b. 1611) was pressed to death on these grounds." Beside this large plaque is a much smaller sign, of fading plastic, reading: "This plaque was originally located on Federal Street, The Old Jail Site, Two Blocks North." I immediately wondered how the plaque came to be relocated here. According to a guide, the museum, which opened at this location twenty-two years ago, has always had the plaque; no further information on its procurement was forthcoming. The effect of the signs is confusing; as with the grave markers for the witches, this is a sign pointing to an absence. But this goes even further: We have one sign pointing to a place that is not the site, and another sign pointing to the inaccuracy of the first sign. Why not keep the plaque at its original, accurate location? Tours do not show visitors that the site of the dungeon has been replaced with a modern (and distinctly not horrifying) office building, revealing that time and the town have moved past their ignoble history. Salem's narrative of campy haunting resolutely denies that any real specter of history might haunt this place.

Meanwhile, there is no marker at 4 Federal Street, the actual site of the jail. The complete obliteration of this site is perhaps most clearly evidenced by the fact that the Heritage Trail does not pass 4 Federal Street; instead, it passes the Witch Dungeon Museum on Lynde Street. Their brochure explains: "The mood is set from the moment you enter the Witch Dungeon Museum. You are there—in Salem Village 1692, and you are guaranteed a unique educational experience with a chill or two" (*Witch Dungeon*). Once again, the attraction emphasizes the "experience" of transportation to the past. One can only imagine what kind of experience the visitor to the actual witch dungeons might have had. Instead, the Witch Dungeon Museum focuses on packaging the witch dungeons as a consumable. It is an attraction that includes actors as well as a suggested visit length; its layout pushes the visitor through the dungeon, so that the visit is short, quite unlike that of the inmates of the actual dungeon. Rather than seeing the actual cells of the real dungeon, visitors "will see the poor conditions and the actual size of the cells that the accused were kept in while awaiting their trials" (Francoeur, Fox, and McAllister 25). Inside these cells are man-nequins representing the witches. Despite the fact that these were clearly inanimate figures, our guide informed us that "in the second cell, the woman is starving to death," as if there were an actual woman in the cell. The Witch Dungeon Museum is not a site of education, nor does it truly evoke the horror that it purports to be representing. It is a site of heritage re-creation serving the purpose of recreation. While education and recre-ation do not have to be mutually exclusive activities, the entertainment of the site comes at the expense of an understanding of the true horror of the events. The museum is yet another example of Salem's ability to tell a "scary" story appealing to a "fun" kind of horror without really engaging with its own truly frightening history.

III. SALEM'S SUCCESS AS A HERITAGE SITE AND CONSUMER PRODUCT

The rapid expansion of Salem's witch tourism in the past fifty years indi-cates an ever-increasing distance from the horrors of the original events, as well as an ongoing economic need to replace other local industries that have failed. Salemites have long been disconcerted by their town's com-memoration of its history. Salem resident Caroline Howard King's late-nineteenth-century memoir, *When I Lived in Salem 1822–1866,* tells of her discomfort with the marketing of Salem. She recalls that when she was a child, she was fearful of passing Gallows Hill. She later reflects: "It may be the influence of those early days which makes it so impossible for me to look with toleration on the witch spoons and witch symbols which are so much sought after now. The whole witch episode seems to me a blot and disgrace upon the history of Salem, an awful tragedy to be regretted and mourned, instead of a thing to be gloried in and perpetuated, and I should be glad if Gallows Hill could be levelled and forgotten" (89). To this day, there is very little regret or mourning in the heritage productions of Salem. If Gallows Hill has been leveled, or its exact location forgotten, there is no way to forget the town's obsession with the events that took place here. King's childhood sense of fear when walking past certain places in Salem is not the kind of fear that modern visitors can ever recapture on a visit to Salem. Salem forces a constant remembrance of its witch history, but it is a rearranged, sanitized, and commodified history that it remembers. Its rec-ollection of history is grounded far more in twentieth-century pop-culture camp than it is in authentic seventeenth-century colonial experience.

Tourist sites can never transport us to the past; no matter how scrupulously accurate and solemn we are in presenting history, we cannot access the past or produce the reality of what seventeenth-century Salemites experienced. But Salem's marketing makes claims about accessing the past and offering an "experience" that Salem simply can't deliver. Moreover, in misrepresenting facts, distorting actual sites, and making light of a horrible history, Salem calls into question the integrity of even the places that are honest attempts to present and explore the witch hysteria in earnest. At most of Salem's sites, the "experience" we are offered is recreational horror packaged to sell tickets; these sites do not present history in a way that encourages us to engage with questions about our past. Rather, we are offered an entertaining and consumable attraction. As John Sears explains in *Sacred Places: American Tourist Attractions in the Nineteenth Century*:

> Modern tourist attractions also continue to serve as arenas of consumption. They are places where the cosmic erupts into the consumer culture which everyone shares, and where, too, the consumer culture often co-opts the cosmic for its own ends. It is this dual nature—the function of tourist attractions as sacred places and as arenas of consumption—that induces many tourists to approach them with a double consciousness, with religious awe or poetic rapture on the one hand and a skeptical, sardonic attitude on the other. (213)

Thus, when we visit Salem, we are made aware both of the site and our consumption of it. The displays, museums, signs, brochures, and souvenirs are all produced for the tourist to encourage the consumption of more displays, museums, signs, brochures, and souvenirs. All of these items are markers to indicate what to see. As Jonathan Culler explains in "The Semiotics of Tourism," "'the real thing' must be marked as real, as sightworthy; if it is not marked or differentiated, it is not a notable sight" (161). The problem with Salem is that there is very little of "the real thing" that remains. As in Culler's conception, "The markers themselves quite explicitly become the attraction, the site itself" (166). Moreover, in Salem, these markers are faulty at best, often not even pointing to the things that they claim to be indicating. Tourism in general, and in Salem specifically, is "a celebration of signification and differentiation which conceals the economic exploitation and homogenization that underlies it" (167). Among the simulacra of Salem, it is quite possible to lose sight of the significance of Salem's history and fall for the haunted-house version of history.

Salem's tourist productions seek to avoid a confrontation with the town's truly haunted history, and instead offer a playful, entertaining, horror-movie-style haunting. Furthermore, Salem's re-creation of itself as "Witch City" frequently destroys authentic historic places in the service of making an entertainment site for tourists. That the tourist industry in Salem is founded on the gruesome murder of twenty people three hundred years ago is ultimately ignored. As one article claims, "In Salem in 1992, a.k.a. 'witch city,' time's alchemy has turned shame into tourism" (Watson 7). During the period of the hysteria, more than 150 men and women were accused of witchcraft and jailed. Nineteen men and women were hanged. One man was pressed to death. Another four adults and one unnamed infant died in their dungeon cells awaiting trial. These are the facts that haunt Salem's history and lurk somewhere behind the simulacra of tourist productions. But the entertained tourist is rarely confronted with the true horror of the events; indeed, why would anyone want to visit such a place?

Creating appropriate memorials on sites of death and tragedy is frequently fraught with moral and ethical concerns. What is surprising about Salem is that there doesn't seem to have been any debate about its development of "Witch City." Current discussions about how (or whether) to rebuild at the site of the World Trade Center show how passionately people feel about proper memorials to commemorate national and personal loss. Tours of Anne Frank's home, visits to actual concentration camps (or the *Schindler's List* tour of the Auschwitz replica created for the film), and even the construction of the National Holocaust Museum in the United States, far from the actual ground of the atrocities, have been critiqued for their callous gift shops and packaged presentations of Hitler's "final solution." Places of bloodshed and death in America, such as the Gettysburg Battlefield and the Trail of Tears have also been contested sites of tourism, with local residents, descendants of original victims (or victimizers), historians, and politicians becoming actively involved in crusades to create (or prevent the creation of) markers and the inevitable accompanying tourist accommodations. So why does Salem seem to have accepted this commercialism, apparently without public concern or debate, and certainly without outrage? Perhaps, compared to the higher death tolls of battles and genocides in more recent history, the deaths of twenty New England colonists seem minor, something to be remarked, but ultimately, not something that will upset too many people. But there are many Americans who claim (with varying degrees of pride, and, perhaps, validity) to be descendants of the original figures of the Salem witch trials. These were, after all, some of the founding citizens of the nation. Is our historical distance from the events in Salem too great for us to mourn properly what happened there? Although it has been some time since anyone has been accused of witchcraft, per se, the terms "witch-hunt" and "witch hysteria" have been evoked to describe numerous troubling periods in twentieth-century history, from 1950s McCarthyism (with Arthur Miller's *The Crucible* making the connection explicit) to the repressed-memory, sexual-abuse scandals of the 1980s and 1990s, to contemporary post–September-eleventh anxiety about Arabs, Arab Americans, and other immigrant groups (particularly dark-skinned ones). The story of the witch trials is still relevant, a frequently invoked cautionary tale in the United States today. So why do the majority of the sites in Salem make light of what happened, costuming the solemn events of three centuries ago in kitsch and creepiness?

Today's Halloween-themed Salem is a haunted place that has buried its real haunting and covered it with an entertainment- and profit-based narrative focused on a fun and amusing kind of fright. The story that Salem tells itself and its visitors is one that indicates the town's refusal to mourn the events that took place there. Visitors come to Salem expecting to learn about a horrible event in American history. Salem's many tourist attractions capitalize on this eager audience by luring them into heritage productions with the promise of offering information or objects related to the witch trials. Many of these sites use this pretext to attract more visitors to something that is in fact unrelated to the trials (i.e., the tours of the "Witch House"), or they misrepresent facts (the plaques on the witch dungeon museum) or ignore the true horror of the events and instead present a campy, horror-movie-style presentation (Dracula's Castle, Boris Karloff's Witch Museum). The factual errors and marketing misrepresentation lead the visitor not to experience the horror of the past but to witness an evasion of it. The sites are built to collect tourist dollars, not to increase understanding.

As James W. Loewen's book *Lies Across America: What Our Historic Sites Get Wrong* explains, historic sites tell stories, not only of the periods they commemorate but also of the periods in which they are created. It is essential that we understand not only what these sites tell us but also what they don't tell us, and what they misrepresent. Salem has some serious problems of misrepresentation. Some individual sites simply misstate facts, others ignore certain elements of the history, and others offer conflicting messages with anachronistic images. The visitor to Salem's tourist productions should not rely on these tourist attractions to teach the history of the Salem witch trials. Rather, as Loewen advises, tourists must question the historic sites they visit so as "to avoid being taken in by the lies our public history tries to tell" (35). Throughout Salem's history as a town, there have been many stories told about the events of 1692; each successive story is haunted by the versions that came before it. Each reinterpretation of Salem leaves its specter to haunt the next tourist or historian, and our own interpretations will appear as another layer in the palimpsest of Salem's haunted history.

NOTES

1. The same might be said of the scholarly industry surrounding the witch trials, as each year seems to bring a new monograph purporting to answer any remaining questions (or to ask new ones) about Salem's "witches." For the most recent publication on the subject, see Norton. For a controversial theory about the connection between witchcraft and encephalitis, see Carlson. For two useful surveys of the history of interpreting Salem's witchcraft hysteria, see Rosenthal and Mappen.

2. Current brochures for both the Witch Dungeon Museum and the Salem Witch Museum claim that their presentations are based on these documents.

3. This site can also be a confusing one for tourists. Right beside the original Nurse house, where Rebecca was arrested for being a witch, on the land that is still a part of the Nurse Homestead, is the 1984 reproduction of the Salem Village Meeting House, constructed for the filming of the movie *Three Sovereigns for Sarah*. Thus, an "authentic" historical site (the Nurse Homestead) also includes a modern reproduction of a historic building (the Meeting House) that is not in its original location.

4. Hunt claims that Rebecca Nurse's remains are in this family burial ground (29). However, Hill indicates that this is not known for sure (174), and a tour guide to the site explained that Nurse's remains have never been located.

WORKS CITED

Boyer, Paul, and Stephen Nissenbaum. *Salem Possessed: The Social Origins of Witchcraft.* Cambridge: Harvard University Press, 1974.

Carlson, Laurie Winn. *A Fever in Salem: A New Interpretation of the New England Witch Trials.* Chicago: Ivan R. Dee, 1999.

Culler, Jonathan. "The Semiotics of Tourism." In *Framing the Sign.* Norman: University of Oklahoma Press, 1988.

Demos, John Putnam. *Entertaining Satan: Witchcraft and the Culture of Early New England.* Oxford: Oxford University Press, 1982.

Fox, Kate, and Jim McAllister, eds. *Salem Massachusetts Visitor Guide and Map 2000.* Commonwealth of Massachusetts, et al. Salem: Destination Salem, 2000.

Francoeur, Rae, Kate Fox, and Jim McAllister, eds. *Salem Massachusetts 1999/2000 Visitor Guide and Map.* Commonwealth of Massachusetts, et al. Salem: Destination Salem, 1999.

Haskell, David. "Salem Haunted, But Not Scared." Salem, Ma. U. P. I. Oct. 15, 2001. Lexis-Nexis. University of Massachusetts Library, Amherst. Accessed Jan. 15, 2002. http://www.library.umass.edu/index.html.

Haunted Footsteps Ghost Tour. Pamphlet. No Date. (2000).

Hill, Frances. *A Delusion of Satan, the Full Story of the Salem Witch Trials.* New York: Da Capo, 1997.

Hunt, Thomas F. *Visitor's Guide to Salem.* Salem: Essex Institute, 1902.

Karlsen, Carol F. *The Devil in the Shape of a Woman: Witchcraft in Colonial New England.* New York: Vintage, 1987.

King, Caroline Howard. *When I Lived in Salem 1822–1866.* Brattleboro, Vt.: Stephen Daye, 1937.

Kirshenblatt-Gimblett, Barbara. *Destination Culture: Tourism, Museums, and Heritage.* Berkeley: University of California Press, 1998.

LeBeau, Bryan F. "The Carey Document: On the Trail of a Salem Death Warrant." *Early America Review* 2.1 (1997). Online. Accessed July 25, 2000. http://earlyamerica.com/reviews/summer97/carey.html.

LeBlanc, Steve. "Executed Salem Witches Exonerated." Boston, Ma.: Associated Press Online Nov. 2, 2001. Lexis-Nexis. University of Massachusetts Library, Amherst. Accessed Jan. 15, 2002. http://www.library.umass.edu/index.html.

Loewen, James W. *Lies across America: What Our Historic Sites Get Wrong.* New York: New Press, 1999.

Mappen, Marc. *Witches and Historians: Interpretations of Salem.* Malabar, Fl.: Robert E. Krieger, 1980.

Mass Hysteria Haunted Hearse Tours. Pamphlet. No Date. (2000).

Norton, Mary Beth. *In the Devil's Snare: The Salem Witchcraft Crisis of 1692.* New York: Knopf, 2002.

Peabody Essex Museum: New England's Roots Start Here. Peabody Essex Museum. Pamphlet. 2000.

Roach, Marilynne K. *Gallows and Graves: The Search to Locate the Death and Burial Sites of the People Executed for Witchcraft in 1692.* Watertown, Ma.: Sassafras Grove Press, 1997.

Rosenthal, Bernard. *Salem Story: Reading the Witch Trials of 1692.* Cambridge: Cambridge University Press, 1993.

Salem Wax Museum of Witches and Seafarers / Salem Witch Village. Pamphlet. No Date (1999).

Salem Witch Museum. Pamphlet. No Date. (1999).

Sears, John F. *Sacred Places: American Tourist Attractions in the Nineteenth Century.* New York: Oxford University Press, 1989.

Upham, Charles. *Salem Witchcraft Volume II.* 1867. Reprint, New York: Frederick Ungar, 1978.

Watson, Bruce. "Salem's Dark Hour: Did the Devil Make Them Do It?" *Smithsonian* 23 (April 1992): 116. Expanded Academic ASAP. University of Massachusetts

Library, Amherst. Accessed Oct. 4, 1999. http://www.library.umass.edu/research/bytitle.htm

Witch Dungeon Museum. Salem Massachusetts. Pamphlet. No Date. (1999).

Witch History Museum. Pamphlet. No Date. (1999).

"Witches Good for Business in the Right Town." Salem, Ma. U.P.I. Oct. 1, 1982. Lexis-Nexis. University of Massachusetts Library, Amherst. Accessed Sept. 14, 1999. http://www.library.umass.edu/research/bytitle.htm

Contributors

CHARLES L. CROW is professor emeritus at Bowling Green State University and has written prolifically on the American gothic and supernatural literary traditions. His *American Gothic: An Anthology 1787–1916* was released in 1999 by Blackwell. With Howard Kerr and John W. Crowley, he edited *The Haunted Dusk: American Supernatural Fiction, 1820–1920* (University of Georgia Press, 1983) and, with Howard Kerr, *The Occult in America: New Historical Perspectives* (University of Illinois Press, 1983). Recently, he edited *A Companion to the Regional Literatures of America* (Blackwell, 2003).

DIANA M. DAVIDSON completed her doctorate from the University of York in the United Kingdom in 2002 and is a Killam Postdoctoral Fellow at the University of Alberta where she teaches popular culture and senior-level courses on AIDS narratives. She is currently writing a manuscript on world literature and HIV/AIDS.

MARY FINDLEY holds a master's degree from Vermont College of Norwich University where her focus was on Gothic literature and its connections to popular culture. She is presently a doctoral candidate at Union Institute and University with a focus on contemporary Gothic literature and the work of Stephen King.

KATHERINE A. FOWKES is an associate professor and the director of media studies at High Point University and is the author of *Giving Up the Ghost: Spirits, Ghosts and Angels in Mainstream Hollywood Films* (Wayne

State, 1998). She is currently teaching a course on monsters, ghosts, and angels in Hollywood films and is also finishing up a screenplay entitled "Sleep."

JEFFREY HAMMOND, Reeves Distinguished Professor in the Liberal Arts and professor of English at St. Mary's College of Maryland, teaches creative writing and early American literature and culture. His books include *Ohio States: A Twentieth-Century Midwestern* (Kent State University Press, 2002), *The American Puritan Elegy: A Literary and Cultural Study* (Cambridge University Press, 2000), *Sinful Self, Saintly Self: The Puritan Experience of Poetry* (University of Georgia Press, 1993), and *Edward Taylor: Fifty Years of Scholarship and Criticism* (Camden House, 1993).

ELIZABETH T. HAYES is the Kevin G. O'Connell Distinguished Teaching Professor of the Humanities at Le Moyne College in Syracuse, New York. She is the editor of *Images of Persephone: Feminist Readings in Western Literature* and the author of several articles on twentieth-century American literature. She is writing a book on U.S. magic realist fiction and drama.

TERRY HELLER is Howard Hall Professor of Literature at Coe College and has written or edited eight books including *The Delights of Terror: An Aesthetics of the Tale of Terror* (University of Illinois Press, 1987), *Henry James's "The Turn of the Screw": Bewildered Vision* (Twayne, 1989), and several volumes of the work of Sarah Orne Jewett.

JOHN J. KUCICH is an assistant professor of English at Bridgewater State College. He is the author of *Ghostly Communion: Spiritualism in American Culture*, forthcoming from University Press of New England. He is presently working on a manuscript about animism and ecocriticism.

JESSICA CATHERINE LIEBERMAN is a visiting assistant professor in the departments of language and literature and fine art photography at the Rochester Institute of Technology. Her essay in this volume is derived from her dissertation.

ALLAN LLOYD SMITH is a senior lecturer in American literature at the University of East Anglia, England, and has previously taught at the universities of Keele and Minnesota. He is the author of many articles on

American fiction, and three books of criticism, *The Analysis of Motives* (on early American psychology and fiction), *Eve Tempted* (on Hawthorne), and *Uncanny American Fiction*. He has recently coedited *Gothick: Origins and Innovations*, and *Modern Gothic: A Reader*.

BRIDGET M. MARSHALL is a doctoral candidate in the department of English at the University of Massachusetts, Amherst. She has presented and published papers on Gothic novels, horror movies, and American popular culture. She was the principal researcher, writer, and curator of a museum exhibit and Web site on the seventeenth-century witchcraft trials of Mary (Bliss) Parsons in Northampton, Massachusetts.

ALISON TRACY is a doctoral candidate in English literature at the University of Washington. Her dissertation, directed by Priscilla Wald, explores the connections between educational praxis and Gothic literature in the early American nation. Her contribution here is derived from her fascination with all things Puritan.

SHERI WEINSTEIN is an assistant professor of English at Kingsborough Community College of the City University of New York, in Brooklyn. Her dissertation, from which her contribution here is derived, is entitled "Mechanical Spirits, Magical Bodies: Spiritualism and Technologies of the Real in American Literature, 1850–1910." She has also published on Henry James and Kathy Acker.

JEFFREY ANDREW WEINSTOCK is an assistant professor of English at Central Michigan University. He is the editor of *The Pedagogical Wallpaper: Teaching Charlotte Perkins Gilman's "The Yellow Wall-paper"* (Peter Lang, 2002) and, with Sarah Higley, *Nothing That Is: Millennial Cinema and the "Blair Witch" Controversies* (Wayne State University Press, 2003).

Index

A RAY AND PAT BROWNE BOOK

Series Editors
Ray B. Browne and Pat Browne

---

*Murder on the Reservation: American Indian Crime Fiction:
Aims and Achievements*
Ray B. Browne

*Goddesses and Monsters: Essays on Women, Myth, Power, and
Popular Culture*
Jane Caputi

Mystery, Violence, and Popular Culture
John G. Cawelti

Baseball and Country Music
Don Cusic

The Essential Guide to Werewolf Literature
Brian J. Frost

Images of the Corpse: From the Renaissance to Cyberspace
Edited by Elizabeth Klaver

*Walking Shadows: Orson Welles, W. R. Hearst, and
Citizen Kane*
John Evangelist Walsh

Spectral America: Phantoms and the National Imagination
Edited by Jeffrey Andrew Weinstock